William Harbutt Dawson

German Socialism and Ferdinand Lassalle

A Biographical History of German Socialistic Movements

William Harbutt Dawson

German Socialism and Ferdinand Lassalle
A Biographical History of German Socialistic Movements

ISBN/EAN: 9783337028893

Printed in Europe, USA, Canada, Australia, Japan

Cover: Foto ©ninafisch / pixelio.de

More available books at **www.hansebooks.com**

GERMAN SOCIALISM

AND

FERDINAND LASSALLE

*A BIOGRAPHICAL HISTORY OF GERMAN SOCIALISTIC
MOVEMENTS DURING THIS CENTURY*

BY

WILLIAM HARBUTT DAWSON

Author of
" *Germany and the Germans,*" " *Bismarck and State Socialism,*"
" *Social Switzerland,*" *&c.*

LONDON
SWAN SONNENSCHEIN & CO., LIM.
NEW YORK: CHARLES SCRIBNER'S SONS
1899

FIRST EDITION   •   •   •   •   •   •   *June*, 1888

SECOND EDITION   -   -   -   -   -   -   *March*, 1891

THIRD EDITION (Revised and Enlarged)   -   *January*, 1899

THIS VOLUME IS

Dedicated

TO THE REVERED MEMORY OF

MY FATHER,

WHOSE LIFE, SHORT IN YEARS BUT LONG IN GOOD AND USEFUL
WORKS, CAME TO AN UNEXPECTED CLOSE WHILE THE
LAST PAGES WERE IN THE PRESS.

CONTENTS.

———◆———

INTRODUCTION.

IN the election to the German Reichstag which took place early last year, nearly eight hundred thousand votes were cast for Socialist candidates, and the Social-Democratic party claimed, not without reason, that altogether nearly a million Socialists took part in the election. That is a stupendous fact. What is its significance? At the time of the election the number of men qualified, by the completion of the twenty-fifth year, to vote was estimated at nine and three quarter millions. Thus one in ten could be regarded as a Socialist. It is, however, a well-known fact that a large proportion of the Socialist army is made up of young artisans, operatives, and labourers from the age of eighteen upward, so that the figures given by no means represent the full strength of the party in Germany. These are facts which will bear a good deal of careful pondering. Let us think of Socialism as we will, it is not to be pooh-poohed out of existence. Here it is, a great power in our civilisation, a momentous factor in national life.

It can hardly be called an idle task to trace the growth of this vast social force in Germany, for not only may Germany be regarded as the classic land of modern Socialism, but other countries, both Continental and Transatlantic, are fed with Socialistic doctrines from this copious fountain. Further, England bears a certain amount of responsibility for the German Socialist movement. Apart altogether from the influence exerted by English political economists and Socialists upon the representatives of scientific Socialism in Germany, it must not be forgotten that many of the active leaders of militant Communism, Socialism, and Social-Democracy—for example,

A

Marx, Engels, and Liebknecht—spent years upon English soil, and made England a base of operations, much to the disgust of the German authorities. The works and agitation of these men prove that their experience of England's free institutions only served to increase their dissatisfaction with the state of things prevailing at home, so that it is not too much to say that England has, innocently and indirectly, contributed very largely to the success of Socialistic propagandism in Germany. Now, however, the influence is reacting, as the study of the nomenclature of Socialists in England will plainly show.

Nowadays few subjects excite more controversy than does this of Socialism, and yet it seems still impossible to treat it in an impartial and strictly scientific spirit. Too many writers on Socialism show a disposition to use their pens as though they were broadswords rather than lancets. A great deal has been said and written in defence of Socialism and quite as much against it, but while the extremes have been followed times without number, the golden mean has far too seldom been found. It seems so natural to the average mind to regard a thing as either good or wholly bad, as either true or quite false, as either meriting full acceptance or complete rejection. This dogmatic spirit inevitably does great harm, and not the least serious result is that public judgment is warped and weighty questions do not receive the attention which they deserve. Yet another reason, however, why Socialism has not had justice done to it is the confusion of ideas that prevails on the subject. Nor is this confusion confined to the least informed part of the community. The fact that a leading London journal could a short time ago insist that " Socialism under whatever guise it presents itself must be crushed with a heavy hand," proves that very curious notions exist even in educated circles. It may, indeed, be allowed that it is not altogether possible to draw a clear dividing-line between conventional and Socialistic economic principles. Social systems may be said to grow into one another as do barbarism and civilisation, and, moreover, it is nearly always easier to say what a thing is not than what it is ; Dr. Johnson recognised this when asked to define poetry,

Still, it should not be difficult to determine the main characteristics of Socialism, those characteristics which cause it to differ
from orthodox economy. True Socialism, as the word implies,
is the antithesis of economic Individualism. The true Socialist
seeks to realise the principle of co-operation in labour and community in the instruments and produce of labour. Association
is to take the place of competition. Labour is to be the principle of society, and to labour both capital and property are to be
made subordinate. Every member of this new society will be
expected to work, and his share in the produce of labour will be
proportionate to his deserts. Socialism—however paradoxical it may
seem—may thus be said to involve as a corollary the highest form of
Individualism, the highest form because it is founded on the principle
of equality. The present individualistic *régime* is based on the principles of complete personal freedom, private property in land and
capital, and free contract in the adjustment of economic relationships.
Socialism, on the other hand, while maintaining the principle of
personal liberty, makes land and capital collective—whether in the
hands of the State or of communities is a subordinate question—it
rejects the system of private undertakership, abolishes rent-income in
all forms, supplants the wages-contract, and regulates both production
and distribution according to plan and method.

While, however, this is Socialism carried to its full logical limits, a
great number of more or less modified forms of Socialism exist, or
the English statesman who recently declared that "We are all
Socialists now," would have been guilty of a misapplication of terms.
It is undoubtedly true that everybody is, if he only knew it, more or
less of a Socialistic turn of mind. Jourdain did not know until someone
told him that he had been speaking prose all his life ; and a parallel
might well be drawn between the *bourgeois gentilhomme* and the unconscious Socialist of modern times. Indeed, no more singular
inconsistency exists than that of subjects of a civilised State declaring
against the Communistic and Socialistic principle. For this principle
has been extensively adopted in all the most progressive countries, and
some of our most highly esteemed institutions are based upon it. The

State post, telegraph, railway, and bank, the free school, the poor law system, the factory laws, sanitary legislation—these are all institutions which must be unconditionally condemned if Communism and Socialism are evil in theory. The fact is, that it is all a question of degree ; it is not a matter of rejecting a principle but of determining how far it should be carried.

It can hardly be necessary, however, to say that the Socialism considered in the following pages is not a modified form. In Germany to-day, the schools of Socialists are more numerous than Liberal factions here. In addition to the Social-Democrats there are International, State, Academic, Christian, Catholic, and Conservative Socialists. Of the chrysalides it is, however, impossible to take account here. Attention must rather be directed to the development of the Socialism which has latterly taken the character and name of Social-Democracy—its why and wherefore, its whence and whither. This Socialism we shall find to be something more than a scientific system. In Social-Democracy not alone the economic, but the political element comes into play, though the political demands are only means to the attainment of economic ends. The political character of the German Socialistic movement will be recognised at every step in the course of our review. Indeed, with one conspicuous exception all the modern leaders of German Socialism have recognised the insufficiency of a purely scientific programme.

In undertaking this task I went upon the well-grounded supposition that Socialism was no exploded theory, no page of ancient and forgotten history. I held rather that it was a power to be reckoned with, a power which if of error must be grappled and fought with outright, if of truth must be allowed ungrudgingly the success which has attended it in the past, and may attend it in the future. Men never commit a greater mistake than when they refuse to acknowledge facts. Let us treat theories as we will, facts must be recognised, and it is in the highest degree unwise to close our eyes to them. Militant Socialism is to-day a great fact. Even the most zealous of anti-Socialists should and must grant this. For the sake of his convictions he ought to admit the folly of trying to persuade himself that there is no antagonist to meet, for while he is doing this the foe is strengthening his position. Only two attitudes can be taken up on this question.

(*a.*) It is possible to refuse to enter into argument, on the principle that there is no disputing with fools. It is hardly necessary to say that this is pure *petitio principii*. When such a standpoint is adopted it is probably because of unfamiliarity with the facts. Those who hold that Socialism is mere folly and nothing else must remember in what a sweeping assertion the contention involves them.

" If Social-Democracy," says one of the most thoughtful critics of the Socialist movement in Germany—" If Social-Democracy were really ' absurdity itself,' and ' evident nonsense,' the fact that perhaps a million of our citizens [these words were written ten years ago] adhere to it would be a reproach to our civilisation, our nation, and our age, a reproach so severe and oppressive that it could not be borne any longer." What holds good of Germany is equally applicable to other countries. By ridicule and denunciation no valuable purpose can be served. They are weapons which never scar an antagonist, but always injure those who bear them.

(*b.*) The other attitude is that of toleration combined with scrutiny. This is a reasonable attitude, and is, moreover, the only one which can to-day be of any avail. Let Socialistic doctrines be fairly met, let them be faced in the impartial arena of scientific combat—let them be vanquished if we will, but in any case let them be faced. It is idle to rest content with the assumption that Socialism is identical with error, and, as a consequence, does not deserve serious notice. Battles are never won by the mere consciousness of superior strength. Achilles overpowered Hector, but he had first to don his armour, and quit the tent. Until he awoke from lethargy, the Trojan chief was invincible.

What has just been said, refers to the critics of Socialism. On the other hand, it is not too much to ask that our advanced Socialist writers should exercise moderation in the treatment of those who, though unable to see with them eye to eye, are not less desirous than themselves of improving the condition of the poorer classes. They may be certain that alone they cannot expect to fight the battle of

social reform and win.   Let it be granted that the well-abused
bourgeoisie, of which so much is said, has not done its duty in the past.
Can there, however, be no indemnity, no amnesty, even for that part of
the class which recognises the responsibilities of the present, the
claims of the future? Is it for ever to be "war and implacable
hatred?" If so, the hope of a beneficent social revolution is a vain
delusion, and all that is certain in the future is the development of inequality into class feuds similar to those which often showed themselves
during the long struggle of the Roman patricians and plebeians. It is
not necessary or desirable to minimise the criminal iniquities of our
social system, but it is a duty imposed alike by patriotism and regard
for morality and progress to work out the reformation of society by
means which will not more than is absolutely unavoidable conduce to
friction and heartburning. Conciliation is called for on both sides—
moderation on the one hand, and willing sacrifice on the other—but
this shown, it were a reproach upon our generation, nay, upon mankind, if, after so many centuries of civilisation and progress, after so
long cultivation of arts and institutions which, rightly employed, should
make for social peace and happiness, we should have to acknowledge
the impossibility of readjusting society by methods that humanise and
elevate rather than degrade.

Here I must take care to say that as these pages have been written
for English readers, innumerable matters of detail, both in history and
biography, as well as unnecessary local colour, have been omitted.
The peculiar character of the task added certainly to its difficulty, but
it is hoped that there will be little cause for complaint on the score
of too great succinctness. The twofold danger of over-conciseness on
the one hand, and prolixity on the other, was always present. If
failure should have attended the author's efforts in this respect, it is
not because his leading purpose has ever been forgotten, that of reducing an almost infinite amount of literary material to such compass
that the patience of an English reader of average forbearance might
not be unreasonably tried. It seemed often, indeed, an ill-paid task,
that of wading through the flood of German literature which has been
called forth by the Socialist movement. A German writer has well

said that " The traces of German Social-Democracy are buried beneath a deluge of wastepaper." No one who has not devoted attention to this subject on the spot, can conceive of the magnitude of the bibliography of German Socialism. Even now books and pamphlets continue to pour from the press, and there is no sign of exhaustion in the supply. What made the task of research less agreeable than it would have been was the character of the literature that had to be consulted. Unfortunately, the Socialist movement has not yet reached, even in Germany, the stage at which impartiality and fairness or even decent toleration can be looked for, and, judging from present appearance, it will be long before the subject is treated in a truly scientific and historical spirit. Of course, the earlier works err more than the later, but even these often leave much to be desired. Invective, abuse, and misrepresentation are frequently found to be the stock arguments of both friend and foe of the Socialist movement, and the reader becomes at last wearied and aggravated. Strange to say, writers who begin by urging the importance of calm inquiry, often end by being as hot-tempered as the rest. At the same time, it must not be forgotten that there are very distinguished exceptions, and it is only necessary to mention the names of Wagner and Schäffle, of Von Scheel and Held, of Lange, Jäger, Meyer, and let me add Prince Bismarck, as those of men who have brought broad and unbiassed minds to the consideration of Socialistic theories. On the whole, however, agreeable exceptions like these are like rare oases in the midst of interminable desert. I have not thought it advisable under the circumstances to publish a list of the works used, for even if there were no objection on the ground of unequal importance, the extent of such a list—which would comprise some three hundred works, not to speak of Parliamentary, pamphlet, and periodical literature—would rule it out of court. As a substitute, I have here and there mentioned the leading works on special branches of the subject, and the writings of all the important Socialistic and Communistic authors referred to are invariably named.

Special prominence has been given, and I venture to think with full right, to the personality and work of Ferdinand Lassalle. Lassalle deserves the distinction accorded to him both by reason of his service to the Socialist cause in Germany and of his most remarkable character. I have elsewhere spoken of Lassalle as having been a product of his age, but this does not exclude the likelihood that without him German Socialism, as we now know it, would have been kept back a generation. Franz Mehring contends that Social-Democracy was not a result of the spirit of the time, but was called forth by the "energetic will of one autocratic man." Such a view I believe to be wrong, and based upon a misinterpretation of history, yet all the same must we allow that Lassalle gave to the Socialistic tendencies of his day an impetus which none but he could have given. This is not the place to speak of the character of one whom Alexander von Humboldt called in his youth a prodigy and regarded in his manhood as a friend ; one of whom Heine spoke as the Messiah of the nineteenth century ; whom Prince Bismarck was glad to meet on terms of familiarity and intellectual equality, and to listen to with something like Boswellian zeal ; and whom hundreds of thousands of German working-men have regarded or still regard as a heaven-sent champion of their cause. This much may, however, be said here, that a man of this sort was no ordinary man, and that no one who takes the trouble to obtain his evidence at first hand, and to form an original opinion deliberately and impartially—regardless of the hatred of enemies and the adulation of friends—will be able to resist the conclusion that he stands in the towering presence of an intellectual giant. If I may be thought to betray admiration for some sides of Lassalle's character, it is because search reveals much grain amongst the husks, much gold beneath the dross. At present justice is seldom done to Lassalle by his countrymen, for public judgment still sways from extreme to extreme. It is, however, refreshing to come across such an unbiassed verdict as that of Professor Adolph Wagner, who has never ceased to preach the duty of judging Socialism upon its merits, and has recorded the following estimate of Lassalle : "There can no longer be any difference of opinion," he says, " with either friend or enemy of the great Socialist agitator as to the fact that, by reason of his activity, he has become a great historical personage." Hitherto comparatively little has been known of Lassalle and his work in England. Indeed, the entire tenour of his social aims has at times been completely misunderstood, or the late Mr. Fawcett could never have spoken of this passionate Nationalist as the founder of the International Association. In view, therefore, of the inadequacy of encyclopedic biographies, and of the fact that Lassalle's historical position is higher now than ever it was, the biographical chapters devoted to this part of my subject will not, perhaps, be thought superfluous. In order to understand the German Socialist movement aright it is absolutely necessary to know the part played in it by Ferdinand Lassalle, and this part cannot be properly understood unless we also inquire what manner of man Lassalle was.

It will soon be seen that this work in no way pretends to be critical. Criticism lay beyond the province of my task, which was purely historical. To have interpolated opinions would have been taking sides, and thus the standpoint of disinterestedness from which it is desirable to approach a work of this kind would have been departed from, and that without benefit to the thinking reader. I had only to chronicle the views and acts of others ; it was not my business to pass judgment, but merely to assemble evidence, so as to enable the reader to pronounce his own verdict. It may be said that a somewhat colourless narrative is the result. Whether that be the case or not, I am persuaded that any other course than the one pursued would have been wrong. As to terminology little need be said. In explaining the doctrines of men like Rodheitus and Marx, a number of more or less unfamiliar expressions have necessarily had to be used, but few, if any, will be objected to on the ground of obscurity. Expressions like land-rent and capital-rent, capital-property and income-property, *bourgeois* society and *bourgeois* economy, labour-power and labour-faculty, surplus-value, capitalistic production, and the like, may at first appear odd to some, but the oddness will soon wear off. The German *Unternehmer* has been rendered undertaker, a word whose value Mill recognised, and *Arbeiter*, when used in a general sense, appears under the variable forms of workman, working-man, and labourer. The term Social-Democracy is of comparatively recent origin, and in the later chapters the term Socialism is frequently used for the sake of variety.

One of the most interesting questions to which the study of German Socialism gives rise is—whither is it leading? That question no one can confidently presume to answer, for speculation must necessarily be based upon supposition. The replies which are, however, hazarded may be grouped into two classes.

(*a*) The prophets of the one school hold that Social-Democracy is heading for Anarchism, and they point to the declaration of the party leaders for proof. But it should not be forgotten that there is such a thing as appeal to fear even when no intention to use violence exists. Probably no great body of men made more noise, and did less damage in proportion to the magnitude of their professions, than the Chartists. I am not prepared to say that German Social-Democracy will ultimately go the way of English Chartism, but we have here at any rate a striking historical parallel, where two great movements have arisen from causes very similar and have developed by very similar means. Whether the parallel will hold good throughout, the future can alone show. Those who look upon the German Social-Democrats as exclusively or largely friends of violence do so from unacquaintance with the facts. This is what a Conservative writer, who is one of the chief authorities on this question, says :

" I recommend influential men to attend Socialist meetings, so that they may get rid of the preconceived opinion that the Socialists are as a rule sluggards, rowdies, and coarse fellows. Nothing of the sort. The majority of them are honest working-men, to whom the warlike attitude in which they stand towards society is painful enough." [1]

" Oh," it is objected, " the Socialists are propagating their doctrines in the army : what does that mean ?" Of course, with universal military service, there must be a large number of Socialists in the army, but it does not follow that a man is unpatriotic because he is a Socialist. It is possible that the Socialists regard themselves as the true patriots, and all other men as enemies of their country, for here the judgment is apt to be wholly subjective. The subject of Socialism

[1] R. Meyer, "Die bedrohliche Entwickelung des Socialismus."

in the army was discussed several years ago by a German Socialist who wrote in *La Nouvelle Révue*,[1] and in the course of a remarkable article it was hinted that the presence of political malcontents in the army might one day prove disastrous for Germany. After contending that the control of the rank and file on the field of battle tends in modern warfare to become increasingly lax and imperfect, and that the soldier, provided with as many cartridges as he can carry, is now his own officer and acts according to inspiration, this writer continued :

"Prince Bismarck, after having gagged the working-men, believes he has obtained their votes; but the working-men have not given them to him. If he entrusts them with arms for the fighting of his enemies or the realisation of his projects, what use will the working-men make of those arms? Will they abide by the logic of their votes? Upon the answer which the future will give to this question depends the existence of the German Empire."

Against the views here indicated rather than expressed we have to place the in general pacific character of the cool-blooded German; the hitherto quiet development of Social-Democracy; the fact that on several occasions the doctrine of violence has been repudiated, even to the extent of expelling its advocates, as Most and Hasselmann, from the ranks of the party ; and the reiteration only last year by the St. Gallen congress of firm adherence to legitimate and peaceful means of agitation. During the French campaign not a few prominent Socialists did yeoman's service under Prussian colours, and both during and after the war the Socialist movement suffered seriously, a proof clearly that if Socialists have taken up arms against the Government it is not because they love their country the less. It is, moreover, significant that when during a debate on the Army Bill in January, 1887, Prince Bismarck remarked that the French Socialists would stand by their country in case of war, a voice cried from the Social-Democratic benches, "And so will we !" To the incendiary speeches which are occasionally made, too much importance should not be attached. At any rate we English people ought not to act as censors in such a

1 *La Nouvelle Révue*, March, 1882 ; article on "Le Socialisme en Allemagne," by "Un Socialiste Allemand."

matter. It cannot be forgotten that most of the important political and social reforms won in this country during the past century—to go no further back—have been accelerated by popular irritation and threat.

(*b.*) The other school of prophets trusts that the social legislation of Prince Bismarck will ultimately succeed in removing the roots of Socialism, and that the movement will thus in process of time die out for want of aliment. It must be admitted that this prediction is the more likely of the two. It is too soon to pass any but a theoretical judgment upon the German Chancellor's social reforms, which are still far from complete. Only after a number of years will it be possible to arrive at a verdict based upon adequate evidence. The departure is an altogether new one, and thus Prince Bismarck may be compared to a mariner sailing in unknown seas. While, however, we must defer our judgment upon his policy, we may at once admit that he is the first German statesman who has really tried during the last sixty or seventy years to do anything to improve the lot of the labouring popu-lation. More than that, he is the first European statesman who has dared to take the social problem in hand with the determination, not indeed to solve it—for that is a task which he himself has admitted will require generations, but to pave the way for solution. It is im-possible to say whether the Accident and Sickness Insurance Laws al-ready passed, and the Old Age and Indigence Insurance Law which is now under consideration, will accomplish all that is desired, but there can be little doubt that Prince Bismarck has discovered where the roots of the social evil lie. He has declared, in words that burn, that it is the duty of the State to give heed, above all, to the welfare of its weaker members ; he has vowed that no opposition and no obloquy shall ever deter him from giving practical proof of that conviction ; and he has already advanced a good step on the way of State Socialism, in which he and thousands of thinking men with him alone see hope for the future of society and civilisation, whether in Germany or elsewhere. The task of pacifying the working classes will not be accomplished in a short time. The roots of the evils existing go too deep for that. Even if success ultimately attend the Chancellor's efforts, it can only be expected after many years, and, it may be added, after the policy of coercion has been abandoned. For the Socialist Law must be pronounced an absolute failure if the vast growth of the Social-Democratic party since 1878 can be regarded as a proof of failure. But the worst of coercion is that when it is once begun, it is difficult to stop, since stopping would be to admit defeat, and to give to those from whom the pressure is relaxed, direct encouragement to persist in their aims. And yet it is questionable whether Prince Bismarck could make a wiser move than to gradually relinquish exceptional legislation and to try to meet the Socialists with the telling argument of social reform. The *Begründung* to the Socialist Law said, " Thought cannot be repressed by external compulsion," and the history of nearly ten years of coercion has proved the truth of this.

Whatever opinion we may after full consideration form of the Chancellor's internal policy, we must allow to the man himself the virtue of sincerity, a virtue not always characteristic in these days of the public acts of statesmen. Further, philanthropy and charity demand that we shall wish him success in the great undertaking upon which he has embarked, an undertaking whose objects are none less than the removal of the wrongs of a vast and ever-increasing class, and the restoration of social peace to a great country.

> " Holder Friede,
> Süsse Eintracht,
> Weilet, weilet
> Freundlich über diesem Land."

W. H. D.

February, 1888.

GERMAN SOCIALISM.

CHAPTER I.

HISTORICAL BASIS OF THE GERMAN SOCIALIST MOVEMENT.

GREAT national movements never attain maturity in a day or a year. Their progress is avalanche-like, gradual, steady, and often imperceptible, "without haste yet without rest," like the march of the stars. Now and then, indeed, strong currents of national feeling carry vast bodies of men and women along with irresistible force, but movements of this kind generally succumb to their own vehemence and passion, and in ninety-nine cases out of a hundred they are short-lived, and fail wholly or in part to fulfil their purposes. Movements which appear and disappear in this abrupt fashion cannot be said to be national in the fullest sense of the word. They indicate a nation's moods rather than its real character ; they may even belie its real character, as the foam the colour of the stream. On the other hand, movements which go right to the heart of a people, which remould its mind, and become part of its very life and being, are slow of growth, yet the slowness of maturity is itself a sign of vigour and an earnest of long life. Such movements alone deserve to be regarded as really national, and in this category falls the Socialist movement in Germany, as well as the Democratic movement in England. Movements of this kind create new eras. But before a new era can dawn countless events must have led up to it ; various forces must have been at play, whose work, often done unseen and in quiet, could have had no other result than the inauguration of a fresh order of things. One social system has its day and is followed by another—which, however, is not necessarily an improvement upon the past—but the new system is born of the old and is not an independent, unconnected growth. In social evolution as in nature, nothing is done *per saltum.* These considerations should be carefully borne in mind in investigating a subject like that of Socialism.

How, then, did Socialism originate in Germany? The causes may be grouped into three classes according as they are philosophical, political, and economical. Though, however, the influence of men like Fichte and Hegel was of great importance during the first half of the century in determining the views of many leading German Socialists now dead—and notably those of Karl Marx and Ferdinand Lassalle—the principal impetus came from political and economic factors, whose operation may be said to have begun with this century. Yet, again, purely economical movements played a part quite secondary to that played by political. Indeed, it will be safe to say that German Socialism owes its existence above all to the political movements which fell to the period between the Napoleonic conquest and the constitutional struggles of 1848 to 1850. From first to last the economic phase of the question has been secondary to the political, for political demands have been constantly kept in the foreground. That this is the case will be clearly seen as we trace the progress of the Socialistic idea. It is customary to look upon the French Revolution of last century as the starting point of modern developments in political and civil liberty. How far this is just to the influence wrought upon the European mind by the English Revolution of the seventeenth century and the American Revolution of 1775 is a question foreign to our purpose. But at the time a new gospel was being preached in France amid thunder, lightning, and tempest, Germany was not ready for the reception of doctrines intended to revolutionise society. Generations of absolute rule, strife within and without, absolute chaos in territorial arrangements, had taken much of the spirit out of her peoples. The States were like the disjointed links of a shattered chain. Even Prussia, if strong as a military power, was weak in so far as her population lacked the qualifications essential to a robust and intelligent national life. Thus political principles which inspired the ardent French mind with passion did not arouse in the German mind the barest enthusiasm. Allowance must, of course, be made for national characteristics. With all his love for the mystical and the theoretical, the Teuton is no wild visionary, and much less is he by nature revolutionary. This fact goes far to account for the meagre success which incendiary doctrines and violent movements have always enjoyed in Germany, and for the shortness of their ascendency even when they may have gained the upper hand. To the thoughtful student of German social questions, perhaps the most remarkable feature of the present Socialist movement is the fact that an earnest agitation in which a million men are concerned is carried on in absolute peace and almost without a hint at violence—making exception for casual rhetorical vapourings, which mean nothing— and that in spite of circumstances which would not fail to incite less phlegmatic natures to acts of fierce retaliation. The pacific progress of Socialism in Germany is not only a fact of importance historically, but it is one encouraging to all who hope for a satis- factory settlement of difficulties which may now appear to defy solution.

Yet another factor must be considered in explaining the slight direct effect produced in Germany by the French convulsions of last century, and that is the social condition of the people. The extremes of wealth and poverty were not then what the development of industry has since made them. Germany was behindhand as an industrial country. While England had been revolutionising industry, Germany had been revolutionising philosophy. The capitalistic system, to use a favourite expression of the Socialists, did not properly exist. Paternal govern- ment, with its guilds and legal institutions for restricting individual action, and for adjusting the relationships of man with man, had done a great deal to delay the era of the " great industry " in Germany, and the class of small independent handicraftsmen continued numer- ous there, after it had dwindled into insignificant proportions in England. The standard of life was altogether lower than now, and the labouring classes were on the whole worse off, but on the other hand the distance between the social status of the employer and that of the dependent workman was far less than to-day. The industrial workman was miserably situated, but he was fairly satis- fied with his condition, which he had learned to regard as suited to his class. All the aspiration he cared to indulge was centred in the hope that he might end his days as he had begun them, and that his children might not fare worse than himself. Similarly, the rural labourers, living in serfdom, were in an unhappy state, but here again there was no memory of happier days to gall them and to put salt into their wounds, and their social condition was at least not worse than their political.[1]

Even if Germany had offered a fertile soil for the doctrines which were proclaimed in 1789, events soon followed which were for a time discouraging to the growth of a free spirit. The new century brought to Germany misfortune after misfortune, until at last she lay at the feet of a relentless conqueror, exhausted and bleeding at every pore. But the darkest hour is that which precedes the dawn. The year after Prussia was vanquished and trodden to the dust at Jena, there was inaugurated in that country a series of legislative reforms which did more than all succeeding military successes to regenerate the nation and create a new and higher spirit of patriotism and independence. The Stein[2] and Hardenberg[3] laws—emancipating the rural population, granting modified freedom in the choice of crafts, introducing peasant proprietorship and a form of self-government, abolishing freedom from taxation, and in short sweeping away feudal rights and privileges—did all their authors expected of them, for they put Prussia upon a new footing and gave her a new lease of life.[4] In a peaceful way these radical reforms did

---

[1] Baron vom Stein writes in a letter to Frau von Berg, April 22nd, 1802 : "I have travelled through Mecklenburg. The appearance of the country displeased me as much as the cloudy northern climate: great fields, of which a considerable part lies in pasture and fallow, extremely few people, *the whole labouring class under the pressure of serfdom*, the fields attached to single farms seldom well-built ; in one word a uniformity, a deadly stillness, a want of life and activity diffused over the whole, which oppressed and soured me much. The abode of the Mecklenburg nobleman, *who keeps down his peasants instead of improving their condition*, strikes me as the lair of a wild beast, who desolates everything around him and surrounds himself with the silence of the grave." Seeley's " Life and Times of Stein," vol. i., p. 132 (Cambridge, 1878).

[2] Baron Heinrich Friedrich Karl vom Stein, one of Germany's greatest statesmen and patriots, born October 26th, 1757, at Nassau. He entered the service of the Prussian State in 1780 and helped more than anyone else to rekindle the national spirit during the time Prussia lay at the feet of Napoleon I. On the signing of the Peace of Paris he withdrew to his estates and died July 29th, 1831, at his castle of Kappenberg, in Westphalia. A statue of Stein, erected by a " grateful fatherland," stands in one of Berlin's squares.

[3] Karl August Prince von Hardenberg, a worthy colleague of Stein in the regeneration of Prussia, was born at Essenrode, May 31st, 1750. As a diplomat and statesman he played a prominent part in the history of Germany during the years 1791 to 1815. He died on the way to Genoa, November 26th, 1822

[4] Theodor von Schön, who travelled in England in 1798, found our agricultural population infinitely superior to the Prussian land-serfs. He writes : " It was through England that I became a statesman. Where the labourer, busy among the cabbages, called out to me in

for Prussia what the Revolution of 1789 did for France ; they sounded the knell of a feudalism which had for centuries kept a large part of the population in servitude.[1]   At last the Liberation Wars ended triumphantly, and the French yoke was thrown off.   During these exhausting wars the German princes had repeatedly promised to their subjects a wide extension of civil liberty, but few of them redeemed the promise.   Some of the South German States, like Bavaria and Baden, received all they had bargained for, but the rest—including Prussia, whose King, Frederick William III., had solemnly undertaken to give his people a constitution[2]—were more or less bitterly deceived. The old police *régime* was continued, the printing press was subjected to stringent control, and popular liberty was gradually hemmed into the old limits ; the disturbed absolute State was, in fact, revived.   In some places the press censorship was so severe that even visiting cards could not be printed until the signature of the censor had been obtained.   The citizens of Berlin were not allowed to smoke in the streets, and when one of the newspapers ventured to suggest that the prohibition might be removed from the adjoining Thiergarten, it

exultation that he had read that my King (Frederick William III.) was about to join the coalition against France along with England—there you have, in the truest sense of the word, public life." Seeley's " Life and Times of Stein," vol. i., p. 376.

[1] " It is impossible not to see that the legislation begun by Stein and afterwards continued by Hardenberg was similar in its durable results to the work of the French Revolution.   It accomplished changes of the same kind and comparable in extent, though by a perfectly regular process." *Ibid.*, vol. ii. p. 173.

The events of this period did not fail to produce popular literature applauding the emancipating measures.   A curious little work was published early in 1808—of course anonymously —with the sufficiently explanatory title, " Der Adel, was er ursprünglich war, was er jetzt ist, und was er künftig seyn soll ; Ein Angebinde zum Geburtstage aller *ächtadlichen* Herren und Damen, insbesondere auch für die Herren von Jena und Auerstädt." (" The nobility, what it was originally, what it is now, and what it should be in future.   A birthday present for all really noble gentlemen and ladies, and particularly for the gentlemen of Jena and Auerstädt.")   The motto is :

" When Adam delved and Eve span
   Where was then the nobleman ? "

[2] On May 22nd, 1815, King Frederick William published an ordinance decreeing that a National Assembly should be formed out of the Provincial Estates, to which end a commission " composed of intelligent public officials and residents of the Provinces" should " without loss of time " be appointed to undertake " the organisation of the Provincial Estates, the organisation of the Representatives of the Country, the elaboration of a written Constitution according to the principles laid down."   Seeley doubts the wisdom of Hardenberg in pledging the king to so much at a time inauspicious to constitutional reform.   At any rate the scheme fell to the ground.   See Seeley's " Life and Times of Stein," vol. iii., part ix., chapter 1.

received orders to preserve silence upon the subject for the future. In-dependence had been won for the nation, but the individual was still unfree. But worse days than ever came for the democratic cause after the political murder of Kotzebue[1] by Karl Sand[2] in 1819. The Prussian Minister-President is said to have exclaimed, when he heard of the Mannheim assassination, "Now a constitution is impossible." The Governments hardened their hearts, and a perfect crusade against democratic movements took place, the starting-point being the Karlsbad resolutions of August and September, which marked the high-water level of the reaction. And yet, in spite of coercion and repression, the aspiration for deliverance grew. One of the "sweet uses" of adversity was to give the oppressed a higher estimate of free citizenship. But there was no organisation, no concerted action—this was out of the question—and for want of union the growing democratic tendencies required long years to their fructification.

Thus it was that the Paris revolution of July, 1830, found the German democracy with lamps out and with cruses dry. The suddenness and violence of the storm, however, did not fail to produce a considerable impression. Baden, Wurtemberg, Bavaria, Hanover, Brunswick—where the reigning duke was deposed—Saxony, and Hesse showed signs of uneasiness. Prussia, however, remained quiet. Here a succession of peaceful years, good if illiberal government, moderate taxation, and a popular king had brought the people into such a frame of mind that hazardous experiments were thought unwise, and the general feeling was one of tolerant satisfaction with the existing state of affairs. At one time it appeared as though Germany would escape serious convulsion. The demands advanced in the States affected by the revolutionary spirit were as a rule very moderate, extending merely to the requirement that constitutions should be granted where they did not exist and be observed where they did. The Federal Diet, however, fanned what had only been smouldering embers into alarm-

[1] August F. F. von Kotzebue, a fertile writer of comedies, born May 3rd, 1761, at Weimar. He was for years in the Russian service, first as administrator and then as political spy, in which latter capacity he lived at Weimar and Mannheim 1817 to 1819. He was stabbed at Mannheim by Sand on March 23rd, 1819, as an enemy of Germany.

[2] Karl Ludwig Sand, born October 5th, 1795, at Wunsiedel, a theological student and a fanatical patriot. After assassinating Kotzebue he tried to take his own life, but did not succeed. He was executed at Mannheim, May 20th, 1820. That Sand was prompted to his murderous deed by religious and patriotic zeal cannot be doubted, but murder is murder, and he died on the scaffold.

ing flames. Meeting at Frankfort-on-Main on November 25th, 1830, it adopted resolutions declaring it to be the duty of every Government to give military help to its neighbours when called upon, restricting the freedom of the Press further than before, and urging the various executives to be chary of surrendering to the revolutionary elements in the population. The measures taken on the strength of these resolutions worked well for a time, and the hour of danger seemed to have passed away, when the Polish revolution broke out, and it was found necessary to adopt a still sharper coercive policy. On October 27th, 1831, the Diet by resolution refused to receive petitions in the future, and prohibited the collection of signatures for the same. Having thus guarded itself against the possibility of popular appeal, it followed a fortnight later with a series of stringent measures, including the complete crippling of the Press. These measures aroused earnest opposition in some of the Diets of South Germany—those of Bavaria, Baden, and Wurtemberg in particular—but the Bundestag looked on with perfect indifference. Finally the dissatisfaction of the disaffected Houses expressed itself in a threat to refuse taxes, and then a course still more extreme was taken. The Federal Diet issued on June 28th, 1832, six ordinances declaring the inability of the estates to withhold the granting of taxes, and upholding the integrity of the Federation, the Bundestag, and the federal sovereigns. The effect of the ordinances was to restrict the authority of the Diets very considerably and to proportionately increase the power of the Bundestag. Popular liberties were entirely destroyed. Protests rose in all parts of the country, but they were without result, for the Governments at once proceeded to give effect to the federal decisions. It was a conspiracy between the Bundestag and the Governments to manacle the elected Chambers and to prevent agitation and the free expression of objectionable views. In some parts of Germany harsh measures were adopted against not alone revolutionary, but advanced Liberal leaders, and the Press was treated with scant courtesy, suppression, confiscation and menace becoming the order of the day.

There is no doubt that the Bundestag and the Federal Governments were themselves responsible for the revolutionary flame which now blazed in various parts of the country. Had a policy of moderation and concession been adopted at the first, it is probable that all difficulties would have been tided over, but temperate counsels were unfortunately unheeded, and when once the hand had been placed to the plough there was no looking back. At last the more fiery members of the revolutionary party determined to make a final effort to kindle insurrection. Confiding in the readiness of the nation to turn upon its unconstitutional rulers, they founded the *Vaterlandsverein* at Frankfort as a centre of agitation and secret conspiracy. The association was joined by South German Radicals, North German students, German refugees living in France, and Polish emigrants, and the end in view was a general revolution in which the Bundestag should be overturned and a German Republic should be proclaimed. The great scheme miscarried ; all that came of it was an outbreak of insignificant proportions at Frankfort on April 3rd, 1833, followed by the wholesale punishment of participants and suspected conspirators, many of whom, however, fled the country. It was evident that past measures had been insufficient to grapple with the revolutionary spirit that was rife, and now, at the convocation of Prince Metternich, a congress of Ministers was held at Vienna during the winter of 1833-1834, and a series of still harsher measures was resolved upon. The Press was placed under stricter censorship, the universities were subjected to control, freedom of speech and publicity of debates were restricted in the Chambers, and the ordinances of the Governments were given the force of law. Repression of this kind may curb men in their acts and the outward expression of the convictions which are in them, but it is seldom successful in curbing the spirit that prompts to action. It was so in this case. The coercive policy was diligently pursued and quieter times followed, but the democratic movement won a moral victory, even though its practical ends were apparently defeated.

What is known as the German Socialist movement dates, however, —if a date must be fixed—from the year 1848. All that preceded was preparatory, but in 1848 Germany may be said to have formally opened her doors to Socialism. It was then that the working classes, —the great *proletariat* which was henceforth to play such an inportant part in the country's political and social history—first learned their power. Until then they had been like an untried Samson, having giant strength, but strength potential and not yet displayed. They were at last to discover what could be done by union. The results achieved by the popular party during the struggles of 1848 to 1850, fell, it is true, far short of expectations, but the significance of what occurred in these years consisted less in the positive successes won by the democracy than in the important lesson learned by the rulers, that the democracy was a power which could no longer be underrated, and much less be overlooked. The effects of this lesson can be traced in all the subsequent political history of Germany and above all of Prussia. It would obviously be out of place to follow all the events which filled the momentous period in Germany's history which extended from 1848 to 1850, and yet the chronicles of the time cannot be altogether passed over. Prussia took the lead in the popular movements which now excited the nation. King Frederick William III. died in June, 1840, and when his son Frederick William IV. came to the throne universal hopes of better days for liberty were entertained. These hopes were strengthened when the king declared that, having as Crown Prince been the first nobleman in the land, he intended as king to be the first citizen ; and moreover gave a definite promise of various reforms. But it was not long before these pleasant expectations were dispelled. As a man, Frederick William IV. had many very good points ; as a king, he had many bad ones. He early displayed a vacillation and a love of mysticism and unpractical theorising in the art of government which boded ill for the aspirations of his subjects. No one doubts that the king meant well when he sought to realise a Christian State, a sort of *civitas Dei* adapted to modern requirements, but all the same his experiments were mischievous. Seven years after his accession the king, in his own way, redeemed the promise of his father to grant a constitution. " Am I not bound as an honourable man,' he wrote to one of his Ministers in 1845, "to fulfil what my father promised ? " But the views of the king and of the nation on constitutional questions were very different. A charter of February 3rd, 1847, made out of the Provincial Estates a United Diet, but its powers were only nominal, and the king let it be known that he had no intention of relinquishing his claim to divine right. " I feel bound," he said in a speech of the following April, " to make the solemn declaration that no power on earth shall move me to convert the natural relationship between sovereign and people—with us especially so powerful because of its inner truth—into a conventional, constitutional relationship, and that I will neither now nor ever allow a written paper to interpose like a second providence between our

Lord God in heaven and this land, in order by its paragraphs to govern us and to replace the sacred fidelity of old." A declaration like this was not likely to give satisfaction to those who had for years been striving after constitutional government, and had hitherto remained quiet in the belief that royal pledges, if long in fulfilment, would eventually be redeemed in full. Nor was such a declaration of the divine authority of absolutism at all calculated to have a pacifying effect if times of ferment came again.

Ten months later, such times came. In February 1848, the City of Insurrection, as Carlyle has called Paris, gave once more to the friends of revolution a signal for activity. The barricades were thrown up, the Tuileries fell into the hands of the populace, the gaols were opened, the city was given over to anarchy, Louis Philippe, the Citizen King, abdicated, and a Republic was proclaimed. The effect of this new outburst of insurrection was felt all over Europe. Thrones tottered or tumbled, and kings trembled or fled. In Germany hardly one person in a hundred had any inclination to take part in revolutionary designs, but a powerful influence was produced on all political parties, extreme and moderate alike. The first thought of many of the lesser sovereigns was that of escaping with a whole skin, and so in some of the minor States terms were speedily concluded with the revolutionary agitators, whose demands, after all, were not inordinate. In Prussia, however, blood was shed, and a settlement was far more difficult. Here the Government was called on to grant a free constitution and liberty of the Press. There was no demand as in Paris for a Republic ; all that was required in the German States was Monarchy firmly established upon a constitutional basis. There were, indeed, Republicans, but their number was small, and their voice was hardly heard. The Paris Revolution was followed by a week of perfect calm in Germany. Had the princes used that precious time wisely, very much of the succeeding trouble might have been averted, but the opportunity for compromise was frittered away, and only when the voice of discontent became angry and menacing, was the gravity of the situation recognised. On March 1st, the Bundestag issued a proclamation to the German people in which it spoke glibly of national unity, pretended to sympathise with the aspirations of the party of consolidation, and promised to promote national interests with greater zeal than in the past. The proclamation fell flat ; people only smiled satirically, for they had heard the same thing before. Petitions and addresses began to pour down upon sovereigns and Governments. The principal demands were constitutional government, freedom of religion and the Press, public administration of justice, right of meeting and of coalition, and universal military service with free choice of leaders. Nor were demands wanting on the part of the Prussian *proletariat.* A cry rose for the organisation of labour, for State guarantee of work for the unemployed masses, and for a Labour Ministry. All sorts of social reforms were spoken of. Some people wished for co-operative associations ; some desired organisations for shortening the hours of labour, for raising wages, and for the emancipation of women ; and yet others only saw salvation in savings banks and loan associations. Demands of this kind, however, were innocent ; it was the political movement which caused the Governments most alarm. The sovereigns of Bavaria, Baden, Brunswick, Hanover, Nassau, Saxony, Wurtemberg, and Prussia all yielded sooner or later to the force of circumstances, and granted or promised reforms, some far-going and all conceived in a liberal and democratic spirit. In Bavaria and the Grand Duchy of Hesse, however, there was a change of rulers. The Bavarian king had, indeed, alienated his subjects by his mad *amours,* and Louis I. was glad to give place to his son Maximilian II.[1] Saxony and Baden were also seriously affected, but the brunt of the revolutionary storm fell upon Prussia.

It soon became manifest that King Frederick William IV. was not a man capable of dealing with a severe national crisis. When a Berlin deputation waited upon him, he answered quite frankly, " When all around everything is boiling, I certainly cannot expect that in Prussia alone the popular temper will remain under freezing point." Nor did it, for the Berlin street fights, which have since borne the name of the March Revolution, formed one of the chief events of that troublous period. The Rhine Provinces gave the signal for insurrection, for there an agitation arose for connection with France in case great constitutional reforms were not adopted in Prussia. This move-

---

[1] Louis (Ludwig) I. of Bavaria, born August 25th, 1786, ascended the throne in 1825. He was a patron of art and science, and was favourably known as a poet, but his weak-minded devotion to the notorious Lola Montez turned the fidelity of his people into disgust. He died at Nice, February 29th, 1868. Maximilian II. reigned until 1864. He was born November 28th, 1811. His successor was the unhappy Louis II., his son, who met a tragic death in 1886

ment encouraged the party of discontent in Berlin. The Press was loud in its demand for constitutional changes and greater civil liberty. It was a time of popular meetings, demonstrations, deputations, addresses and petitions, but these were shortly to give place to bloody conflicts between the mob and the military. The king at last broke silence. Pressed on all sides, and heartily desirous to see the peace preserved, he issued, on March 14th, a Cabinet Ordinance in which he announced his desire to aid in the re-organisation of the confederation and to rule in a liberal spirit, and he also convened the United Diet for April 27th. Unfortunately for the king's designs, the Austrian help upon which he had relied was not to be had, for the day before the issue of the ordinance Metternich had fallen. But apart from this, the royal proclamation did not give pleasure to the democratic party. It required the nation to wait a while longer in patience, and the nation was already tired of waiting. The excitement in Berlin grew intenser than before, and the king was compelled to make further concessions. On March 18th, he published the famous proclamation in which he promised a constitution and freedom of the Press, convened the Diet for April 2nd, and proposed the re-organisation of Germany and the federation of the States on a new and more national basis. The populace became enthusiastic, and in the afternoon of this day a great assembly gathered before the Royal Castle, for the purpose of acknowledging the king's munificence. King Frederick William repeated his assurances, and the people answered with frantic cheering. All went well until the presence of a body of military was observed in the courtyard. Why was it there? Soldiers were out of place when a king was amongst his people. And so suspicion was excited, and while one part of the crowd called for the removal of the soldiers, another made them a butt for sarcasm and affront. This treatment enraged the infantry, and, accidentally or purposely, several shots left their ranks. No one was injured, but the scene soon became one of confusion and uproar. The cavalry stationed in the adjoining Lustgarten regarded the shots as a signal for action, and approached with the intention of clearing the streets. The people now believed that they were the victims of a pre-arranged plot, and while one set of voices loudly spoke of treachery, another cried, "To arms! The barricades!"

A time of anarchy and carnage was at hand, and it lasted until

dawn of the following day. The king passed the dreadful night of
Saturday, March 18th, in close deliberation with his Ministers, most of
whom were opposed to a policy of surrender, and strove to nerve the
irresolute monarch to determined resistance. But the king insisted
upon taking his own way, and on the morrow he issued a proclamation "To my dear Berliners," in which he prayed for the cessation
of hostilities. "Hear the paternal voice of your king, inhabitants of
my faithful and beautiful Berlin," said the desperate monarch, "forget what has happened, as I will from my heart forget it, for the sake
of the great future which will, with God's blessing of peace, open up
for Prussia, and through Prussia, for Germany. Your loving queen
and truly faithful mother and friend, who lies very ill, unites her sin-
cere and tearful entreaties with mine." A deputation of citizens
waited on the king in the forenoon, carrying the ultimatum of the populace, which was that the barricades would not be removed or arms be
laid down until the troops had been withdrawn from the city. The
monarch hesitated, but finally yielded to the popular demand, much to
the disgust of both his advisers and the military. Three hundred
persons had fallen to the fire of the troops during the struggles around
the barricades, and in order to humiliate the king still more the
popular leaders resolved to give distinguished burial honours to these
"heroes of the Revolution." The bodies, garlanded with flowers, but
with wounds displayed, were conveyed on cars or biers into the courtyard of the castle, and there the attendant mourners sang a dirge and
demanded the appearance of the king. Frederick William came forward as required, his consort on his arm, and baring his head before
the ghastly scene repeated all his promises once more, after which
the corpses were removed. Revolution had conquered in Berlin, and
both king and military lay prostrate before it. The Prince of Prussia,
who had been wrongly suspected of having commanded the guards in
the attacks on the populace, had meanwhile left Berlin on a "secret
mission" to London. When this became known the mob formed the
resolution of burning down his palace, with which the Royal Library
would have been destroyed. This idea was, however, abandoned,
and the more harmless one of declaring the building to be national
property was conceived. Accordingly "Nationaleigenthum" was
painted in large letters on the front of the palace, and everybody was
satisfied.

On the 20th, panic spread over Berlin again. Nothing had been seen of the guards, which had been withdrawn the previous day, and their absence gave rise to the fear that the king was meditating another surprise. People talked of a plan which had been detected of falling on Berlin ; and supposition soon passed into conviction. No one slept in Berlin that night. The cry " To arms," was raised anew, the barricades appeared once more, and when the sun rose on the morning of the 21st, it looked down upon a city armed and arrayed as for conflict. A very small matter would have sufficed to rekindle the smouldering embers of anarchy, but no soldiers came upon the scene, and the alarm passed gradually away. A strange scene was witnessed in Berlin that day, when Prussia declared herself to be the leader in the movement for the regeneration of Germany. In the forenoon, King Frederick William, accompanied by his Ministers, and a vast following of citizens and students, marched from the castle, and carrying German national colours—which adorned the castle, palace, and houses on the route—passed along the Linden. Here and there the king stopped and addressed the assembled populace on the purpose of the singular demonstration. Before the nationalised palace of the Crown Prince he said : " I bear colours which are not mine, but I usurp nothing thereby. I seek no crown, no dominion, and only desire Germany's unity, Germany's freedom, and order—that I swear to God. I have only done what has already often happened in German history : when order has been trodden under foot, powerful princes and dukes have seized the banner, and placed themselves at the head of the entire nation ; and I believe that the hearts of the princes will beat in unison with mine, and that the will of the nation will support me." There were voices which greeted this declaration with cries of " Long live the German Emperor ! " but the king rebuked all such ebullition of feeling. On the same day the king issued an " Appeal to my people and to the German nation," wherein he justified the step he had taken and laid down principles for a Prussian and a German constitution. " I have to-day assumed the old German colours," he said at the close of this interesting composition, " and have placed myself and my people under the venerable banner of the German Empire. Prussia is henceforth absorbed in Germany ! "

The burial of the victims of the street fights took place on March 22nd, and the procession to Friedrichshain was made up of members of the governing authorities, trades unions, guilds, the civic guard, municipal officials, students, and citizens, while half Berlin lined the road to the burial ground. The two hundred coffins had the day before been exhibited before the churches on the Gendarmenmarkt, and they were now conveyed with solemn pomp, and amid the strains of funeral marches and the flutter of innumerable banners, to the woody knoll which had been chosen as the last resting-place of Berlin's revolutionary martyrs. The procession passed the Royal Castle, from which, as from private houses, black banners hung, and the king with bared head looked down upon the weird scene from a balcony, giving, as it were, to the March Revolution a final mark of royal sanction. For several months Berlin continued in a state of extreme excitement. When the political demands were no longer thought to be in danger, the social aspect of the revolution became more conspicuous. The condition of the working classes was miserable to begin with, and the period of anarchy had made it still worse. In order to provide work for the unemployed the municipal authorities began undertakings involving large expenditure, though their value to the city was small. All sorts of excesses were committed, and for a time the Ministry felt powerless to grapple energetically with the forces of disorder. It was feared that any attempt to unduly curb the populace would lead to a renewal of the March horrors, and so small evils were tolerated in the hope of staving off great ones. At times rank mob-law prevailed. One day towards the end of May a crowd of some thousands of labourers flocked to the residence of the Labour Minister and demanded work. The bewildered Minister could not give an answer on the spur of the moment, and offered a gift of money, but this acted like oil upon flames. "We are not beggars," cried the excited mob, "we are free working-men ; we do not want alms, but work," and they refused to accept the gift. The difficulty was tided over by a compromise ; work was promised in three days' time, and as the unemployed were meanwhile without means they were lent money sufficient for the purchase of food. Events like this were of frequent occurrence. It was emphatically a time of ferment and insecurity, for none knew what the following day might bring forth. And still with the exception of a rude civil affray in October, the crisis passed away without further appeal to arms. The fire of insurrection gradually burnt itself out.

It is manifestly impossible to refer here to the efforts made at this time to reorganise Germany—to the proceedings of the National Assembly at Frankfort, which led to the election of the King of Prussia as "hereditary Emperor of the Germans," an honour declined, or to the measures taken by Prussia and Austria, separately and jointly, with a view to a new, if not a better federation—for these solely concern German constitutional history. Notice must, however, be taken of the several further risings which make up the revolutionary record of the time. On April 12th, 1848, Friedrich Hecker,[1] the chief member of the Opposition in the Baden Second Chamber, and a jurist held in high esteem, proclaimed a German Republic at Constance. The town was enthusiastic, but only twelve hundred persons were so zealous in their Republicanism that they were prepared to appeal to arms. Hecker led his followers forth, and on the 20th there was a collision with the Government troops at Kandern. The commander of the latter, General von Gagern, was shot dead, but the insurgents were compelled to take flight. Hecker escaped to Basel, and abandoned his ambitious scheme in disgust and despair. The struggle was, however, continued by Gustav von Struve,[2] who, supported by a handful of ill-armed men, boldly proclaimed the Republic at Freiburg on April 22nd. Two days later General Hoffmann fell on the town and drove the insurgents out with great loss. Meantime, Georg Herwegh,[3] a lyrical poet and an ardent Republican, had been endeavouring to raise reinforcements, but when his men had been dispersed at Dossenbach on the 27th by a party of Wurtemberg soldiers, the insurrection collapsed. The same month a Polish rising occurred

1 Friedrich Karl Franz Hecker, born at Eichtersheim, in Baden, September 28th, 1811, studied law at Heidelberg, and became an eminent jurist. As a member of the Second Chamber of Baden he acquired through his eloquence and popular sympathies a leading position, and on the revolution breaking out in 1848, he plunged into insurrectionary schemes. He took part in the American War of Secession.

2 Gustav von Struve, born October 11th, 1805, at Munich. He was first envoy's secretary at Frankfort, and later advocate at Mannheim. He early gave in adherence to the Republican party. When his attempts in Baden failed, he went to Switzerland and afterwards to America. In 1863 he returned to Germany, and he died in Vienna, August 21st, 1870.

3 Georg F. Herwegh, lyrical poet, born at Stuttgart, May 31st, 1817, and studied at Tübingen. He early joined the revolutionary movements in Germany and Switzerland, and for years lived in the latter country and in France as a political refugee. His last years were spent in Paris, South France, and Baden-Baden, where he died April 7th, 1875. He was a friend of Heine, Beranger, and George Sand. Herwegh was a German William Morris.

in Posen, but it was suppressed by Prussian troops. A second attempt to overturn the Government was made in Baden by Struve—Hecker had in the meantime gone to America—in September. During the night of the 20th-21st of that month Struve with five hundred men occupied the village of Lörrach and issued thence proclamations "in the name of the Provisional Government of Germany," one of which, beginning "German Republic! Prosperity, education, liberty for all!" declared the abolition of all military burdens and feudal services, personal and monetary; the forfeiting of all property in the hands of the State, the Church, and citizens taking the side of the princes, which property was provisionally to pass into the hands of the parishes in which it was situated; and furthermore announced that a progressive income-tax would take the place of all existing imposts, and that military service would be compulsory between the ages of eighteen and forty. At the head of three thousand adherents Struve left his village retirement in order to take possession of his new dominion, but General Hoffmann, now Minister of War, hurried with troops from Karlsruhe, and the insurgent leader withdrew to Staufen, which he prepared to barricade. On the 24th the Government troops were before the town, which was in a few hours reduced, and the rebels had to escape as best they could. Struve left Staufen when he saw that all was lost, and tried to raise a fresh band of followers. Arrived at Wehr, where the news of his defeat had preceded him, he was betrayed by men tempted by the reward offered by the Government, and was handed over to General Hoffmann.

An unimportant rising also took place at Dresden on May 3rd, 1849, the causes being the reaction and the arbitrary dissolution of the Chambers. The few troops which formed the garrison were overpowered, and King Frederick August was compelled to retire to Königstein. The revolutionary party formed a Provisional Government, at the head of which were Heubner, Todt, and Tschirner, Republican Deputies, but their incapacity spoiled any slight chance of success which the movement might have had. The king despatched troops to Dresden, and these being seconded by a small Prussian force, the rising was speedily put down. In the same month of 1849, Struve, released from prison, made a final attempt to bring Baden over to his side. At one time his prospects looked more favourable than before. The king's troops were defeated, a new Ministry was formed with the title of Executive Committee, and a treaty was concluded with the Palatinate—itself at the time convulsed—for unity. Hecker, the author of the first rising, was invited to return from America and take part in the Government, and he at once set out, but before he could arrive in Germany the revolution had been suppressed, and he, therefore, recrossed the ocean without delay. Prussian troops crushed the insurgents in the Palatinate by the end of June, though only after severe fighting, and the Baden revolution was quelled in the following month. The Prussian forces had suffered a total loss of over six hundred men and several officers. Many of the revolutionary leaders illustrated in their fate the saying of Mirabeau, "Ceux qui font les revolutions à moitié creusent leur tombe," for they were summarily tried by court martial, and shot for high treason.

What, then, were the results of this appeal to revolution? The immediate results were everywhere very small. In Prussia the promises made by King Frederick William IV. were not fulfilled, for directly popular passion subsided, the king's enthusiasm for constitutional reform disappeared. The insurrectionary outburst spent itself like the eruption of a recurrent volcano, yet all the same rulers and ruled had learned to know, if not to love, each other better for the struggle in which they had been engaged. The Prussian Diet met on April 2nd, 1848, and the Camphausen[1] Ministry laid before it proposals for a new constitution, the alleviation of Press restrictions, the granting of the right of meeting and full religious freedom, and the reform of the legal courts. These proposals were accepted, but after sitting a week the Diet was dissolved and a fresh assembly was called for May 22nd, for the revision of the constitution. A draft constitution was introduced, but it was rejected as being too aristocratic. The dispute between the king and the Diet was prolonged until the end of the year, and finally under the Brandenburg[2] Ministry, a constitution was promulgated on December 5th.

This constitution was liberal enough as it was introduced—provid-

1 Ludolf Camphausen, born January 3rd, 1803, near Aix-la-Chapelle; he withdrew from public life in 1849.

2 Count Friedrich Wilhelm von Brandenburg, born in Berlin, January 24th, 1792, son of King Frederick William II., from his morganatic union with the Countess von Dönhoff. Died vember 6th, 1850. His Ministry was called the *Galgen-Ministerium* (Gallows Ministry), ecause the final letters of the members' names together form the word *Galgen*: Brandenburg, Strotha, Manteuffel, Ladenberg, Pommer-Esche, and Rintelen.

ing for two elective chambers ; responsibility of Ministers to the Diet ; personal, religious, and Press freedom ; right of association ; equity before the law ; and independence and publicity in the administration of justice ; but the Government had no sooner made the offer than, like Pharaoh, it rued it. The constitution was again revised and expurgated until when finally promulgated on January 31st, 1850, it bore no resemblance to the original draft. To make matters worse for the democratic party, the king in taking the oath, six days later, declared that the constitution was not a right but a favour bestowed by the crown ; that the oath-taking—which was likewise an act of free will and not a royal duty—did not preclude the possibility of future revision ; and that all royal privileges, the divine office of the king, and the allegiance of the people remained unaltered ; while the constitution would necessarily have to give way if it were found to be incompatible with government. It was the same nearly everywhere. The pledges given were not redeemed in full, but in spite of this a tremendous impulse had been given to the advanced democratic movement, and Republicanism, Communism, and Socialism were no longer empty phrases only having a meaning for the few. Not even the powerful reaction which followed was able to efface the impression made upon the mind of Germany by the momentous events of 1848 and 1849.

It may be said that what has preceded is a chronicle of Anarchy and not of the growth of Socialism. But the truth is that revolution has throughout all history been a handmaid of great political and social developments. Socialism emerged from the convulsions and the ferment of these years as a fresh goal of popular aspirations. It was Socialism which remained after the earthquake, the tempest, and the fire had passed away. Succeeding events greatly stimulated the new movement. Politically the working-man became free, for the equality of all citizens in the eyes of the law passed from the region of theory to that of fact. The development of industry, however, exerted quite a contrary effect, for it perpetuated and increased the economic and social subjection of the labouring classes. The more the capitalist system was extended, the more social inequalities multiplied. The law made equal and capitalism made unequal. Thus the position of the labourer became ambiguous. As a citizen and a subject of the State he was perfectly free, sharing the civil rights of the wealthiest, but as a member of the community of industry he occupied

c

a position in reality dependent and unfree. It was inevitable that this anomalous condition of things should conduce to social discontent and class antagonism. The labourer saw his employer filling his money-bags, while he, the producer of wealth, was seldom able to earn more than covered his every-day needs. Before this time the working classes had in one part of the country expressed their dissatisfaction by serious riots and the destruction of industrial property. This was in Silesia, where in 1844 a rising of weavers took place, the immediate cause being want and misery. For many generations linen-weaving had been a prosperous industry in the Silesian mountain districts, and thousands of hand weavers were engaged until far into the second quarter of this century. Gradually, however, the power machine changed the whole character of the industry ; manufactories sprang up, and the house-weavers like Demetrius saw their craft taken away from them, or if they were able still to compete with the power-loom it was only by the acceptance of wages which scarcely procured them food. By the year 1844 the Silesian weavers were reduced to a condition of absolute despair. The wretched inhabitants of the mountain parts were only able to earn eighteen shillings for work which occupied them five or six weeks, each of ninety or a hundred hours' labour. At last they could bear their suffering no longer, and in the desperate hope of improving matters they rose against those whom they regarded as oppressors. As Carlyle wrote :

> " Hungry guts and empty purse
> May be better, can't be worse."

Factories were stormed, and in several places both buildings and machinery were utterly wrecked by enraged mobs. This violence might not have taken place had the manufacturers shown a more humane spirit, but many of them simply laughed at the misery of the supplanted weavers, and these men were singled out for exemplary punishment. The rising failed to accomplish any good result. A handful of military quelled the disturbances and a number of rioters were killed or wounded.

The industrial revolution which was effected in Silesia during the early part of the century took place in other parts of Germany, but the want suffered by the victims was not so intense as there. Never theless, the wages of labour were everywhere miserably low.[1] To take a few instances, the ordinary rates paid at Breslau up to 1850 were for textile factory operatives, 1s. for men, and 6d. to 7d. for women daily; for work-people in tobacco manufactories, 6s. to 7s. weekly for men, and 5s. 7d. to 6s. 7d. for women; in paper manufactories, 6s. 6d. to 7s. 6d. weekly for men; mechanics, 10s. 6d. to 12s. per week; day labourers, 10d. in summer and 7d. in winter daily; while printers earned as much as mechanics. The factory operatives had not, however, continuous employment, and they were only paid according to the time worked. In 1845 railway labourers received in Lower Silesia 3s. 7d. per week. It was found that a poor rural family, consisting of five persons, was only able to expend 16s. monthly on rent, food, local taxes, and school-money. A labourer of Eilenburg, in the province of Saxony, with wife and two children, had weekly receipts of 6s. 9d., and food alone cost 6s. 5d. On the Lower Rhine in the same year an operative could earn 9d. to 1s. 6d. per day, with irregular work, and a day labourer 8d. to 9d. In Bavaria wages were often still lower. In 1847 tailors, shoemakers, linen weavers, bakers, and joiners received 1s. 7d. to 2s. weekly, besides food and lodging, while butchers, glaziers, plasterers, and millers were better off with 2s. to 4s. Labourers received from £10 8s. to £13 yearly, and their household expenses amounted on a minimum calculation to more than the latter sum. On the land labourers could earn 8d or 10d. a day without food and lodging, and 6d. or 8d with. A herdsboy was worth 16s. to £1 a year with food and lodging, a maid £1 16s. to £3 12s., a hind £2 8s. to £6 with the same perquisites. A similar condition of things prevailed in Saxony, the Palatinate, Baden, and other States. Even in Berlin in 1857 skilled mechanics and artisans only received 12s. to 18s weekly, while masons received 2s. 3d. to 2s. 9d. a day, day labourers 1s. 2d. to 1s. 6d., though with piece work as much as 12s. and 18s. a week. Children up to sixteen years old were worth in the manufactories 7s. 6d. with long hours. The work done was generally exhausting, and the food which the wages allowed so insufficient that the life of the labourer was far shorter than that of more favoured people. Statistics of the years 1829 to 1839 for Dresden show that only 17 out of 100 members of the higher classes died before the age

[1] See appendix to "Die Arbeiterfrage und das Christenthum," by Bishop von Ketteler (Mayence, 1864.)

of 50 years, while 28 died amongst lower officials, 38 amongst day
labourers, 47 amongst tailors and shoemakers, 50 amongst cabmen,
55 amongst bookbinders, weavers, printers, and watchmakers, 58
amongst carpenters, 66 amongst joiners and glaziers, and 88 amongst
masons.   Statistics of the years 1820 to 1852 prove that in the same
place the average duration of life was as follows amongst various
classes : clergy, 65 years 11 months ; teachers, 56 years 10 months ;
tradesmen, 56 years 9 months; carpenters, 49 years 2 months ;
masons, 48 years 8 months; coopers, 47 years 6 months; shoemakers,
47 years 3 months ; joiners, 46 years 4 months ; smiths and lock-
smiths, 46 years 3 months ; tailors, 45 years 4 months ; stone-cutters,
compositors, type-founders, and pewterers, 41 years 9 months ; and
lithographers and engravers, 40 years 10 months.   The mortality
of Prussians was in general very high at this time compared with that
of the inhabitants of England or France.   Statistics for the years
1844 to 1853 show the following to have been the comparative
death rates : [1]

	Prussia. One in	England. One in	France. One in
1844	38·85	47·86	43·55
1845	36·73	43·36	45·29
1846	34·05	40.47	41·39
1847	31·59	43·37	40·22
1848	30·12	39·82	40·82
1849	32·74	38·15	35·25
1850	36·31	45·48	44·71
1851	37·82	44·72	42·77
1852	30·39	43·70	42·25
1853	32·76	42·52	43·02
Average	33·85	43·79	41·73

Living under such conditions it is not surprising that the working
classes became dissatisfied with their lot.   But what made this lot
still harder to bear was the fact that the capitalists were becoming
wealthier.   As the labourer compared the present with the past state
of society, he found that the rich had grown richer and the poor
relatively poorer.   How was this, and was it right?   Being an un-
lettered man he knew nothing of political economy, and was not

[1] " Bevölkerungsstatistik." Wappäus (Leipzig. 1859.)

aware that the principle of free competition, which made his labour a pure commodity purchasable for the cost of its production, claimed divine origin and might not be impugned. Ignorant of this, and only knowing that the capitalist grew wealthier while he himself made no progress, the labourer willingly heard of projects of social regeneration which promised to place the producer of wealth on a higher level of comfort. Many of the assurances held out to him were extravagant, and he knew it, but there was at least the possibility of gaining something. In any case he had nothing to lose by following this prophet, the social reformer, and so he became a devoted believer.

The development of industry and the increase of national wealth in Germany have thus been accompanied by the spread of Socialistic and Communistic doctrines. These are moments which must be placed alongside the influence of French thought and of German philosophical speculation, the convulsions of the first half of the century, the democratising of political institutions, and—with safety it may be said—the decline of religious belief.[1] All have gone together, all

[1] Speaking in the debate on the Socialist Bill in October, 1878, and alluding to the atheism prevalent amongst Socialists, Prince Bismarck declared that he would not desire to live a day longer if he had not what Schiller calls the " belief in God and a better future." " Rob the poor of that, for which you cannot compensate them," he added, " and you prepare them for the weariness of life which shows itself in acts like those we have experienced " (*i.e.*, the murderous attempts of Hödel and Nobiling upon the life of the Emperor William). Less near the mark, however, was the Chancellor when he attempted to explain away the spread of Socialism in the following manner (Reichstag, October 9th, 1878):—

" I do not wonder at it at all," he said. " A country with such mild laws, with such good-natured judges ; a country in which there is a conspicuous love for criticism—especially when it concerns the Government ; a country in which an attack on a Minister and the censure of a Minister are acts regarded in the same way as if we lived in the year 30 ; a country where the recognition of anything which the Government does brings a man immediately under suspicion of servility ; a country in which the bases of operations chosen by Socialism—the great towns —were very carefully prepared by the work of the Progressists, and in which the discrediting of our authorities and institutions had already reached a high point, owing to the Progressist agitation :—such a country was attractive. In short the Socialists found here a country in which they could say, ' Let us build tents here.' The Germans have a great inclination to discontent. I do not know whether anyone of us has known a contented fellow-countryman. I know very many Frenchmen who are completely satisfied with their lot and with their vicissitudes. When they take up a craft they set before themselves the task of attaining, if possible, by the age of forty-five or fifty, a certain competence, and if they succeed their only ambition is to retire and live independent for the remainder of their days as *rentiers*. But compare the German with the French : his ambition is not directed towards the enjoyment of a moderate income after his fiftieth year, his ambition is boundless. The baker will not merely be the most well-to-do baker in the town ; no, he will own a house, and he desires like his great Berlin ideal to be eventually a banker and a millionaire. This is a characteristic

have played their parts, and contributed to the great Socialist movement which to-day agitates Germany.

which has its good side : it is the German assiduity which never fixes its goal too near ; but
so far as contentment in the State is concerned, it has a very dangerous aspect, especially as
regards the lower classes of officials.   Where is the official who does not wish, in the education
of his children, to take them a step higher than he has gone himself ?   The consequence of
this discontent is that a large part of our subordinate officials are infected with the disease
of Socialism."

CHAPTER II.

EARLY SOCIALISTIC AND COMMUNISTIC THEORISTS.

MUCH of the Communistic and Socialistic literature which was published in Germany during the first half of this century has been lost sight of and forgotten, owing to the perfect inundation of works which has followed since Socialism became a great power in the State. In order, however, to a proper comprehension of this subject, and to a right estimation of latter-day Socialists, it is necessary to learn something of the theories advanced and the work done by the early champions of Socialism in Germany. Passing over Fichte, who, though a philosophical Socialist of revolutionary views, can hardly be said to have exerted great influence as such upon the thought of his day,[1] the leading authors of this school during the first half of the century are found to be Karl Rodbertus, Karl Marx, Friedrich Engels, Heinrich von Thünen, and Karl Marlo (Professor Winkelblech), to whom may be added one of the early captains in the camp of Communism, Wilhelm Weitling, a German refugee, who lived long in Switzerland. As the first two of these writers will require extensive notice, it will be convenient to overlook them for the present.

[1] In 1793 Fichte wrote in " Beiträge zur Berichtigung des Urtheils über die französische Revolution " : " He who will not work may, indeed, eat if I choose to give him something, but he has no legally valid claim to eat. He should not employ the powers of another for himself. Every man possessed originally the right of appropriating raw material, and thus the right of possession was introduced." In his work " Der geschlossene Handelsstaat," (Tübingen, 1800), Fichte develops a complete Socialistic State system. This small work Fichte begins with the remark that while the opinion that the State should be the absolute guardian of man, making him "happy, rich, healthy, orthodox, virtuous, and, if God will, eternally blessed," has been sufficiently controverted, on the other hand the new version of the State's duties and rights is too limited. Fichte defines the province of the State to be the allotment to its members of the property they may call their own and the protection of all in their possessions. He takes the standpoint of equal rights. Every member of society claims to live as comfortably as possible, and as no man is more a man than his fellows, all have equal rights in making this claim. Fichte knew as well as anyone that his Socialist State was ideal and could never be realised. In his dedication to Herr von Struensee, a Prussian Minister of State, he admits the likelihood that his scheme will be " without result in the practical world," and says he will be contented if his work only leads others to reflect upon the subject it handles.

JOHANN HEINRICH VON THÜNEN.

Taking the other authors in chronological sequence, the first to be noticed is Johann Heinrich von Thünen, of Jeverland, who lived 1783-1850. He was the son of a landed proprietor, and became himself the owner of a large estate near Rostock. He was early intended for the pursuit of agriculture, and his studies at home and at Göttingen University were directed to that end. Political economy became his favourite study, and in 1826 he published the first volume of his classical work, " Der isolirte Staat."[1] It is still a matter of debate how far Von Thünen was a Socialist, but many of the opinions to which he gives expression are of a decidedly advanced nature. Thus, over sixty years ago, he complains that the remuneration of every industrial undertaker is far too high in proportion to the share of profits which falls to the labourer ; and writing at a time when constitutional government could not be said to exist in Germany, he pleads earnestly for the representation of the working-classes in the Legislature.

In a letter written to a relative in 1830 Von Thünen tells how, during a recent conversation on social questions, the future seemed suddenly to open out to him, and " I saw in the coming centuries another frightful struggle begin, which required for its completion perhaps five hundred years of ruin and misery. I mean the struggle between the educated middle-class and the common people, or more properly between the capitalist and the artisan. In the present crisis all is certainly done *through* the people, but nothing *for* the people. Only the middle-class has acquired rights, and can defend these rights in the future, while the artisan has nowhere obtained admission to the Legislature, and thus he cannot even maintain his present degree of culture."[2] An interesting passage in one of his private letters shows, too, how earnestly he studied social questions. Writing in 1830 he says :

" All writers on political economy are agreed that the sum of the means of subsistence necessary to the maintenance of life is the natural wages of labour. Science necessarily governs the opinion of all men, and so we find that all Governments and all legislative re-

---

[1] "Der isolirte Staat in Bezug auf Landwirthschaft und Nationalökonomie," (vol. i., Hamburg, 1826, Rostock, 1842 : vol. ii., 1850.)
[2] "Johann Heinrich von Thünen : ein Forscherleben,' by H. Schumacher (Rostock, 1868.)

presentatives embrace this principle, and every endeavour after higher wages is regarded and punished as sedition. Man is never more terrible than when he is in error : he can then be unjust and cruel, and his conscience is quiet because he believes he is doing his duty. But will the people ever share the view of the political economists ? Will they become convinced that the frightful inequality in the remuneration of mental and physical work, and of the services of capital, is founded in the nature of the case ? Excited by such considerations, and regarding the subject as from this point of view one of the greatest importance, I was driven with such force back to my former investigations, continued for some years, into the relation between interest and wages, that for four weeks I could think of nothing else, though my health suffered seriously as a consequence. At last the longed-for light broke on me, and great was the reward of my exertions."

Writing on August 20th, 1846, he tells how he endeavoured to do something practical for the working class : " On August 4th we left Marienbad. The afternoon previously we paid a visit to Privy Councillor of Justice von Voss. I felt it a sacred duty to lay my views on the lot of the working class before this opulent man. At first it was impossible to give the conversation this turn, and when Minister von Uhden and a Privy Councillor entered the room every prospect seemed to have disappeared. I then felt suddenly filled with a holy anger : putting modesty aside I spoke up and said what I had to say."

More than all, Von Thünen proved his own faith in his precepts by adopting upon his Tellow estate the system of profit-sharing, which was a great benefit to his labourers. He died September 22nd, 1850.

Von Thünen's inquiries led him to the conclusion that the wages of a labourer only cover the costs of his maintenance, and the interest on the capital employed in his bringing up : for his labour, his exertion, he receives nothing but his life, *i.e.*, his necessary subsistence. " For this price," he writes, " the capitalists can always maintain labourers, and enjoy the fruits of their labour. As the labour of the slave only costs the master his support and the interest on his cost-price ; as the work of a machine only costs the manufacturer the cost of maintenance and the interest on its cost-price, so the labour of the free man only costs the capitalist the man's food and the interest on the capital which his bringing-up has required."[1]   This state of things Von Thünen regards as revolting, and he explains it by the supremacy of capital, which makes the labourer a tool in the hands of the employer.   For twenty-five years this thoughtful student investigated the problems of rent and wages, and he regarded it as the great achievement of his life that he found what he termed the *naturgemässer* (as opposed to the *natürlicher*) *Arbeitslohn* (wages) to be the square of wages and production so long as there is still land which can be occupied and cultivated.[2]   He writes : "If the maintenance of a labouring family during a year = A bushels of rye, and the yearly produce of the family's labour = P bushels of rye, then the *naturgemässer Arbeitslohn* (the wages that are according to nature) = $\sqrt{AP}$.   Here man appears as the lord of creation : what he can win from nature by his labour is his property.   Capital itself is a product of labour, and the remuneration which the capitalist receives is only wages from earlier performed labour."[3]   Von Thünen thinks that the only way to raise the wages of labour is to increase the cost of bringing up the labourer, and thus he advocates the better education and training of the workman's children, the requisite cost being regarded as an indispensable need.   At the same time he imposes the condition that the labourer shall not marry until he possesses the means of bringing up a family.   The result of this arrangement will be a diminished supply of labourers and higher wages.   He seeks, in fact, to hasten the era of reason.   The labouring classes must learn that the remedy for their unfortunate condition lies largely with themselves, for it is at bottom a question of population.   "The Isolated State" was greatly valued by Karl Rodbertus, who wrote on September 29th, 1840, that the oftener he read it the more invaluable it became to him. The work continues to be regarded as a classical hand-book to the study of questions connected with the cultivation of the land.

WILHELM WEITLING.

A very noteworthy figure in the early history of German Communism was that of Wilhelm Weitling, born in 1808 at Magdeburg, the son of

[1] " Der isolirte Staat," part ii., p. 415, (edit. 1863).
[2] Von Thünen's definition of rent is as follows : " What remains from the revenues of an estate after deduction of the interest on the value of the buildings, stock of timber, enclosures, and all objects of value which can be separated from the soil, I call land-rent."
[3] " Der isolirte Staat," vol. ii., p. 7.   " $\sqrt{AP}$ " is engraved on Von Thünen's gravestone.

a soldier. Weitling, who was poorly educated, but possessed considerable natural gifts, was apprenticed to a tailor, and as a journeyman he travelled through Germany during six or seven years. Living at Leipzig in 1830 he entered heartily into the political movements of the time, and attempted to gain entrance for his advanced views in a local newspaper, but his advances were generally received with coldness. He next went to Vienna, and finally removed in 1837 to Paris, Germany having become too warm for him. Before this he had once visited the French capital for a short time, and he now remained in France nearly four years. At this time the theories and systems of Fourier and Cabet were exciting much interest, and it is only natural that the current controversies should have set Weitling thinking. His thinking led to writing, and in 1838 he published his first work with the title, "Die Menschheit wie sie ist und wie sie sein sollte" (" Mankind as it is and as it should be "), the cost being borne by the German Socialists in Paris. In the summer of 1841 Weitling proceeded to Geneva for the purpose of carrying on an agitation which might produce more results than any efforts exerted in Paris could do, and in the September following he issued the first number of a Communistic magazine, " Hülferuf der deutschen Jugend " (" Cry for help of German youth"). The motto of this monthly print was " Against the interest of individuals in so far as it injures the interest of all, and for the interest of all without excluding one individual," and the theories advanced were, as might be expected, very far-going. Not only did Weitling agitate by means of the Press, but he formed Communist Associations in various parts of Switzerland, in spite of the opposition of the Government, which from the first kept a vigilant eye upon him. In 1842 appeared his " Garantien der Harmonie und Freiheit "(" Guarantees of Harmony and Freedom"), the tone of which is revolutionary, and three years later he published " Das Evangelium eines armen Sünders," ("The Gospel of a Poor Sinner"). In the latter work no fewer than a hundred passages are quoted from Scripture as furnishing justification for radical proposals of social reform.

Before this time, however, Weitling had taxed the patience of the authorities to the utmost, and early in June, 1843, his house was searched with a view to the discovery of compromising documents. The police found copies of "Guarantees," and also a portion of the manuscript of the still unpublished " Gospel." He was imprisoned, and in September was brought before the Zurich Criminal Court. The charges against him were that he had, in the works referred to, made himself guilty of blasphemy and attacks on property, and that he had founded associations for the propagation of Communistic doctrines. Weitling did not deny any of his principles ; on the contrary, he freely admitted that he was a Communist, and added that he had been made so by the study of the New Testament. The sentence of the court was six months' imprisonment—less two months already suffered, though the Crown Solicitor proposed a year and a half—and lifelong expulsion from Switzerland. The result of an appeal against this sentence was the addition of four months to the term of imprisonment and the reduction of the term of expulsion to five years.[1] Weitling's agitation in Switzerland was at an end. He tried residence in Berlin and Hamburg, and agitated zealously in both places until the police compelled him to take flight. Eventually he left the country in 1849 and after a brief residence in England crossed the Atlantic. Following the example of Cabet, he endeavoured to give practical effect to his Communistic theories, and indeed succeeded in founding a colony with the name Communia in Wisconsin. Its existence was, however, short and inglorious. Proceeding to New York he secured a situation as clerk, and for years pursued a more or less uneventful career, dividing his leisure time between political agitation and the study of astronomy. He died in New York on January 25th, 1871, three days after having taken part in a reunion of German, English, and French members of the International Association in that city. Wilhelm Weitling may rightly be called the Father of German Communism.[2]

Weitling, whose Communism is mainly based on the theories of Fourier and Cabet, looks for social harmony to a labour society, having no State, no church, no personal property, no distinction of nationality or class. In this society all men are to be labourers, and

[1] While in prison Weitling wrote a collection of poems published at Hamburg in 1844 with the title, " Kerkerpoesien." The poems were written, he says, " partly in order to comfort, and partly in order to occupy myself." As might be expected, the tone of many is fierce and warlike, though others show a despondent frame of mind.

[2] Marx wrote in the Paris *Vorwärts* in 1844 : —" Where could the *bourgeoisie* (of Germany) —their philosophers and theologians included—point to a work similar to Weitling's 'Guarantees of harmony and freedom,' in regard to the political emancipation of the *bourgeoisie* ? Let the jejune and feeble mediocrity of German political literature be compared with this incomparable and brilliant *début* of the German working-men."

all are to share equally in the produce of labour. Every member of society will be secured a comfortable existence, and none will have power to injure the welfare of another. Knowledge will be the supreme authority, and progress will be the vital principle of this society. Complete harmony will reign, and both police and laws will be superfluous. "A perfect society," he says, "has no government but an administration, no laws but duties, no punishments but remedies." He is opposed to the appropriation of land, because it is only to be morally justified so long as every man has full freedom and is in a position to acquire land. When these conditions are no longer fulfilled, property is not a right but an injustice, because it is the cause of want and misery to thousands. "This truth," he says, "is as clear as the sun. Open your gaols and penitentiaries, I tell you, for they contain many honest people. Open them and tell these, ' You did not know what property was, and we did not know ; let us together tear down these walls and hedges and rails, let us fill up these ditches, so that the cause of our division may disappear, and let us be friends.'" Weitling declaims violently against a system of distribution which gives to those who have " by the sweat of their brows won the produce of the earth " only a niggardly share of the produce, and he is convinced that the time will come when the labourers will reap all the fruits of their exertions.

Yet he cannot understand the passiveness of the working classes. "When the deer injure your fields," he exclaims, " you make war against them in order that you and your cattle may have the necessary subsistence, and none of you would be so cowardly as to diminish the food of his cattle or suffer want himself ; then why do you not resist the deer which make ravages on the produce of your labour ? You always seek the cause of your want in your surroundings, while it is in palaces, resting on thrones and soft carpets." Weitling was no political economist by study, but he saw that, with the prevailing system of production, the multiplication of mechanical contrivances tends to reduce the value of labour, and thus to lower the position of a large part of the labouring class, and that the poorer a working-man becomes the more impotent he is in the hands of the capitalist. This is why he advocates pure Communism, which, he says, is " the common right of society to be able to live without care in uninterrupted prosperity." Yet Weitling despairs of seeing his plans realised by the pursuance of argumentative means. He therefore preaches the sacredness of revolution. He is hardly in favour of transitional measures ; he would like society to swallow his reforms all at once. It never does, he tell us, to scotch a serpent . it must be killed outright. He allows that the first two years of the new order of things will be irksome for the dispossessed classes : still, that should not prevent the immediate carrying out of the principle of equality which is the very foundation of the reformed society. " The duke who leads the army to war, the dictator who organises the working-men, both must be treated in regard to their needs just like the youngest drummer or the stonebreaker on the highway." Weitling goes so far as to draw up a legislative programme for the first Government which shall succeed the revolution. The poor are first to be cared for. Houses unfit for habitation are to be burnt or otherwise destroyed, with all delapidated furniture, and the poor are to be lodged temporarily in public buildings or with the rich, not, however, before their rags have been exchanged for new clothes. All bonds, promissory notes, and bills are, with rights of inheritance and titles of nobility, to be declared null and void. Labour is to be organised. All members of administrative bodies, officers, and soldiers, and all persons maintained by the State are to live in community, and differences of rank are to cease The gold and silver in stock will be expended in the purchase of food and war material abroad, and the internal administration will be carried on without money, taxes being raised in natural products. The goods of emigrants and all land lying unused, but capable of being cultivated, will be confiscated. State and church lands will be employed for the benefit of the community, and the clergy in future will be maintained by the parishes requiring their services. After caring for agriculture and the army, the administration must devote especial attention to the erection and improvement of schools.

It is impossible to follow Weitling farther into Dreamland. The verdict which he pronounces upon his own scheme is as follows : " If these ideas were put into execution we should find only brothers and sisters everywhere, and nowhere an enemy." Weitling's most remarkable book is " Das Evangelium eines armen Sünders." In this work he makes Christ's Christianity the basis of his Communistic doctrines. " Poor sinners," he says, " this gospel is for you ;—make it a gospel of freedom." He shows the levelling tendency of Christ's teaching, as seen in the proclamation of liberty, equality, and community of goods, and in the denunciation of money-grabbing and usury; and while many of his interpretations and applications are palpable exaggerations, there is no mistaking the downright earnestness and honesty of this singular man. He fiercely denounces the modern "Christian propertied classes," and the "Christian jurists," as he calls them in irony, for departing from the doctrines preached by the founder of Christianity. His opinion of Christ is shown in the following passage :—"But this Christ, if we are to love him, must be a friend and brother to us poor sinners (the *proletariat*) ; he must be no supernatural, inconceivable being, but like ourselves must be subject to frailties. That he was, as we shall find in this gospel, and therefore we love him." Weitling anticipates the teaching of later German Socialists as well as Communists of the Bebel school when he says :

" Imagine a future in which there is no longer money ; in which the administration of the people superintends the distribution of its labour and its enjoyments ; in which all useless labour is abolished, and no one could be intentionally idle, because he would not have the opportunity, or as now have nothing to eat ; imagine education training our youth into honest men and women, and men having only to work a short time daily in order to secure the means of existence ; imagine the care of the sick being provided for far better than can be conceived nowadays ; imagine no labour and no labourers being despised, but everyone being equally respected ; yes, picture to yourselves such a state of things, which Christ and the Communists of to-day regard as possible, and it will be seen that no act can then be called robbery, that robbery will become an impossibility, that brutality, intemperance, idleness, &c., will naturally disappear from a society so constituted."

Robbery would not be robbery, says Weitling, for if a man were to take his neighbour's coat and shoes, all the owner would have to do would be to go to the warehouse and procure others.[1] "Consequently," he adds, "the Christian has no right to punish a thief, because so long as there are thieves Christianity has not become practical amongst us." Every attack by the poor upon property should be justified and not condemned. In the same way he defends revolution,

[1] An argument which he justifies by the passage in St. Luke vi., 30 : "Give to every man that asketh of thee, and of him that taketh away thy goods ask them not again."

though he will only have recourse to force as a last remedy; so long as freedom of thought and speech, and freedom of press, are not interfered with, revolution will be unnecessary.

It is hard or impossible to judge a man like Weitling harshly. Wild as his theories for the most part are, he wrote in the full conviction of their justice. His rugged, outspoken utterances, interspersed with passages of Scripture and injunctions upon the rich to mend their ways, carry the mind irresistibly to the burning declamations of Piers the Ploughman. "Property is the source of all evil," he exclaims in one place, "deliver us, O Lord, from the evil!" So thoroughly devoted to Communism was he, that the very idea of personal property was abhorrent to him, while money and the love of it were alike intolerable evils. "Do you hear how they cry for money from one corner of the earth to the other?" he asks. "The prince and the robber, the merchant and the thief, the advocate and the swindler, the priest and the charlatan, all cry 'Money!' And dost thou, beggar, cry for money, too? Knowest thou and rememberest thou not that the hour is coming when it will be a shame to cry for money, and a sin to wish to extort it?" Weitling holds a unique position as a Religious Communist.

KARL MARLO (WINKELBLECH).

Karl Marlo is the name under which a little-known but highly-readable German Socialist, Professor Winkelblech, wrote, prior to and after the year 1850, a large work bearing the title "Untersuchungen über die Organisation der Arbeit, oder System der Weltökonomie." Karl Georg Winkelblech was born, the only son of a Protestant clergyman, at Ensheim, April 11th, 1810. From both his parents he received scrupulous care, and the instruction bestowed upon him by his mother appears to have exercised great influence upon his thought and life. Winkelblech used, indeed, to say that his mother was the only preceptor from whom he learned anything.[1] After completing his school education at Mayence, Karl Georg was sent by his parents to an apothecary, who was requested to make a man of him. That he had little taste for this avocation may be judged from the fact that he always carried a volume of Goethe, Schiller, or Lessing in his

[1] Preface to the 2nd edition, "Untersuchungen über die Organisation der Arbeit," (Tübingen, 1885), based on family notices.

pocket.   Winkelblech appears to have wakened from his youth's reveries when, in 1828, his father died.   He now, at the age of eighteen, determined to take life more seriously, and to make his way in the world.   Quitting the apothecary's shop, he went to Giessen, and matriculated there as a student of philosophy, hearing lectures on chemistry by Liebig,[1] who took a great liking to the plodding Ensheim youth. The study of antique philosophy also engaged his attention.   After remaining at Giessen for several years, Winkelblech succeeded in securing the position of assistant lecturer on chemistry at Marburg, whose chemical chair was filled by an old and sickly professor, and his success was such as to warrant his early promotion to an extraordinary professorship.   In the course of the year 1838, Winkelblech visited Paris, and during a stay of three months made many friendships amongst professors there.   In the following year he accepted a professorship at the Higher Industrial College at Cassel (*Höhere Gewerbeschule*).   It was some time, however, before he devoted himself to the economic studies in which he was to achieve his chief success.   Only after travelling in Norway was he induced to make the study of economic and social questions the work of his life.   In the preface with which he introduces his "History and Critique of Economic Systems," Winkelblech tells us that a casual meeting with a German workman in that country led to this change in the course of his career.   The man had vividly described the sufferings of the labouring population, and his words caused the peripatetic philosopher to ask himself if these things need be.   Hitherto in visiting the seats of industry he had, as he says, allowed furnaces and machines to monopolise his attention, and had not thought of men ; he had been taken up with the products of human industry, and had overlooked the producers ; and thus he had no idea of the misery which underlay our vaunted civilisation.   "The convincing words of the workman caused me to see to the full the vanity of my scientific endeavours, and in a few moments I had formed the determination to investigate the sufferings of our race, their causes and remedies."   Winkelblech prosecuted his inquiries for a long time, and the result was the conviction that the evils of society were caused by its institutions, which rested on a false basis, and that the prevailing

---

[1] Baron Justus von Liebig, the famous chemist and naturalist, born May 8th, 1803, at Darmstadt, filled chairs at Giessen (1842-1852) and Munich, dying at the latter place April 18th, 1873.

economic principles were largely founded on error. Thus a new
system was necessary, and to the development of this he resolved
to devote his remaining years. Winkelblech died January 10th, 1865.
He married, in 1840, a daughter of the astronomer Professor Gerling,
of Marburg.

Winkelblech proceeds from the view that political economy is not
merely a science of material wealth, but has to do, first of all, with
the interests of industry. He sees in the decay of guilds, and the un-
limited sway of great capitalists, two great evils. Formerly the position
of the journeyman was transitional, leading to the goal of mastership.
Now, however, there are no longer masters and assistants, but under-
takers and labourers, and the number of independent employers tends
to become ever smaller. Thus the wages received by the labourers
depend upon their number relatively to that of the undertaker class.
If the supply of labour exceed the demand, wages fall to such an extent that the labourer is barely left the means of obtaining the necessaries of life. If the demand exceed the supply, wages may rise above
the limit of indispensable needs, though the surplus will not continue
long. The industrial revolution which has followed the introduction
of machinery, and the massing of capital in few hands, has led to the
creation of an extensive *proletariat*, which has no chance of attaining
social independence. The employment of this *proletariat* is uncertain,
and always severe. Labour is seldom a matter of choice, for the labourer must be content with the industrial circumstances of his locality,
and thus it is impossible to expect that work can be a pleasure. Work
tends, too, to become more and more monotonous as the division of
labour becomes greater, and the daily duration of work depends largely
on the will of the employer. But this unenviable position might be
tolerable if the workmen were certain of an assured existence. This,
however, is not the case. The caprice of the undertaker, or a change
in the demand of consumers, may, in an instant, deprive a workman of
his employment, and thus of his means of subsistence, for he is unable
to provide for the future, the needs of the day being barely met by
the day's earnings. The position of labourers is still worse in large
industrial towns, where they are huddled together in hundreds of
thousands, for there, wealth, splendour, and extravagance are seen on
every side, while the working population is poorly housed and poorly
fed. The family life of the *proletariat* does not deserve the name.

" What care and training can the children enjoy, when their parents
are employed twelve hours or more in the factory ; and what domestic
life can there be, when all the members of the family are kept by their
work from home all day, and almost solely assemble in the dwelling
for sleep ? "   The mother is prevented from giving to her children the
attention they should receive, and girls are unable to learn domestic
arts.   Worse than this, the dissolution of the family leads to
immorality, and the female sex is degraded.   As girls receive their
training in workshops, they learn unchastity, and finally their wages
are based on the presupposition that prostitution is carried on as a
supplementary vocation.   Not only does morality suffer, but the physical
well-being of the *proletariat* is ruined, owing to crowded habitations,
overwork, and insufficient food.   Winkelblech does not attempt to conceal the vices which are to be found amongst the *proletariat*—such
as drunkenness, improvidence, and hostility against the higher
classes—but he holds that they are inseparable from the conditions
under which the poor live.   " After all," he says, " if the *bourgeoisie* is
not guilty of these vices it is guilty of others, as dishonesty, selfishness,
an inordinate desire for gain, indulgence, and disregard of social and
other duties."   His conclusion is that the dependence of the modern
proletariat upon the undertaker class is only another form of the
serfage of the Middle Ages and the slavery of antiquity.   The position
of the *proletariat* is, in many respects, less favourable than that of the
slave or serf, for these had, at any rate, an assured existence, and the
proletariat has not.   The serf was bound to the soil : but does not the
workshop of the undertaker keep modern labourers similarly bound?
The slave might only acquire property in so far as the will of his lord
allowed, but though the modern labourer is free to possess what he has
the means of acquiring, the right is only an apparent one, for it cannot
be used.   Finally, it is questionable whether the serf had to work half
as hard for his living as the free labourer of an industrial town.

Winkelblech would heal the ills of society, and improve the condition
of the working classes, by the adoption of a compromise between
Liberalism and Communism.   Among his demands are collective
property in land, side by side with private ownership, co-operative
production, the handing over of means of communication to public
bodies, and State participation in mining, forestry, fishing, and even
trading and banking.   But he would also restrict private undertakership

and speculation wherever the interests of society require it, and he would grant to the labourer the right to work and to the incapable adequate means of subsistence. Like Malthus, he regards the question of population as the kernel of the social problem. Thus he advocates marriage restrictions—only those shall be allowed to marry who can show the possession of adequate means, a requirement which shall be reinforced on the birth of the fourth child—and he is prepared to punish with hard labour the man who brings into the world mouths which he cannot feed. He would also encourage religious orders, nunneries, and all institutions in which celibacy is fostered. Winkelblech's work fell flat—Germany was not ready for it—and for years it was entirely neglected. Schäffle[1] was one of the first authors to redirect attention to this ingenious writer, to whom, in "Kapitalismus und Socialismus," he pays a high tribute.

FRIEDRICH ENGELS.

No mean place in the history of the Socialist movement is taken by Friedrich Engels, though he is in reality a Communist of the most pronounced stamp, and as such has done yeoman's service for his cause. Engels, who was born in 1822 at Barmen, was for forty years the inseparable associate of Karl Marx, whom he first met in Paris after his expulsion from Germany. Marx, not less than Engels, highly valued from the very first day the friendship thus formed, and if Engels appears to shine but as a lesser star in comparison with the great light which Marx undoubtedly was in the Communistic firmament, it is quite certain that this lifelong companionship was mutually beneficial. Engels may be called the *alter ego* of his friend, whose opinions on all political and social questions were his own. Rarely have two minds represented such union as was seen throughout the entire intercourse of these true comrades in arms. When Marx died, in 1883, he left, in a very unprepared state, a host of manuscripts, forming a continuation of the first volume of "Capital," which was published in 1867. It

[1] Albert Schäffle, political economist, born February 24th, 1831, in Wurtemberg. Originally a journalist, he turned his attention to political economy, and became professor of the science at Tübingen in 1861, and Vienna in 1868. For a time he filled the office of Austrian Minister of Trade, but on his retirement, because of a ministerial change, he withdrew to Stuttgart, and resumed literary work. His chief work is "Bau und Leben des sozialen Körpers," (4 volumes, 1875-8), and next in importance is "Kapitalismus and Socialismus" (1870).

was, therefore, fortunate that a man was to be found who had been so schooled in the ideas of Marx that he could undertake the formidable task of editing the posthumous works. This is certainly not the least of Engels' achievements in the cause of Socialism. Engels underwent his baptism of fire as a political agitator at the time of the Elberfeld rising of 1849. For his share in causing this trouble he was ordered to leave Prussian territory, a fate which came to Marx as well. Before this he had come into prominence through the publication, in 1845, of a volume on the condition of the English working classes,[1] the result of nearly two years' study on the spot. In this work he advances the outspoken Socialistic opinions which have ever since been associated with his name. The work is dedicated to the working classes of Great Britain and Ireland, and in the dedication the author pays a high compliment to the British workman, not the least of whose good qualities are said to be sympathy with every progressive movement and freedom from "that blasting curse, national prejudice and pride." "I found you to be more than mere Englishmen, members of a single isolated nation," says Engels, "I found you to be *men*, members of the great and universal family of mankind, who know their interests and those of all the human race to be the same."

We here see the cosmopolitan sympathies shared by Engels in common with the Communist party, and they are further shown by his ceaseless endeavours on behalf of international co-operation amongst working-men. Besides associating with Marx in the establishment of a German Working-men's Association in Brussels in 1845, and in its later direction, Engels was joint-author of the Communist Manifesto, published early in 1848, and was one of the founders of the League of Communists formed in the preceding winter. He has written a number of works, large and small, on different phases of the social problem. Besides that on the English working classes may be named "Herr Eugen Dühring's Umwälzung der Wissenschaft: Philosophie, Politische Ökonomie, Socialismus,"[2] a criticism of Dühring's scientific works; "Die Entwickelung des Sozialismus von der Utopie zur Wissenschaft,"[3] and "Der Ursprung der Familie, des Privat-

---

[1] "Die Lage der arbeitenden Klasse in England." (Leipzig, 1845.)

[2] Leipzig, 1878. The works criticised are "Cursus der Philosophie," "Cursus der National- und Sozialökonomie," and "Kritische Geschichte der Nationalökonomie und des Sozialismus."

[3] Hottingen Zurich, 1883. (Dated London, September 21st, 1882.)

eigenthums, und des Staats :[1] Im Anschluss an Lewis H. Morgan's Forschungen," [2] and he was joint-author with Marx of " Die heilige Familie, oder Kritik der kritischen Kritik. Gegen Bruno Bauer & Consorten." [3] He has further contributed largely to Socialistic publications. From his pen, too, appeared the noteworthy " Outlines for a critique of political economy," in the " Deutsch-Französische Jahrbücher," (Paris, 1844), wherein Engels claims to have first maintained the proposition that " the natural, that is, the normal price of labour-power coincides with the minimum of wages, that is, with the value-equivalent of the means of subsistence absolutely necessary to the life and propagation of the labourer." [4]

As to theory, Engels may be said to hold precisely the same views as Marx, but as he has gone out of the purely scientific track, and has given to his theories a practical application, it is advisable to glance briefly at the teachings of his social works. Modern Socialism, Engels tells us in his critique of Dühring, is the result of the opposition of classes, the propertied and the unpropertied, the *bourgeoise* and the wage-earners, and of the anarchy which prevails in production, though theoretically it owes its origin to the French movements of last century. " Socialism is the expression of absolute truth, reason and justice, and needs only to be discovered in order by its own power to conquer the world." He dates the scientific development of Socialism from Marx's discovery of *Mehrwerth* or surplus-value. It was then shown that the appropriation of labour which is not paid for is the primal form of the capitalistic mode of production, and the exploitation of the labourer entailed by it ; that the capitalist, even when he buys the labour of his workmen at the full market value, derives more value from it than he pays for ; and that this surplus-value forms the basis and substance of the capital now in the hands of the propertied class. Engels accepts all the conclusions which follow from the theory of an appropriated surplus-value, for while he shows the effects of this appropriation, he advocates measures which will put an end to it. He is thoroughly antagonistic to the present mode of pro-

[1] Hottingen, Zurich, 1884. Engels says the work was undertaken by Marx, but was afterwards placed in his hands.

[2] "Ancient Society, or Researches in the Lines of Human Progress from Savagery through Barbarism to Civilisation," by Lewis H. Morgan. London : Macmillan & Co., 1877.

[3] Paris, September, 1844, and Frankfort-on-Maine, 1845.

[4] " Das Elend der Philosophie, by Marx, (Stuttgart, 1885, pp. 26, 27, note.)

duction, and not less so to the prevailing system of competition. In competition expression is given to the state of war which prevails throughout modern society—*bellum omnium contra omnes.* For this war, which is one of life and death, exists not only between class and class, but between the individual members of classes, for everybody is in the way of everybody else ; working-men compete amongst themselves just as the *bourgeois* classes do. Even the associations to which the labouring classes have recourse are unable to save them. The *proletariat* is, in fact, helpless, for the *bourgeoisie* keeps a firm hand on all the means of existence and the Executive Power supports this monopoly. The relationship of the *proletariat* to the *bourgeoisie* is that of slavery. The *proletariat* seeks subsistence from the *bourgeoisie*, and offers in return its labour, thus giving itself over absolutely into the hands of the enemy. The labourer is nominally free, but in reality he is not, for he is compelled to accept whatever conditions the employer chooses to enforce. The competition which goes on amongst the labourers themselves makes matters worse for them, but better for the capitalists. This competition has only one check, and it is that no labourer will work for less than he requires for his existence, for if he has to hunger, he might as well hunger idling as working. Still, even this check is relative rather than absolute, for the standard of life varies amongst labourers, and according to this standard of life will the minimum wages be determined. Then, again, where every member of the family works, the individual is able to subsist on less wages than would be necessary were he isolated, for a saving of cost is effected by community. While the minimum wages depend on the competition of labourers amongst themselves, the maximum wages are fixed by the competition which goes on amongst the capitalists. The *proletariat* produces commodities for the *bourgeoisie*, which sells them at a profit. If the demand is so large that it cannot be met, all disposable labour is employed, and thus the competition of labourer with labourer ceases and gives place to a competition amongst the capitalists for the required labour-power. Average wages, or wages just exceeding the minimum, exist when neither capitalists nor labourers have any reason to compete against each other : when just as many labourers are employed as can produce the commodities required. The extent to which the minimum is exceeded will depend on the average needs and the degree of culture reached by the labourers. The labourer is, in fact, a commodity, the price of which varies according to the demand for it and the cost of producing it. If there is a large inquiry for labourers their price rises, and if the demand falls, so, too, the labourers fall in price, while a superfluity of labourers causes a part of them to "remain in stock," just as ordinary commodities, which are not saleable, remain on the shop shelves. Population is thus influenced by the economic position occupied by labour. If the price of labour (that is, the labourer's wages) rises, marriages increase, and more children are produced, until the demand for labour is met. When the supply is excessive, prices fall again, and the consequence is that hunger and disease sweep away the superfluous population. One of the evils of the system which makes the labourer a commodity, is the position of absolute dependence in which the working classes are placed. If a manufacturer employs labourers for nine hours a day, there is nothing to prevent him, at a time when the offer of labour is large, from compelling them to work another hour on pain of dismissal. Thus he has the benefit of an hour's extra labour daily, without the necessity of paying for it. In proportion as the condition of the labourer is less independent does the power of the capitalist to exploit him increase. Thus the weaker the members of society are, the less hope of help have they.

The labourer is both legally and in fact the slave of the capitalist class. "All the difference from the old, out-spoken slavery is that the present labourer appears to be free, because he is not sold all at once but piecemeal—per day, week, or year—and because one owner does not sell him to another, but he must sell himself in this way, as he is not the slave of a single person but of the entire propertied class. But for the labourer it is in reality all the same, and if this appearance of freedom secures him on the one hand a certain degree of real freedom, he suffers on the other hand from the disadvantage that no man guarantees him support, that he may be cast away at any moment by his master, the *bourgeoisie*, and be left to die of hunger if the *bourgeoisie* has no longer any interest in his employment, that is, in his existence. The *bourgeoisie*, however, is far better off with this arrangement than with the old slavery, for it can turn away its people when it likes without losing invested capital, and, moreover, it gets labour done far more cheaply than is the case with slaves." [1]

---

[1] "Die Lage der arbeitenden Klasse," pp. 103, 104.

What, then, will Socialism do for the working classes? Engels answers that it will do away with the class differences which are a consequence of the unequal distribution of the produce. Society is at present split up into opposing camps—the privileged and the prejudiced, the exploiting and the exploited, the ruling and the ruled— and the State, whose duty it should be to give protection within and without to the community at large, merely props up the dominant classes by forcibly maintaining the conditions of their supremacy. The existence of a ruling class is now as much an anachronism as slavery is. Both have become superfluous, though they had formerly full justification. "We should never forget that our entire economical, political, and intellectual development presupposes a condition of things in which slavery was necessarily and universally recognised. In this sense we are justified in saying 'Without the slavery of antiquity no modern Socialism.' It is very easy to inveigh in general terms against slavery, and to pour out highly moral anger at such enormities. But unfortunately all that is said by this is, what everybody knows, that these ancient institutions are no longer in accord with present conditions, and the feelings which these conditions have produced."[1]

So long as the really productive part of the community—the labouring classes—could secure no leisure, owing to excess of labour, for the common affairs of society, as State affairs, sciences, and art, a special class must attend to these things, and, adds Engels, this class has never failed to heap heavier and yet heavier burdens upon the working classes. But now there is no need for this ceaseless physical strain ; there might be sufficient leisure for all to take part in social affairs ; and for that reason the ruling class has become unnecessary —nay, more, a perfect hindrance to social progress, and should, therefore, be abolished. He says : "A surplus in the produce of labour over the cost of maintaining the labour, and the formation and increase of a social productive and reserve fund out of this surplus, were and are the basis of all social, political, and intellectual progress. In past history this fund has been the possession of a privileged class, which with this possession acquired also political supremacy and intellectual leadership. The impending social revolution will make this social productive and reserve fund—that is, the whole mass of raw material, instruments of production, and food—in reality social, when it takes

1 See Engels' " Herr Eugen Dühring's Umwalzung der Wissenschaft."

it from the privileged class and assigns it to society as a whole as
common property." On purely economic grounds Engels holds that
a revolution in the present mode of production is imperative. One of
the natural and inevitable results of this system is the recurrence of
commercial crises, which are especially injurious to the working
classes. As the production and distribution of the means of existence
follow no rule, and do not take place for the immediate purpose of
satisfying social needs, but of making the capitalists rich, a crisis may
occur at any time. Chance governs the actions of the individual
producer, whose dealings are quite independent of the dealings of
others. Everybody is ignorant of what is being done by everybody
else, and the result is confusion. This anarchy in production compels
industrial capitalists to perfect their machinery more and more on
pain of being superseded, and this perfection of machinery makes
human labour increasingly superfluous. As Marx says, machinery is
the most powerful instrument of war which capital possesses against
labour, for the labourer's own product is made a means of his bondage. Though, however, production increases, the sale does not
expand correspondingly, so that trade in time comes to a standstill,
the markets are surfeited, produce lies unsaleable, manufactories are
stopped, public credit is shaken, bankruptcy follows bankruptcy, and
the labouring classes suffer the greatest want. All these evils will disappear with the abolition of the capitalistic system of production and
the consequent extinction of the capitalist class. Nor does Engels
regard this consummation as impossible. The *proletariat* has only
to become strong enough and the means of production will be social-
ised. When this is done, however, the *proletariat* as such will exist
no longer, for all class distinctions will cease, and therewith the State
as it now is. A society which is based upon the existence of mutually
opposed classes needs the State in order that privilege and monopoly
and power—the threefold principle of class—may be maintained.
When the State is no longer the representative of one favoured section, but represents in reality society as a whole, it becomes superfluous, for so long as there is no class to prop up, and none to keep
down, repressive power is not needed. Production will then be carried
on according to rule and plan, and all the needs of society will be
provided for. "The first act wherein the State appears as really
representative of all society—the taking possession of the means of

production in the name of society—will be its last act as a State. Government over persons will be succeeded by the management of things and the direction of processes of production. A free society cannot need or tolerate the existence of a State between itself and its members."[1] Thus will be realised the Free People's State. Society possessing the means of production, the producer will no longer be at the mercy of the produce, but will enjoy the full fruit of his labour. The struggle for existence will end, and in this respect man will for the first time be distinguished from the lower animals, for the first time will be really Lord of Nature, for the first time really free. It is the high mission of the *proletariat* to effect this emancipation of mankind, and scientific Socialism is the instrument it will employ.

KARL GRÜN.

Another eminent Socialist, who both as author and agitator exercised great influence during the first half of the century and later, is Karl Grün. Grün was born September 30th, 1817, at Lüdenscheid, in Westphalia. He was, like Lassalle and Marx, a follower of Hegel, whose philosophy he endeavoured while resident in Paris to implant in the mind of his friend Proudhon, though with very qualified success. He relates, indeed, in the charming collection of letters and studies which goes by the name of " Die soziale Bewegung in Frankreich und Belgien,"[2] how Proudhon, who did not understand German well, would answer an unwelcome argument with " I do not comprehend you." "And yet," adds Grün *naïvely*, " I was plain enough." Grün was very early drawn into the arena of politics. Early in 1842 he became the editor of a Mannheim journal, and as such succeeded —though the task was not a difficult one—in winning the dislike of the Baden Government. The result was that before many months had expired he unexpectedly received notice to quit the Grand Duchy. This expulsion was, however, an act of doubtful legality, for Grün had never once given the Press censor occasion for dissatisfaction.[3] All the explanation to be had was that his political views were objectionable. For several years Grün devoted himself to literary work, but

[1] " Herr Eugen Dühring's Umwälzung der Wissenschaft."
[2] Darmstadt, 1845; a more interesting work on the French Socialists and Communists could not be imagined.
[3] " Meine Ausweisung aus Baden," Zurich and Winterthur, 1843.

when the stormy days of 1848 came he threw himself into the thickest of the fray.   He took part in the rising in the Palatinate in 1849, and being captured was put into prison.   On regaining freedom he removed to Belgium, and later he resided in Vienna, where his death occurred in 1887.   Grün has written a number of works on social and literary subjects.   His " Sociale Bewegung," already mentioned, was not without influence in stimulating the Socialist movement in Germany.   Monographs on Goethe and Schiller have also been written by him.   A few years before his death he withdrew from active work on behalf of the Socialist cause, but he remained faithful to his principles to the last.   The name of Karl Grün is held in high respect by the younger generation of Socialists in Germany.

CHAPTER III.

KARL RODBERTUS AND THE WAGES PRINCIPLE.

FAME is often very fickle in the distribution of honours. While the less deserving is favoured, the more deserving is very frequently passed over. Karl Johann Rodbertus is a singular instance of the caprice of fame. There are, it may be said, four men who by common consent are regarded as the founders of modern scientific Socialism in Germany. These men are, Karl Marx, Rodbertus, Ferdinand Lassalle, and Frederick Engels. Of these Marx is almost universally chosen for the distinctive title of Father of the Socialistic movement, so far as scientific theory is concerned, while Rodbertus, his senior in age and in literature, is with great injustice passed by. Only within recent years has even the attempt been made in Germany to give to this deep thinker his proper place in science, and even now an amount of neglect is visible which speaks ill for the fairness of writers on Socialism. Some of the German historians of the Socialistic movement pass Rodbertus by in silence, and others only deign to give him bare mention. To Adolph Wagner,[1] the leading representative of the State Socialistic school, is due the credit of having discovered the importance of Rodbertus as an economic writer. Wagner generously speaks of him as "the first, the most original, and the boldest representative of scientific Socialism in Germany,"[2] and as "the most distinguished theorist of the purely economic side of scientific Socialism."[3] Rudolph Meyer goes further and contends that Marx "has, as can be proved, built up the greater part of his critique" from the publications of

[1] Adolph Wagner, born March 25th, 1835, at Erlangen, has since 1870 been professor of political economy at Berlin. He has, however, taught at Vienna, Hamburg, Dorpat, and Freiburg. Wagner is the leading representative of State Socialism in Germany, and naturally a zealous supporter of Prince Bismarck's social policy, which he is even prepared to place upon a still broader basis.

[2] Introduction to "Briefe von Ferdinand Lassalle an Karl Rodbertus-Jagetzow," (Berlin, 1878), also "Tübinger Zeitschrift für Staatswissenschaft," 1878, pp. 199-237.

[3] *Ibid.*

Rodbertus which appeared before 1835, and that Lassalle has done the same, the only new thing being the positive proposals of these two imitators.[1]

As only a small part of the life of Rodbertus—the "Ricardo of Economic Socialism," as Wagner has called him—was passed in public activity, we know comparatively little about the person of the man. He was born on August 12th, 1805, at Greifswald, in old Swedish Pomerania, where his father was a Swedish Councillor of Justice and professor of Roman law at the university. In 1808 Professor Rodbertus retired from his chair and removed to Beseritz, in Mecklenburg-Strelitz, the estate of his wife, and here he continued for the remainder of his life. His son Karl passed through the Gymnasium of Mecklenburgisch-Friedland, then went to Göttingen University, where he studied from 1823 to 1825, going in the latter year to Berlin to study law, and remaining there till 1826. His term as auscultator was passed in the provincial and municipal court at Alt-Brandenburg, and passing the necessary examinations he became referendary at Breslau in 1829 and the following year at Oppeln, where he studied political economy, afterwards to become the science after his own heart. He prosecuted his studies further at Heidelberg, where he divided attention between political economy, history, and philosophy. Meanwhile, he had travelled in Switzerland, France, and Holland, and when in 1834, at the age of twenty-nine, he returned home, it was as a studied man who had also seen a good deal of the world and its ways. Purchasing the estate of Jagetzow, in Pomerania, he removed thither from the paternal estate of Beseritz in 1836. He took part in provincial administration, and at one time was elected a member of an agricultural commission appointed to consider the question of taxation. In 1847 he was returned to the Provincial Landstag. The independence which was always a characteristic of Rodbertus was shown at this time by his declining the offer of King Frederick William IV. to advance him to the nobility. He satisfied himself with taking the name of his estate, and signing himself as "Rodbertus-Jagetzow." Rodbertus was a member of the commission appointed to draw up electoral laws for the Prussian National Assembly, and in May, 1848,

---

[1] "Der Emancipationskampf des vierten Standes," Berlin, 1874, vol. 1, pp. 43, 44. This is an excellent work of reference, which may well be consulted by those who desire a closer knowledge of the practical development of Socialism in Germany.

he was returned to the new Assembly, the election being by universal franchise. His part in the proceedings of that body is of purely national interest, and need not detain us. Suffice it to say that he was an active figure in the political history of 1848 and 1849 in Prussia. Rodbertus did not regard the movement of the former year as political but as social, just as at a later time he refused to believe that Lassalle's political agitation would find sympathy amongst the people. In June, 1848, Rodbertus took office in the Auerswald-Hansemann Cabinet as Minister for Public Worship and Education, but differences caused him to resign in a fortnight. He was thrice elected in 1849, once for the First Chamber and twice for the Second. On April 13th he introduced a motion for recognising the Frankfort Imperial constitution and he carried it on the 21st, but the Second Chamber was a few days later dissolved, and the end of his political career soon followed. Though a democrat of the first water in early life, he was able to support much in Prince Bismarck's policy during his later years.

It was a good thing for science that Rodbertus was defeated when he tried to enter the North German Reichstag, for the result was a resolution to devote himself closely to the study of political economy in its bearing upon social questions. Thus for the remainder of his long life he wrote almost incessantly on economic subjects. He was able to bring to the consideration of these subjects the qualifications, rarely combined to such a degree as with him, of wide and generous sympathies and deep learning. For though Rodbertus was a true student—he never read without a pencil in his hand, and his fondness for exchanging views is proved by a voluminous correspondence—he was also thoroughly practical. The sincerity of his efforts on behalf of the working classes is nowhere better shown than by his refusal to co-operate with Lassalle in agitation. Like Owen, he held that the social problem was not a question of politics but solely of economics, and he would not hear of a combination of the two.[1] Resisting all attempts to draw—it may rather be said to thrust—him into the political arena, he remained in the study, believing rightly that he could there do better and more lasting service to the cause dear to

[1] He writes to his friend Rudolph Meyer, August 16th, 1872: "That I hold the social question to be a purely economic question, with which those having in view only the secondary aims of Sabbath-hallowing and soul-catching *(Seelenfang)* should have nothing to do . . . . this you have long known better than anyone from myself."

him. In 1873 his health gave way, though he had been ailing for some years. But physical weakness and pain troubled him far less than did his failing sight, which prevented him from pursuing study and literary work as he wished. The winter of 1873-1874 he passed he Italy, and he returned, to all appearance, much better in health. The following winter tried him severely and it was with difficulty that he struggled through. The end came in December, 1875, being hastened by exposure to the weather. On the 2nd of the month he was out of doors superintending the beautifying of his estate, and on the 5th he died.

Rodbertus was a man of lofty character, a man of whom any science and any country might be proud. He held what are known as advanced views on some of the deeper questions of life, and we find him writing on one occasion that he has worked himself into an entirely new contemplation of the world, and that though he is "anything but a Materialist," he is not an adherent of the Christianity of the day. It would, however, be unsafe to attribute to these last words a far-reaching significance, for the letters of Rodbertus would not allow of it. As a political economist he stood upon decidedly Socialistic ground, as an examination of his theories will show. But he took up this position only after deep study of political economy, history, and philosophy, and after gaining wide experience in practical agriculture ; and although he was a Socialist when Socialism was not common amongst men of science, he never deserted his guns or even sought to apologise for his heterodoxy. When a friend once recognised his great service to science he replied, indulging in a little banter at his own expense, "In your kind opinion of me you quite forget what a wicked heretic I am in our science—what a black economic soul I really am." But odium did not affect him and he could say in the last year of his life: "I swear yet with few exceptions to every word which I have written on political economy, and I am firmly convinced that when I shall have published 'Capital' and 'The Social Question' my theory will be preached in fifty years from the roofs, and then practice will soon follow. Unfortunately," he adds, "I began the elaboration of the social question too early, when no one believed in it, and thus I was quite disregarded, which is not encouraging to a writer who by dint of great exertion is enabled to establish and create something new."[1]

[1] Letter to J. Zeller, March 14th, 1875.

The last years of the scholar's life were taken up, as were the last years of Kant, with preparations for a great and final work, which should worthily crown his labours. He wished to collect all the scattered fragments of his social theories into a complete system, and to the very last he did not despair of completing the task. In the letter from which a passage has just been taken he says that though he is old and sick, and has lost the sight of one eye, " which is a great obstacle to work," he trusts in " God and my good constitution." But though his face was turned to this goal, the journey thither was slow and death overtook him on the way. His widow wrote to a friend shortly after his death : " My heart longs for the recognition which he deserves, not only, however, as a man of science, for I should like to see his rare and amiable qualities appreciated. The years in which he abstained from taking part in public affairs vastly increased his stores of learning, and it pains me beyond measure that they should have been laid in the grave with him." Even yet Rodbertus has not received the recognition he deserves, but posterity certainly promises to be more discriminating than were his contemporaries.

In seeking to understand the economic theories of Rodbertus in so far as they bear directly on Socialism, it will serve no good purpose to follow his works in chronological sequence, for this would only lead to confusion. Nor will it be wise to attempt an analysis of the works individually. The plan adopted disregards the disjointed character of Rodbertus' writings, and contemplates his system as though it had been connectedly worked out. In order to a better comprehension of the system, quotations will be freely given, and the author's own language be often followed pretty closely, even when extracts are not made.[1] Rodbertus speaks of his economic theories as a " logical de-

---

[1] Kozak in his " Rodbertus-Jagetzow's socialpolitische Ansichten," a work which should be read by all wishful to learn in greater detail the economic views of this gifted author, enumerates some thirty writings from the pen of Rodbertus, ranging from systematic works down to essays and correspondence. The importance of Rodbertus as a political economist and a social reformer will justify the giving of as complete a list as possible of his works :

"Zur Erkenntniss unsrer staatswirthschaftlichen Zustände," (Neubrandenburg, 1842).

" Für den Kredit der Grundbesitzer : eine Bitte an die Reichsstände," (1847).

"Die neuesten Grundtaxen des Herrn v. Bülow-Cummerow," (1847).

" Die preussische Geldkrisis," (1848).

"Mein Verhalten in dem Conflict zwischen Krone und Volk : an meine Wähler," (Berlin, 1849).

" Sociale Briefe an von Kirchmann," (two letters appeared in 1850 and a third in 1851).

E

velopment of the proposition introduced into science by Smith, and established more firmly by Ricardo's school, that all commodities can only be considered economically as the product of labour, and cost nothing but labour." This proposition he places at the beginning of his first great work, "Zur Erkenntniss unsrer staatswirthschaftlichen Zustände," published in 1842. It will thus be expected that Rodbertus looks for the solution of the social problem to some reform which will place labour in a fair and just position as against capital. He describes his purpose as follows :

"The chief aim of my investigations will be to increase the share of the working classes in the national income, and that on solid grounds taken from the influences of the vicissitudes of trade. I wish to allow

" Die Handelskrisen und die Hypothekennoth der Grundbesitzer," (Berlin, 1858).

"Offener Brief an das Comité des deutschen Arbeitervereins zu Leipzig," (1863).

"Zur Frage des Realkredits," (first published in the *Norddeutsche Allgemeine Zeitung*, 1868).

"Zur Erklärung und Abhülfe der heutigen Kreditnoth des Grundbesitzes," (Berlin, 1868-1869).

" Für das Rentenprinsip," (*Norddeutsche Landwirthschaftliche Zeitung*, 1870).

" Der normale Arbeitstag," (*Berliner Revue*, 1871.)

" Briefwechsel zwischen Rodbertus und dem Architekten H. Peters," (published in 1878 : it had reference to the operation of the normal workday).

" Ein Brief von Rodbertus an Rudolph Meyer," (September 18th, 1873, published in Meyer's " Emancipationskampf des vierten Standes," 1874 : giving his mature views on the property question).

" Rodbertus' Antwort an einen Kathedersocialisten," (published in the same work and relating to the same question).

"Briefwechsel zwischen Rodbertus und dem Minister für die landwirthschaftlichen Angelegenheiten Dr. Friedenthal," (in O. Beta's " Die wirthschaftliche Nothwendigkeit und politische Bedeutung einer Deutschen Agrarverfassung," 1878).

" Briefe und socialpolitische Aufsätze von Dr. Rodbertus-Jagetzow," (Berlin, 1882).

"Aus dem literarischen Nachlass von Karl Rodbertus-Jagetzow, herausgegeben von H. Schumacher-Zarchlin und Adolph Wagner": 1. " Briefe von Ferdinand Lassalle an Karl Rodbertus-Jagetzow, mit einer Einleitung von Adolph Wagner," (Berlin, 1878); 2. " Das Kapital," (edited by T. Kozak, Berlin, 1884).

"Zwei verschollene staatswirthschaftliche Abhandlungen," (Vienna, 1885, published by Marx Quarck).

Appendix to J. Zeller's edition of " Zur Erkenntniss "—" Die sociale Bedeutung der Staatswirthschaft," and " Der normale Arbeitstag," (Berlin, 1885).

In addition a large number of articles and letters have appeared from the pen of Rodbertus in Hildebrand's *Jahrbücher*, the *Tübinger Zeitschrift*, and other publications. Of works on Rodbertus and his theories may be named :

" Rodbertus-Jagetzow's socialpolitische Ansichten," T. Kozak, (Jena, 1882).

" Bismarck, Wagner, Rodbertus : drei deutsche Meister," Moritz Wirth, (Leipzig, 1883.)

"Rodbertus der Begründer des wissenschaftlichen Sozialismus," Georg Adler, (Leipzig, 1884)

these classes to share in the increase of productivity, and to abolish the law—which otherwise might one day become fatal for our social conditions—that, however the productivity may increase, the labourers are ever thrown back by the force of trade upon a rate of wages which does not exceed the necessary subsistence ; a rate which shuts them out from the culture of the age, since this would take the place of the servitude which keeps them down, a rate which forms a most flagrant contradiction to their present legal position, that formal equality with other classes which is proclaimed by our most important institutions. By securing for the labourer a larger share in the national income, I wish at the same time to do away with the frightful industrial crises which occur periodically, and which consist wholly in the disproportion between purchasing and productive power—but not, as Say and Ricardo think, because want of purchasing power is want of productive power, and not, as Malthus and Sismondi think, because the productive power may surpass the purchasing power *per se*, but because the purchasing power remains behind the productive power, owing to the fact that participation in its results is not regulated, for purchasing power is, differently expressed, nothing but a share in the results of the productive power or in the national income."[1]

For this argument it is necessary to prove that the wages of labour are not paid from capital, but, standing on the same level as rents,[2] are with these a share in the produce, and thus in the income of the period for which they are paid. For if wages are paid out of capital they cannot be increased beyond the limits of this capital without striking at the roots of national production and prosperity, but if paid out of the national income they may be increased without capital being touched : (1) either wages may be increased at the cost of rents ; or, and this is the proposal of Rodbertus, (2) without rents being reduced such precautions may be taken that the labourer shall benefit by the increased productivity which science causes. In establishing his initial proposition that commodities only cost labour, Rodbertus excludes the share of nature and of mind in production from the idea of cost. All the cost to man consists of physical force and time.

---

1 " Zur Erkenntniss unsrer staatswirthschaftlichen Zustände," pp. 28, 29, note.

2 It may here be anticipated that Rodbertus adopts two kinds of rent, rent from land and rent from capital (*Grund-* and *Kapitalrente*). The terms will be noticed later. He also divides property into three kinds, property in land, capital (both of which fall under the head of *rentirendes Eigenthum*), and income.

Material is necessary, but this nature supplies ; mind must also show labour the way, but here again the element of cost is lacking ; tools are requisite, but tools resolve themselves into labour.   The full cost of a commodity falls into three parts : the labour directly bestowed upon its manufacture ; the labour bestowed upon the material in its earlier stages ; and a certain amount of labour corresponding to the wear of the tools employed.   But it is a mistake to regard the food consumed by the labourer during his work as part of the cost of the commodity ; it is rather a part of the produce of his work.   This error arises from the habit of reckoning wages to capital in the same way as material and tools, while they stand in reality on the same level as rent and profit.   Material and tools stand in the relation of capital to the product, for they are produced in order to serve for future production, but food is only produced in order that the labourer may live, not in order that power of future production may be given, and thus it is the income of the period in which it is produced.   When the process of production begins there exists no natural stock of food out of which to pay wages.   The undertaker has, indeed, to have a fund out of which to remunerate his workmen, but it is not a food supply which must, like materials and tools, exist before production is begun ; it is merely a money-fund—a fund of notes or orders (*Anweisungen*) on any desired commodities, which are handed out to the labourer in reward of his labour.   The labourer receives these orders only because he has supplied a certain product, and the man with whom he exchanges them for food recognises in the money a guarantee for its substitution in the product of the workman's labour.   Thus the labourer is paid not out of capital but out of the produce of his own labour, and it is only division of labour and exchange that cause confusion.   This brings Rodbertus to his conclusion that wages are, equally with profit and rent, a share in the produce, in the income ; so that, as he says, " The bread on which the labourer lives is certainly worse than that of the *rentier*, but it is equally as fresh."   To regard wages as part of capital is to place the labourer on a level with the material and the tool ; he is made a mere machine, and his food is like the fodder of the ox, or the coal which feeds the engine.

Having thus placed wages upon the same level as rent and profit, Rodbertus reaches another stage in his argument, viz., the relationship which this share in the produce bears to the other shares.   Here, however, we stumble over his theory of rent. He defines rent as that income which is derived by virtue of a possession and without labour, and he divides rent into rent from land and rent from capital. The food and means of subsistence paid to the labourers from the produce of the land are their wages, and the rest of the commodities produced are the rent retained by the owner of the land : this is land-rent. Similarly, capital-rent is all the income which remains to the capitalist after deduction of the wages paid to his labourers. Originally, however, the land-owner and capitalist were one. " Only with the rise of the modern towns, with the legal distinction between country and town, with the exclusive right of the latter to carry on most industries, with the necessary result that the raw products must change owners, was a separate capitalist class with the idea of capital formed, and therewith the possibility given that where the landowner himself employed capital he might calculate a part of his income as falling to this."[1] If the capitalist, instead of employing labourers himself, prefers to hand over materials and tools to another in return for a part of the rent-income, the undertaker appears, and the recompense which he gives to the capitalist is interest on capital. Thus capital-rent falls into interest for the capitalist and profit for the undertaker. Consequently, land-rent, interest, and profit form together the overplus which remains after wages have been deducted from the total national produce. He draws no distinction between land and capital-rent as to character or origin, but remarks : "While Zachariae[2] said that land-rent is 'a deduction from the wages which, if land had no owner, would wholly fall to the labourer,' I extend this proposition and maintain that capital-rent is also a deduction from the wages which, if capital had no private owner, would wholly fall to the labourer," and he adds that it is entirely the institution of private property in land and capital which has given to the owners of land and capital a property in the produce of labour, and which now "compels the labourers to be satisfied with a small share in their own produce."

How, then, is the produce divided? Rodbertus lays it down that (1) "With a given value of produce, or with the produce of a given quantity of labour, or with a given national produce, the height of rent is in inverse proportion to the height of wages, and in direct propor-

[1] "Zur Erkenntniss," pp. 77, 78.
[2] Heinrich Albert Zachariae, born November 20th, 1806, at Herbsleben, Gotha, became professor at Göttingen in 1835, and died April 29th, 1875, at Canstatt.

tion to the height of the productivity of labour in general. The lower wages are, the higher rent; the higher the productivity of labour, the lower wages and the higher rent. (2) Let the height of rent be given with a certain value of produce, and the height of land-rent and that of profit on capital stand in inverse proportion to each other, and to the height of the productivity of the labour expended on raw product and manufacture respectively. According as the land-rent is higher or lower will profit be lower or higher, and conversely; the higher or lower the productivity of the labour expended on raw product or manufacture, the lower or higher land-rent or profit, and conversely the higher or lower profit or land-rent. (3) The height of profit on capital is entirely determined by the height of the value of the produce in general, and that of the raw product and manufactured product in particular, or by the relationship of the productivity of labour in general, and of the labour bestowed on raw production and manufacture in particular ; in addition, the height of land-rent depends on the magnitude of the value of the produce or the quantity of labour or productive power which is employed with a given relationship of productivity to production."[1] Thus the higher the value of the raw product, the greater its share in the return, and *vice versa ;* but as value decreases with the increase of productivity, a higher productivity in agricultural than in industrial labour will cause a fall in land-rent as compared with capital-rent, and conversely. It follows from what has been said that so far as the division of the rent is concerned, the landowner can only benefit at the expense of the capitalist and *vice versa.* But all produce is the produce of labour, and with free competition the value of every commodity gravitates towards the value of the labour expended upon it ; so that the relationship between the values of the raw and manufactured products is, on the whole, only regulated by the amount of labour expended upon each. Rodbertus points out that a change in the sum of a nation's productive forces, in other words, a change in the number of labourers—apart, of course, from an alteration in productivity, or in the division of the produce—only changes the sum of the national produce and the amounts (not the proportions) which fall to rent and wages. According as the sum of the productive forces employed increases or decreases, will more or less rent be received by the land-owners, and more or less

[1] Third " Social Letter, ' (1851), edition 1875, pp. 123, 124.

profit by the capitalists. Wages will not be higher with increased production, because, productivity and division being supposed the same,
the increased produce falling to the labourers will be shared by the
larger population. Yet an increase of rent in consequence of the increase of productive forces does not influence land-rent and profit on
capital in the same way. It increases the former, but does not increase the rate of profit. This is because the increased land-rent must
be reckoned on the same area, since land does not grow, while increased profit falls to an increased capital. Land-rent is thus in the
fortunate position of being able to increase in three ways, at the cost of
wages, by the diminution of the labourers' share in the produce ; at the
cost of profit on capital, by encroachment upon the capitalists' share ;
and by the increase of rent as a whole. There is, however, a way in
which both kinds of rent may increase without one of them suffering,
and it is by the depression of the wages share in the produce.
Whether wages fall simultaneously below the level of necessary sub
sistence depends upon the productivity of labour. They may form a
less share of the produce, and still be sufficient to maintain the
labourer. The reason why wages are at the mercy of land-rent and
capital, is that labour is made an ordinary article of merchandise,
which it should not be. The workman gives his labour to the undertaker according to the law of supply and demand, and receives,
according to the same law, the exchange equivalent in wages. This
distribution of the national produce according to the "natural" laws of
exchange, entails the consequence that with the increasing productivity
of labour, the wages of the labourer form an ever-decreasing proportion of the produce. Labour is bought and sold for its cost price, viz.,
food. "As if the employer *gave* the labour," says Rodbertus, "and
did not *receive* it." The labourer when he receives, in his day's wages,
the food necessary for the day, does not receive the produce of his
day's labour : he has to be satisfied with less than the day is worth.
The slave is compelled to do this by force, and the free labourer
by hunger. He complains that the shares of the landowner, the
capitalist, and the labourer in the produce are not regulated by social
foresight, by a rational social law, but are left to the arbitrary working
of so-called "natural" laws. "It depends on the chances of the
market how great the share of each class in the national produce
will be."

Rent being, according to the theory of Rodbertus, all income which is received without labour and entirely by virtue of a possession, it follows that this category of income includes the landowner's rent, the capitalist's interest, and the undertaker's profit.   Since there is no income which is not produced by labour, rent rests upon two inevitable provisoes. (1) There can be no rent unless the labour produce more than is necessary in order that the labourer may continue his labour, for without this surplus it is not possible that a person can draw an income, unless he work himself.   (2) There can be no rent unless institutions exist for depriving the labourer of this surplus, wholly or in part, and giving it to others, who do not themselves work, since the labourer is primarily in possession of the produce of his labour. Economic grounds, the same grounds which account for the increased productivity of labour, prove that labour gives this surplus, and it is law which takes it from the labourer and gives it to another.   This is especially seen in the case of slave-labour, where the labourer is allowed just so much of the produce as is necessary to the continuation of his labour.   Nowadays, the arbitrary measures of the slave-owner have been replaced by the wages-contract between labourer and employer, but, says Rodbertus, " this contract is only formally and not actually free, and hunger fully takes the place of the whip.   What used to be called food, is now called wages."   Where and when this happy-go-lucky plan of distributing the produce is followed, it is impossible to expect that satisfactory results will attend the increase of the productivity of labour.   The wealth of society may increase to such an extent that all its members might live in abundance, and yet the fact may be that the majority are plunged into poverty.   Rodbertus, writing nearly forty years ago, calls attention to phenomena which are to-day attracting great attention.   He found that the process of impoverishment was then steadily going on amongst a large class of society.   "It has reached such an extent, that a very large part of the people is no longer able to live upon its own means, but is in some way or other thrown on the support of the other part of society. . . . This fact runs parallel with another equally indubitable, and making the first still more striking : the national wealth has simultaneously increased.   Not only has the national income become greater, because the population has increased, and the increased population has therefore produced more, but if the increased national wealth be divided

between the increased population there is a larger sum per head." [1]
These remarkable facts go together : (1), the impoverishment in a
nation increases out of proportion to the growth of population, while
simultaneously (2) the national income increases at greater ratio than
the population, and the national wealth also tends to grow.

This phenomenon Rodbertus holds to be unique in history. There
have been times when a universally increasing impoverishment has
taken place—as the time of the decay of the Roman Empire—times,
too, when an individual class has suffered temporarily—this is often
the case with both landed proprietors and capitalists—but never before
have we had a continually increasing partial impoverishment of
society, a steady growth in the impoverishment of one and the same
class of people, while all the time the national wealth has increased.
This brings Rodbertus to a theory of pauperism and commercial
crises. According to the exchange-value possessed by a person is the
extent of his purchasing power, and according to his purchasing power
is the amount of the use-value which he can convert into exchange-
value. There must be in exchange a purchasing power equal to the
use-value produced for society, or else a part of the same cannot
become exchange-value by passing into the hands of consumers. If
every producer received the value of all he produced, increasing productivity could not bring about stagnation in trade until more commodities had been produced than society needed. For the purchasing
power would be equal to the use-value produced, and until the needs
of all consumers were satisfied there could be no over-production.
But the purchasing power of the labourers is not equal to the use-
value they produce ; it rather decreases with increasing productivity.
The consequence is that over-production enters in before the needs of
society are satisfied. As a matter of fact, the production may not be
excessive, but the purchasing power of the labouring class is exhausted
before its wants are supplied. Thus commercial crises occur, and
thus pauperism is created. These phenomena he attributes to the
existence of a "cruel law," according to which " When commerce is
left to adjust the distribution of the national produce at will, certain
circumstances connected with the development of society have the
effect that with the increasing productivity of social labour, the wages of
the labouring classes become an ever-decreasing part of that national

---

[1] First " Social Letter," (Berlin, 1850), p. 9.

produce." Here he does not mean merely the amount of nominal wages—the quantity of food, clothing, &c., purchasable with the money received—but the proportionate share which the labourer derives from the total produce. Two assumptions are necessary to the correctness of this theory ; the one that the productivity of labour has increased and is still increasing, the other that the share of the labourer has in reality not increased proportionately, has remained stationary, or has fallen. These historical suppositions proved, however, it follows necessarily that wages as a quota of the national produce have fallen simultaneously with an increasing productivity. He holds that both assumptions are correct,—that agricultural [1] and industrial labour is increasingly productive, and that wages have in Europe failed in general to rise much or for a long time above the limit of necessary wants, but form an ever-decreasing part of the produce of society, with the consequence that rent increases and the recipients of rent flourish at the expense of the labourers. The labouring classes were formerly the victims of legal privilege, now they are the prey of a ruling class. Their toil begins with the rising and ends with the setting of the sun, but no exertion can alleviate their hard lot. Is it not a just claim that those who create the wealth should receive a fair share, and enjoy some of the advantages which it offers to society?

Rodbertus recognises that we are at present living in an anomalous state of things. The working classes possess full personal freedom, and are received in the State union with rights and duties similar to those of the propertied classes. The State is now society, and the change is pregnant with significance. That system has, he says, been abolished in which, as in antiquity, the greater part of society stood outside the State as aliens or slaves. So, too, has disappeared that system in which, as in the Middle Ages, all society stood within the State, but in which the State was a conglomeration of associations wherein the State rights and duties of members of society were fully defined. The existing condition of society is one in which all citizens have equal rights. Thus all the concomitant institutions and arrangements of earlier social orders cease with the disappearance of these to be longer valid. The working classes can no more be excluded

---

[1] Rodbertus devotes his third "Social Letter" (Berlin, 1851) to a refutation of Ricardo's theory of rent and of his contention that the productivity of agriculture tends to diminish a contention which he calls a "phantom of Ricardo's, set up for the purpose of supporting his theory of rent.

from the consideration of the State, and they acquire the new right of being entitled to share in the resources of society. " Incontestably the free citizen who fulfils his duties to society has a legitimate claim to a commensurate share in the common produce, unless the idea of a claim without debtor be conceded." But Rodbertus holds it to be good policy as well as mere justice to recognise this claim.

"The working classes," he says, "who have hitherto gone so willingly in the yoke of an unremunerated labour, are now not only kicking against the insupportableness of their suffering, and the torment of inadequate attempts at a remedy, but are, under a feeling of their right, about to throw the whole load from their backs. The imminent danger exists that they will prefer to destroy the civilisation of society, so that they may no longer have to bear the suffering of this civilisation. The imminent danger exists that again a storm of barbarism—this time proceeding from society itself—will lay waste the seats of culture and wealth. It is madness to think of relying upon armies for protection against the danger of this second migration of nations. The barbarians who had served in Rome's armies conquered Rome."[1] And, again, we find him exclaiming, " What contradictions in the sphere of political economy in particular, and what contradictions in the social system throughout! The social wealth increases and the companion of this increase is the increase of poverty." The social condition of the working classes should be raised to the level of their political condition, but all that has been done so far, has been to press it lower down. Rodbertus has no patience with the egoism which, " clothing itself too often in the garb of morality," says that the vices of the working classes are the causes of their misery and of pauperism. People call out to the labourer " *Ora et labora*," and enjoin upon him the duty of temperance and providence, but the fact is, says Rodbertus, that thrift is an impossibility, and to preach thrift where there is no chance of saving is pure cant and cruelty. Not, indeed, that morality is not to be enjoined on the working classes. Morality should never cease to enforce its Categorical Imperative everywhere, powerless as the human will is to attain to perfection, but the policy of merely reiterating the duty of morality is useless. He who gives bread to the hungry man, he remarks, protects him far more surely from stealing than he who repeats the

[1] First " Social Letter," p. 79.

command, "Thou shalt not steal." Nor has he much more respect for the *Laissez-faire* school of economists. The production of commodities being a social matter, and depending upon the labour of all the members of society, an endeavour should be made to find a proper standard for distribution. He sneers at the argument of "natural laws." Only in nature do natural laws act of themselves intelligently. For society, which is not natural, laws must be made.

We thus see that the aim of Rodbertus is to secure the labourer a larger and fairer share in the produce. He takes care to repudiate the doctrine of those who would adopt the rough and ready remedy of giving the labourer all the produce. In his third "Social Letter," he expresses himself explicitly on this point :—" While I maintain that land-rent and profit on capital—and therefore farm-rent and under-takers' profit—are the product of the labour of others than the recipients, in consequence of their being in possession of land and capital ; and while I also maintain that the institution of property in land and capital causes the labourers to be deprived of a part of their produce, I do not at all mean to contend that those who employ a number of labourers productively with capital should not be remuner-ated for their social services. Common-sense will never allow itself to be deceived. Not only knowledge but also moral power and energy are needed in order to the successful division of the operations of a number of labourers engaged in production. The same qualities are also necessary, in order that the demands of the market may be under-stood, funds be employed correspondingly, and the requirements of society be promptly satisfied. It is seldom that a capitalist or a landowner is not somehow active in this manner. The productive labourer does not perform services of this kind, nor from the nature of his employment can he. And yet, these services are absolutely necessary in natural production. For this reason, no one will doubt, so long as social services continue to be remunerated, that capitalists and landowners, undertakers and directors of undertakings, are as much entitled to reward for the useful and necessary services they render to society, as is the labourer for his useful services of a differ-ent kind. They are as much entitled as a Minister of Commerce and Public Works is—provided he does his duty. Further, these services, like those of judges, schoolmasters, physicians, &c., can only be remunerated from the produce of the labourers' work, since there is an other source of material wealth." Rodbertus, moreover, does not desire to do away at once with property in land and capital, though only admitting the "relative necessity for the present day" of this institution, and denying an absolute necessity; what he first seeks to do is to prevent the increasing stream of social wealth from emptying itself further in rent.[1]

Rodbertus proposes to abolish the present wages-contract and to introduce in its place a normal workday with a normal form of wages; then to introduce labour-note money, the issue of which should be entirely in the hands of the State: and finally to establish a system of warehouses for commodities to be paid as wages. These contrivances would provisionally leave property in land and capital as at present, except that for the future the labouring classes would share in the increasing productivity; but the ultimate goal is the replacement of this form of property by a property in income alone, which would inaugurate a new and a higher State order than any that has gone before. And here a word in passing as to Rodbertus' idea of the State. In his theory of the State Rodbertus advances from the elementary organism of the family to the tribe. This is the era of the hunters of the plain, when men worked merely to live and did not live to work. All the produce of labour belonged to the labourer. The vanquished enemy was killed, for there was no food to support him. Then came the gradual formation of the State. Agriculture of a primitive kind was introduced —the cultivation of the land and the rearing of cattle—and now it was possible to win in one day more food than was needed for the day's demand. There was leisure to spare, and so the dawning appeared of a new era, when mental as well as physical pursuits could be followed. There was now introduced the institution of slavery. The conquered were no longer put to death ; they were put to labour, they were made to produce food for the victors. The slaves were supplied with food and enjoyed protection, but they and their labour were the absolute possession of their masters. The State which was thus based on slavery Rodbertus calls the heathen-antique type, and he

---

[1] Rodbertus holds that the collective property which the Social-Democrats seek would lead to far greater injustice than is caused by individual property, and he says in one of his letters, "The working-classes here follow Lassalle. But I had by letter brought home to him the absurdities and injustices to which such a property must lead and (what was particularly disagreeable to him) that *he* was not the originator of this idea, but that he had taken it from Proudhon's '*Idée générale de la révolution.*'"

reckons to this group four forms—those of the Pharaohs and the Incas, the Indians, the Persians, and the Greeks and Romans. But in process of time the man became free and only the soil and the tools remained in the hands of the master. This is the era of the Christian-Germanic group, comprising the Ecclesiastical State, that of the Estates, the Bureaucratic State, and the Representative State, the last being the State of the present. Rodbertus says that we are on the eve of a new era, and that the coming State will differ as much from the present form, and be as superior to it, as the present differs from and is superior to its predecessors. This difference and superiority will consist in the institution of a new form of property and a new relationship between the various classes of society. He, in fact, imagines a state of society in which the only individual property is that of income, both land and national produce belonging to the entire nation in common. With such an ideal order of things, commodities would only cost labour, and it would only be possible to express the value of commodities according to the measure of time, for the length of time taken to produce a commodity by labour would be its cost.

To deal, first, with the transitional change. Rodbertus would take nothing directly from property in land and capital. All he desires to do is to adopt such measures as may prevent the increasing national productivity from falling in the future exclusively to rent and profit, so that wages may receive a due share. For this purpose the State must ascertain the present value of the national produce in metal money, and the quota which the present national wages fund forms, then the sum of the wages must be commuted into national produce estimated according to labour, and must for the future be retained at the proportion thus found. Before going further, we must understand what Rodbertus means by his normal workday, which is based on his initial principle that economic commodities cost labour and only labour. The term normal workday does not mean with him what it means with most Socialists, a legally determined number of hours' work daily. He expressly says in one place that the expectation that such a normal workday will protect the labourers from the greed of their employers, and secure them fair wages, is entirely without foundation. Nor does he regard the legal limitation of the period of labour in the case of adult males as tenable on practical grounds, or defensible when regarded from the standpoint of personal right, though he makes an exception with females and children. " As much as I am for the subordination of the individual to the State," he says, " I still maintain that the State has no right to say to a free man, ' You shall work no more than so and so many hours daily : ' for this is virtually what it means—to forbid undertakers to allow work more than a certain number of hours daily, is to forbid work-people to work more than a certain number of hours." He recognises, indeed, that too long labour is an evil, but he asks the reason why the working classes must labour so long for the satisfaction of their bare needs ; and this brings him again to the *crux* of the whole social problem. The law which makes the share of the labourers in the produce continually smaller, and the further law which forces wages down to the cost of necessary subsistence, would work more unjustly than before. Besides, a normal time-day in the ordinary acceptance of the term would not be fair, for good and bad labourers would be placed on the same level, to the total disregard of the rights of employers. The proper thing is to increase wages, and then if the workman finds that he can earn in four hours enough to keep him for the day, there will be little fear of his working twelve. Even if the State were to restrict the hours of labour to eight, and to decree that wages should not be reduced, the material position of the working classes would not be improved. " Legislation which *only* restricts the hours of labour merely lops the branches of a poison-tree. Legislation which at once fixes a definite amount of labour, or rather a definite performance (*Leistungsquantum*), lays the axe at its roots, plants in its place a healthy, fruitful tree, which it can then allow to shoot and blossom as freely as it will." Thus the day must be normal not only as to time but as to performance. Three points have to be borne in mind in considering this question : time, perform- ance, and income. As to time, the Legislature in fixing a normal workday would probably begin by assuming that in a certain number of hours—say six or eight, according to the industry—a workman can and must earn as much as his position as a citizen requires. On the basis of this standard of time he would fix a standard of performance or work done, and then on the basis of the latter he would finally fix an adequate standard of income. In that way the workman would for an average quantity of work done receive a normal income. A " perfect normal workday," according to Rodbertus, presumes therefore " Normal performance in the normal time and normal wages for the normal performance." According to this rule he would let men work as long as they might desire, though the State should contrive that the normal performance of a workday of eight, nine, or ten hours gave wages corresponding to the social position of the workman and the existing state of national productivity. Either the State might fix this standard of wages itself, or employers and workmen might agree upon a scale under the supervision of the State, but the wages-scale would, like the scale of work, require periodical revision in accordance with the increasing productivity of labour. Recapitulated the objects which the normal workday would aim after are : (1) Justice between employer and employed, in that an average performance would be required for the normal day ; (2) justice between workman and workman, in that the workman would be paid according to his work, the good workman receiving more and the bad workman less ; and (3) justice between the working classes and society, in that the former as a part of society would benefit by every succeeding increase in the national productivity, instead of the benefit going solely to the landowners and capitalists.[1]

Rodbertus makes his proposal clearer by an example. Let it be supposed that the labouring population of a country turns out produce equal in value to 10,000,000 normal hours of labour—normal labour being now an invariable standard of value—and that of this amount 3,000,000 fall to wages, 1,000,000 to the State for national purposes, and 3,000,000 each to rent and profit on capital. Suppose, too, that the wages represented by 3,000,000 hours of labour are only equal to the bare cost of subsistence. After twenty years the productivity has, perhaps, doubled, so that the same number of labourers turn out double the former produce. In other words the 3,000,000 hours of labour represent twice the cost of subsistence. Under the " iron law " of wages the labourer would, however, continue to receive the amount of wages equal to the cost of living. Thus measured according to normal labour the wages would only be half what they were before, for instead of forming $\frac{3}{10}$ths of the whole produce they would now only be $\frac{3}{20}$ths. If, however, wages formed a fixed quota of the produce they would still form $\frac{3}{10}$ths of the whole, and the real wages would be equal to twice the cost of living.

[1] Rodbertus had trained a Pomeranian landowner, a tenant, and a farm inspector into his normal workday scheme, and they found that it " worked very well." This was before 1848, but the catastrophe of that year came " raw and cold, and destroyed the life of the young plant."

A further advantage of the normal workday would, in the opinion of Rodbertus, be the discovery of a better measure of value than is furnished by either gold or silver, viz., labour itself. The retention of metal money as a measure of value would lead to difficulties, owing to the fluctuations to which the precious metals are subject, and so Rodbertus requires not only that the value of all produce shall be reckoned according to normal work-time ; but that wages in every trade shall be paid according to normal work-time. The product of a normal day's work would represent one workday, whatever the time taken to its production, and thus the product of one trade would be equal to that of any other : in other words, " products of equal work-time would be equal to one another in value," labour being in this way the measure of all value. The workman would now be paid for so much normal labour performed, and his wages would represent a certain value of produce.

According to this mode of calculating value, the entire raw products of a country would have a value equal to the direct labour bestowed upon them, *plus* the indirect labour represented by the wear and repair of tools. The half-manufactured products would have a value equal to the direct and indirect labour expended on them, *plus* the value of the raw products. The value of the manufactured commodities, finally, would be equal to the direct and indirect labour expended on them, *plus* the value of the half-manufactured products. Thus the value of the national produce would, in the end, be equal to the sum of the normal labour directly and indirectly performed. From the aggregate value would be learned the value of every single category of production, from this the value of any desired quantity of a product. The constituted value of a bushel of wheat would be found by dividing the aggregate value of the wheat by the number of bushels in an average harvest. But, further, to the proper execution of this plan of a normal workday, with its corollary of a labour standard of value, it would be necessary to introduce a new paper money running in hours and fractions of hours of labour. The labourers would be paid in this money, for which they would be entitled to purchase, in accordance with its value, any desired commodities. A commodity which had cost one hour's work would be purchasable with a one-hour ticket or certificate. This paper money would be an ideal money, inasmuch as it would be a perfect measure of value, and would ensure absolute

F

security, since it would only be issued when the indicated value really existed.[1]   To meet the possibility of the fraudulent use of tickets, the State should alone issue the new money, and for safety it might rely upon the difficulty or impossibility of imitation in the manufacture of the paper, and also upon the penal law.   The danger of the State deceiving the nation, by appropriating commodities without authority, might be guarded against by the proper organisation of the State authorities and the control offered by publicity.   The State would then grant loans in the paper money to employers according to the amount of labour they employed, and these loans would be repaid in produce calculated according to normal labour.   Warehouses would be established for the produce thus paid, and the tickets paid to the labourers would be accepted here in exchange for commodities desired by the holders of the tickets.   It would not, however, be absolutely necessary that these warehouses should be established ; the labourers might be paid in labour-money, and the State might merely receive it at banking houses in exchange for metal money.   Either plan would allow of the labourers receiving their fixed share of the produce, first in money and then in commodities.   If they worked twelve hours a day, and their share of the produce were a third, they would be paid for four hours, and the remaining produce and the paper money corresponding to it would fall to the capitalists and landowners.

Let us now see how the system would work.   Keeping to the figures and proportions taken before, we will suppose a national produce of 10,000 000 hours of labour, of which 1,000,000 fall to the State, while 9,000,000 are divided equally amongst landowners, capitalists (together to be called the propertied classes), and labourers.   This latter amount thus represents the distributable produce, and with it alone have we

[1] In constructing this system, Rodbertus claims to have proceeded upon entirely independent lines.   "In 1842," he writes, "when I explained the idea of a constituted value and a labour-money in 'Zur Erkenntniss,' I did not know that a practical experiment had ever been made in France or England.   Up to the present time I have been unable to learn anything in detail as to Owen's bank, and the description of Reybaud ["Etudes sur les Réformateurs"] is clearly vague and faulty."   ("Das Kapital," p. 156.)   He also takes care to prevent confusion with Chitti's "Des crises financières," a work he never read, and only heard of through a critique.

In "The Social System," by John Gray (Edinburgh, 1831), and "Lectures on the use of Money," by the same, (Edinburgh, 1848), we have a somewhat similar scheme to that of Rodbertus explained.   Compare the following passage :—"Money should be merely a receipt, an evidence that the holder of it has either contributed a certain value to the national stock of wealth, or that he has acquired a right to the same value from some one who has contributed to it."

to do. It is evident that the commodities produced cannot all be such
as the labouring classes will require. The propertied and labouring
classes must, therefore, be divided into groups according as they con-
sume, let us say, articles of luxury and useful commodities. Following
the plan adopted by Moritz Wirth in his critique of Rodbertus, a table
may with advantage be drawn up as follows :

GROUP I.	GROUP II.
A Propertied classes ⎫ Producing useful Commod- AA Labouring classes ⎭ ities.	B Propertied classes ⎫ Producing Articles of BB Labouring classes ⎭ Luxury.

Let the value of the combined produce of a fixed period be 9,000,000
hours, work-time being the measure of value. The produce of A—AA
consists, we will say, of 3,000,000 hours (useful commodities), and that
of B—BB consists of 6,000,000 hours (articles of luxury). The labouring
classes require the useful commodities, the propertied classes require
the articles of luxury ; but how to adjust this exchange? As the
labourers' share of the produce is a third of the whole, A pays over to
AA labour-money to the amount of 1,000,000 hours, and similarly B
pays to BB labour-money amounting to 2,000,000 hours. AA and BB
exchange their money, together 3,000,000 hours, for the warehoused
produce of A. Now the labourers are in possession of the useful
commodities produced. A has cleared out, and has received labour-
money representing 3,000,000 hours, and B retains a full warehouse of
articles of luxury. The propertied classes A must, however, be supplied
from the produce of B. Of the labour-tickets of A a third are retained
for future use, and two-thirds are exchanged for articles of luxury
held by B. Now B has 2,000,000 hour-tickets and 4,000,000 hours'
value of articles of luxury for division. The net result may be shown
as follows (in millions) :

| | ORIGINAL PRODUCE | | AFTER DIVISION. | |
	Useful Commodities.	Articles of Luxury.	Useful Commodities.	Articles of Luxury.
A Propertied classes	3	—	—	2
AA Labouring classes (now labour tickets)			1	—
B Propertied classes	—	6	—	4
BB Labouring classes (now labour tickets)			2	—

9   9

In addition A is in possession of 1,000,000 labour tickets (hours) and B is in possession of 2,000,000 tickets for the future payment of the labourers. If the productivity were doubled the distribution would follow the same proportion. If the production became excessive, and more commodities were produced than could be consumed, the only effect would be to reduce the amount of labour done to the requisite production. Everyone would still have all he needed, and in addition more leisure would be afforded for intellectual pursuits. Rodbertus, therefore, holds that his system of distribution excludes the possibility of commercial crises, though Wirth shows that with a reduction of wages—that is, with a diminution of the labourers' share in the produce—a crisis would occur.

Though Rodbertus thinks that property in land and capital could be dispensed with, there are circumstances which make it impossible to expect that this can take place for a long time. These reasons are not, however, economic. Already the largest productive concerns are directed by officials : why not by the State equally well ? The reasons are social, for apart from the question of right it must be remembered that property exercises an educational and cohesive power in society which cannot safely be allowed to slip away unless an adequate substitute be found. Nevertheless, the supplanting of this form of property is the ultimate goal he has in view, for the ideal form is property in income only. He finds that with division of labour only two alternatives are open : either the present system of property in land and capital, in which the social produce of the labour of many persons belongs to one individual, or else a " social property in land and capital," with a share for everyone in the value of the common produce. The term " social property in land and capital " has two meanings. It may stand for a system (1) according to which the State owns the entire national soil and produce, or (2) for the Association system of production, in which the State furnishes the land and capital requisite to the carrying on of independent agricultural and industrial undertakings, a transitional form of which system is seen in profit-sharing. In the latter case the social property would be really private property in another form, and the effect would be to resolve the State into innumerable small productive or trading associations, working like commercial companies ordinarily do. This plan he regards not only as undesirable but as incapable of realisation. The

other form which society without private property might take is that
in which the land and capital are liberated from private possession,
whether by individuals or communities, and belong to the entire nation
as such.   Here the entire national produce would remain social until
it came to be distributed as national income for consumption by the
individual members of society.   One may imagine, says Rodbertus, a
communism in regard to the land and capital of a nation without
communism in distribution.   Here only property yielding rent—rent,
that is, in the wider sense of the word—would be abolished, and not
property altogether.   Property would rest then on its true basis,
labour, and would not consist in "the individual property of the
labourer in his direct produce—which is, with the division of labour
and with property in land and capital, impossible—but in the individual property of the labourer in the entire *value* of his produce."
Division of labour might retain the same form as at present.   Farms,
factories, industrial undertakings of all kinds might be carried on as
now, but it would be on the common account; and they might even
produce the same commodities as now, only care would be taken to
adjust production to the national demand.   The State would own the
land and capital absolutely, but its control over the produce would
only continue until the distribution took place : it would exercise no
supervision over the incomes of persons, neither over the persons
themselves as owners nor over their free wills.   There would be full
personal freedom, with the exception of the absence of power to
acquire property in land and capital.   Life, talent, and capacities
would be untouched, and private associations for the beneficial
employment and enjoyment of income might exist without restraint.
There would be no oppression of the weak by the strong, for the
system is based, not on subjection and slavery, but on the free and
universal fulfilment of those duties upon whose performance the State
depends.   Freedom would be greater, equality more general, and property itself more secure in a system of communism in land and capital
than in any system which allows these to remain in private hands, for
only when this form of personal property is abolished will social
despotism disappear.   There would, however, be compensation for
the proprietors disappropriated.   Their rents would be ascertained,
and they would be redeemed in course of time at their value, but as
productivity increased the amount of the country's indebtedness to
the proprietors would become gradually smaller.

"Not Individualism but Socialism completes the series of emancipations which began with the Reformation."[1] This is Rodbertus' conclusion. He is convinced that only when the social system thus described comes into operation will right and liberty truly prevail. After all, he says, the new form of property does not differ more from property in land and capital than this does from property in human beings. And still he does not seek to minimise the difficulties that stand between him and his goal. "The way is long," he remarks in one of his letters, but for that reason it is desirable that the journey shall be begun without delay. Justice and prudence alike urge the necessity for movement, since the social question is fast taking this form: "Are the proprietors of the soil to be driven out, as in a migration of the nations, by those who are without property?" But the cost! "Certainly, the solution of the social problem will cost more than the printer's ink of a police order, simply because it *is* the social problem." He is confident that this problem will never be settled "in the street by means of strikes, paving-stones, or petroleum," that social ills will not be "relieved, much less healed, by camomile tea."[2] Permanent social peace, a strong Executive Power, enjoying the confidence and attachment of the working classes, and extensive preparations made in quiet and order, are all necessary preliminaries to the final settlement of a difficulty which becomes more dangerous the longer it is ignored.

No one, however, could be more sensible of the vastness of the task involved in the realisation of his scheme than was Rodbertus himself, and that is why he was to the last desirous to see a temporary compromise effected, a compromise the object of which should be to give to the labouring classes a just share in the produce of their labour.

During the life of this eminent theoist a question of precedence arose as between himself and Karl Marx, and since his death it has excited a good deal of controversy. It is not to be denied that in Germany a majority of leading political economists give Rodbertus the credit of having first established the theory of surplus-value which is the basis both of his own system and that of Marx.[3] Rodbertus

[1] "Das Kapital," p. 221.

[2] Letter of November 6th, 1875.

[3] Adolph Held must be mentioned as a decided opponent of Rodbertus' claims. See his "Sozialismus, Sozialdemokatie, und Sozialpolitik." (Leipzig, 1878), pp. 59-65.

does not, it is true, use the term surplus-value, but his whole argument rests upon the contention that a portion of the labourer's produce is retained by the capitalist, who buys labour at exchange-value and makes profit by giving the labourer only so much of the produce as is necessary to his maintenance. While Marx will secure the surplus-value to the labourer by the rough and ready method of expropriation, Rodbertus, with what some people have dared to think a higher sense of justice, will secure it by abolishing, by legitimate means, personal property in land and capital, and making income the only form of individual property. Rodbertus felt strongly that the author of "Capital" had been unfair to him, and he did not hesitate to say so. He writes to his friend Wagner on July 8th, 1872, "You will find that since 1842 —when I published my first greater work—I have unalterably followed the same thoughts ; and that others, as for example Marx, have hit upon much that I had already printed." And again to his correspondent Zeller he writes on March 14th, 1875 : "You will find that the same [line of thought] has been extensively used by Marx in his 'Capital' and by Dühring [1] in his last important work, but certainly without quoting me." He goes so far as to say, in a letter to Rudolph Meyer, that Marx has "plundered" him, and in another he observes : "Where the increased value of capital arises I have shown in my third 'Social Letter' essentially as Marx does, only much more briefly and clearly. But Marx's work is not so much an investigation into capital as a polemic upon the present form of capital, which he confuses with the idea of capital itself, whence his errors spring." [2]

Marx, on the other hand, would not admit plagiarism. He even patronises Rodbertus, for referring in "Capital" [3] to the third "Social Letter," he observes: "I shall return later to this writing, which, in spite of its false theory of rent, sees through the nature of capitalistic production." Engels, the editor of the third edition of "Capital," is good enough to add : "It will here be seen in what a friendly way Marx judged his predecessors as soon as he found in them actual progress, a new and correct idea." Had Rodbertus lived to add a comment to this comment on a comment, he might have shown that Marx had good reason to treat his authority with respect. Engels says further in his preface to the German edition of

[1] See the reprint, "Zur Beleuchtung der socialen Frage," (1875), p. 104, note.
[2] In "Briefe, etc., von Rodbertus-Jagetzow," (Berlin, 1881).
[3] Vol. i., edition of 1883, p. 543, note.

"Das Elend der Philosophie," published after Marx's death, that the charge of Rodbertus is absolutely unfounded, for Marx never saw "Zur Erkenntniss,"—only having read the three "Social Letters," and these not before 1858 or 1859—and did not even know of the charge of piracy. But it was only in 1859 that Marx's "Zur Kritik der politischen Ökonomie" appeared. It is only fair to weigh well all that Engels says on the subject in the preface to the second volume of " Capital." Here he stoutly denies either that Marx plagiarised, or that he knew anything of the charge which Rodbertus publicly made against him as early as 1879, and which Rudolph Meyer had advanced on his own account five years before in his " Emancipationskampf," a work of which, as Engels says, Marx was in possession. Engels refers as follows to the position of Marx in relation to the surplus-value theory :

"The existence of that part of the value of the product which we now call surplus-value was established long before Marx, and it was with more or less clearness said wherein it consists, viz., the produce of the labour for which the appropriator has paid no equivalent. But no one got any further. Some people—the classical *bourgeois* economists—investigated at the most the proportion in which the product of labour is divided between the labourer and the owner of the means of production, and others—the Socialists—found this distribution unjust, and sought by Utopian measures to remedy the injustice. Both, however, remained embarrassed in the economic categories as they had found them. Then Marx came forward, and took up a position in direct opposition to all his predecessors. Where they had seen a solution he saw only a problem. He saw that there was here neither dephlogisticated air, nor inflammable air, but oxygen—that it was not merely a question of the confirmation of an economic fact, or of the conflict of this fact with eternal justice and true morality, but of a fact which was calculated to revolutionise economics altogether, and which offered the key to the comprehension of capitalistic production in its entirety—to him who knew how to use it. Proceeding on the basis of this fact, he investigated all the discovered categories, just as Lavoisier on the basis of oxygen had investigated the discovered categories of phlogistic chemistry. In order to know what surplus-value was, he had first to learn what value itself was, and Ricardo's theory of value had above all things to be subjected to criticism. Marx thus investigated labour in its value-forming quality, and for the first time determined *what* kind of labour forms value, why and how it forms value, and proved that value is nothing but congealed labour of *this* kind—a point which Rodbertus to the last had not grasped. Marx then investigated the relationship of commodities and money, and showed how and why, by virtue of the property of value indwelling in them, commodities and the exchange of commodities must produce the antithesis of commodities and money : the money theory he thus founded is the first exhaustive one, and tacitly it is now universally accepted. He investigated the transformation of money into capital, and proved that it rests on the purchase and sale of labour-power. In thus substituting labour-power, the value-creating property, for labour, he solved at once one of the difficulties on which the Ricardo school had been shipwrecked, viz., the impossibility of bringing the reciprocal exchange of capital and labour into accord with Ricardo s law that value is determined by labour. By distinguishing between constant and variable capital he succeeded in exposing and thus explaining the real process of formation of surplus-value in all its details, which none of his predecessors had done ; and he also proved the existence of a difference in capital itself, with which Rodbertus was no more able than the *bourgeois* economists to do anything, though it furnishes the key to the solution of the most complicated economic problems. He investigated surplus-value further, found both its forms—absolute and relative surplus-value—and showed the different, yet in each case important, part which they have played in the historical development of capitalistic production. On the basis of surplus-value he developed the first rational theory of wages which we have had, and for the first time gave the characteristics of a history of capitalist accumulation and a representation of its historical tendency." [1]

So far the defence of Engels on behalf of his friend. Few people have attempted to detract from the great credit due to Marx for producing a work of such originality as " Capital," and yet it is only a fair contention to say that Rodbertus had a clear idea of what is now spoken of as the Marxian theory of value long before the publication of that work or its precursor the " Kritik." Such a claim does not involve a charge of piracy, and much less does it seek to minimise the importance of Marx as a founder of scientific Socialism. So far as the reading world is concerned, the question of priority is not

[1] Preface to vol. ii. of " Das Kapital," pp. 19, 20.

of very great moment, and indeed Rodbertus and Marx may both wear laurels as Socialist economists of light and leading, yet science likes to apportion to every man his proper place in the Valhalla of fame. What has been said will have prepared us for a nearer consideration of Marx's views.

CHAPTER IV.

KARL MARX AND SURPLUS VALUE.

KARL MARX was born at Treves, in the Rhine Province, on May 5th, 1818, the son of a high mining official. Like so many men who have achieved eminence in science and literature during modern times, he was of Jewish blood, both his parents being Hebrews. He belonged, indeed, to a family which could boast of an unbroken line of rabbins from the sixteenth century. The proper name of the family was Mordechai, but the grandfather of Marx discarded this patronymic. Originally the father of Karl Marx was an advocate at Treves, and it is said that when the town fell to Prussia in 1814 he received orders from his new rulers either to be baptised into the Christian Church or to cease legal practice. Of these alternatives the former was chosen, and both parents renounced their religion.[1] Perhaps this incident may explain the unseasonable bitterness and ridicule frequently employed by the advocate's son when he went out of his way to attack Christianity. Karl Marx studied jurisprudence at Jena and Bonn ; but at Berlin and elsewhere philosophy, political economy, and history engaged his attention. When quite a young man he attracted notice on account of his genius and rare scholarly attainments. Life seemed to offer to him brilliant prospects, for had he either followed an academic career or elected to enter the service of the State—the two vocations for which he was thought to be best fitted—he could not have failed to make his mark. Where, however, relatives and friends proposed, Marx and circumstances disposed. He drifted first into journalism and then into authorship combined with political agitation. After completing his studies he lived at Treves as a private man for some time, and in 1843 he married the sister of a later Prussian Minister, Herr von Westphalen. Before this time he had shown a decided inclination for politics in articles contributed to the *Rheinische Zeitung* of Cologne, of which journal he became editor in 1842. This position enabled him to criticise the proceedings of

[1] G. Adler, " Die Grundlagen der Karl Marx'schen Kritik der bestehenden Volks-wirthschaft " (Tübingen, 1887), p. 226.

the Prussian Government with an unsparing hand, and he made himself so unpleasant that a special censor was sent from Berlin for the purpose of reporting upon the movements of Marx and the hostility of his newspaper. As, however, the bitterness of the attacks only became greater, the Government resolved to go to the root of the matter and suppressed the journal early in 1843. Marx had meanwhile devoted great attention to social questions, and had developed strong Socialistic tendencies, so that when in that year he removed to Paris, partly for the sake of the further study of political economy, but also in order to learn more about French political movements past and present, he was recognised as the exponent of very advanced views on social and economic questions. In Paris he soon found himself mixed up with political movements and organisations. His literary work at this time included the co-editorship with Arnold Ruge[1] of the "Deutsch-Französische Jahrbücher," the first number of which contained contributions by Heinrich Heine,[2] Michael Bakunin,[3] Georg Herwegh, Ludwig Feuerbach,[4] Johann Jacoby, Friedrich Engels,

[1] Arnold Ruge, an author of considerable importance, was born on September 13th, 1803, in the island of Rügen, and studied philosophy at Halle, Jena, and Heidelberg. He was early involved in political movements and in 1825 he received sentence of imprisonment for five years. He also took part in the convulsions of 1848, and the following year had to quit Germany for England, where he lived as teacher and author. Ruge was national in sympathies and by no means a Socialist. He died December 31st, 1880. His literary work was very extensive, and covered the domains of politics, philosophy, fiction, and poetry.

[2] Heine was born at Düsseldorf in 1799 or 1800 (the year is variously stated), and died February 17th, 1856. Like Marx he was of Jewish descent. He had to leave Germany on account of the publication of rabid democratic writings in 1831, and from that year to his death he resided in Paris.

[3] Michael Bakunin was born of a rich noble family at Torschock, in the Government of Tver, Russia, in 1814. He entered the Russian army in 1838 and in 1840 proceeded to Berlin, whence he was recalled, but he refused to obey the summons. Remaining in Germany he took part in revolutionary agitations and was one of the leaders of the Dresden rising of 1849. Captured by Prussian soldiers, he was lodged in Königstein and was in May, 1850, sentenced to death, though his penalty was changed to one of lifelong imprisonment. He was, however, surrendered to Austria in 1851 and was again sentenced to death for political crime, the same commutation once more taking place. Finally he was handed over to Russia, and for some years he was imprisoned on the Neva. After the Crimean War he was transported to East Siberia, whence he succeeded in escaping to Japan and Europe. Until his death at Bern in 1876 he took part in Anarchist movements.

[4] Ludwig Andrew Feuerbach, a German philosopher of note, born at Landshut, July 28th, 1804. He studied theology at Heidelberg, and becoming a Hegelian he went to Berlin for the purpose of hearing Daub. Here he forsook theology and devoted himself entirely to philosophical studies. He intended to follow an academic career, and became *Privatdocent* in 1828,

Moses Hess,[1] and Lazarus Bernays. Marx and Ruge did not, however, agree long, and financial difficulties caused the venture to be
abandoned. With Heine Marx also conducted the journal *Vorwärts*.
In Paris he made the acquaintance of many noted publicists and men of
science, and amongst them of Proudhon, with whom he often had
arguments which lasted through the night.[2] But no exchange of
views could bring these two men together, and when the personal
acquaintance in Paris ceased the gulf widened. Thus when the
"Philosophie de la Misère" was about to appear Proudhon wrote to
Marx, "J'attends votre ferule critique," and it was not long before he
had it. Marx in 1847 answered Proudhon's "Philosophy of Misery"
with his scathing "Misery of Philosophy," and this, as he writes, "put
an end to our friendship for ever," at which no one who reads the
critique will wonder.

More important in its influence upon the future work of Marx was
the friendship which he contracted in Paris with Friedrich Engels.
This veteran Communist records that when he came to converse with
Marx, he found a man who in all theoretical questions shared his own
views. The two formed an intellectual partnership on the spot, and
from 1844 until the death of Marx in 1883, they were always found
harnessed together in the work of Communistic agitation, furnishing
an example of personal attachment rarely observed in politics or
literature. It was not long before Marx made himself as obnoxious to
the French Government as he had been to the Prussian, and in 1845
M. Guizot gave him notice to quit. He went next to Brussels, where
Engels joined him, and the two formed there a German Working
Men's Association, having as an effective organ the *Deutsche*

but his heterodox views on the subject of the immortality of the soul were an obstacle to his
progress and he withdrew from the teacher's chair. Feuerbach wrote many philosophical
works and took great interest in social politics. He died September 13th, 1872. Karl
Grün has written a biography of the philosopher and a *critique* of his system.

[1] Moses Hess was born January 21st, 1812, at Bonn, the son of a well-to-do Jewish tradesman. He was a prolific writer on Socialism and Communism, and he proved the strength of
his revolutionary principles by taking an active part in the South German rising of 1849,
being sentenced *in contumaciam* to death for complicity in the affair. Leaving Germany he
spent the rest of his life in Switzerland and France. He died April 6th, 1875.

[2] "During long debates, often lasting through the night, I infected him, to his hurt, with
Hegelianism, which, owing to his imperfect knowledge of German, he could not study
properly. What I began Herr Karl Grün continued after my expulsion from Paris, and he
as professor of German philosophy had the advantage of me that he knew nothing about it
himself."—See appendix to "Das Elend der Philosophie," edition 1885.

Brüsseler Zeitung. Their activity attracted the favourable notice of a German Communist League located in Paris, which, desirous of securing such powerful allies, sent delegates in 1847 to Marx in Brussels, and to Engels in Paris, asking them to enter the organisation, and promising that a congress should shortly be convened in London, when they would be able to make their views known. The invitation was accepted, and the congress was held in the summer of 1847. As a result of this congress, and of another held at the end of the year, the new and startling theories of Marx were generally accepted, and he was asked to undertake with Engels the drawing up of a Communist Manifesto, which appeared early in the following year. The motto of the old League, now changed to the League of Communists, had been "All men are brothers," but a new watchword was taken, " *Proletariat* of all countries, unite," a watchword which was not only effective as such, but served to proclaim the international character of the organisation and its mission. In his introduction to a German edition of the Manifesto published shortly after the death of Marx, Engels says generously that the fundamental idea running through the work is "solely and exclusively" that of his friend. The Manifesto was printed in various languages, but it was long before it attained the unique fame of being the creed of modern Communists. The reputations of both Marx and Engels were, however, greatly increased by the masterly composition.

While Marx was, in 1848, engaged upon a work on labour, the February Revolution broke out, and its effects were felt far and wide. In Brussels the authorities feared disturbance, and doubting the desirability of the presence of Marx in the city, they had him arrested on March 3rd, and compelled him on the following day to change Belgian for French soil. Marx was not at all unwilling, and he proceeded direct to Paris, where he found himself surrounded by a host of former associates. A manifesto was at once drawn up for circulation in Germany, in which seventeen demands were advanced by the Communist party. These demands comprised the proclamation of a Republic ; payment of members of Parliament, so that working-men might be eligible for election ; the conversion of "princely and other feudal estates," with mines, &c., into State property ; the appropriation of all means of transport, as railways, canals, steamships, roads, and posts, by the State ; the restriction of the law of succession ; the intro.

duction of heavy progressive taxes and the abolition of excise duties ; the establishment of national workshops ; State guarantee to all work-people of an existence and provision for the incapable ; and universal and free education.   Of the six names which appeared below this manifesto that of Marx was the first.   Shortly afterwards Marx re-turned to Germany, and along with Engels, Wolff,[1] and Freiligrath [2] founded the *Neue Rheinische Zeitung* at Cologne, the first number ap-pearing on June 1st, 1848, under his own editorship.   Once more he was able to employ the poignant weapons of censure and condemnation against a Government whose constitution not less than whose acts he was unable to tolerate.   The new Cologne journal quickly took the lead of the Opposition Press, and it was only by the exercise of re-markable skill that Marx escaped the fate which had befallen him five years before.   Then came the unconstitutional acts of November, which led the *Neue Rheinische Zeitung* to urge the people to forcible resistance against the Executive.   For his part in the publication of such advice, Marx had twice to appear at the Cologne Assizes, but he was each time acquitted.   The defence which he made on February 9th, 1849, is a masterpiece of trenchant legal argument.   It was not long before the objectionable Rhenish print was got rid of on another pretext.   In May, 1849, there were risings in Dresden and the Rhine Province, and Marx was not slow to give them his editorial benedic-tion.   This led to the curtailment of his career as a German journalist. The newspaper was suppressed, and the last number appeared, printed in red ink, on June 19th.   Freiligrath contributed a " Farewell " poem, which breathed defiance from first line to last.   The journal is made to promise a speedy resurrection when the forces of revolution have done their work :—

> " Farewell, but not for ever farewell,
>   Thou cannot kill the spirit, my brother ;
>   In thunder I'll rise on the field where I fell,
>   More boldly to fight out another."

Marx was expelled from Prussia.   He first went to Paris, but he was soon refused residence there, and he turned his face towards

1 Wilhelm Wolff, born at Tarnau, June 21st, 1809, died at Manchester, an exile, May 9th, 1864.   He was a great friend of Karl Marx, who dedicated to him the first volume of "Das Kapital" as to a "daring, faithful, and noble champion of the *proletariat.*"

2 Ferdinand Freiligrath, a popular lyrical poet, originally a tradesman.   He was born June 17th, 1810, at Detmold, and owing to political reasons left Germany in the fifties, and resided many years in England.   Died March 18th, 1876, at Canstatt.

England, where he had travelled for six weeks with Engels in 1845. From this time Marx lived continuously in London—making exception of the casual visits paid to Germany and other countries for the purpose of agitation—and here there gathered round him in time quite a colony of ardent Communists, many of them gifted men, and nearly all fellow-outlaws, who received inspiration from him, and were always content to follow his skilful leadership. He found London an exceptionally favourable place for the further study of political economy, for not only was the British Museum at hand with its vast literary stores, but his entire surroundings were such as enabled him to examine more closely than was possible elsewhere the economic doctrines and institutions which he regarded it as his life's task to combat, and if possible to subvert. He resolved to begin his work again from the very commencement, and the resolution was never regretted. Still, his studies were for a long time broken, for it was necessary to earn a livelihood while pursuing them, and the duties of correspondent to the *New York Tribune*, which Marx fulfilled for eight years, consumed a large part of his time. During this period, however, his economic views were ripening, and we see the first fructification in the " Critique of Political Economy,"[1] which bears the date January, 1859, a work containing the principles which were afterwards to be developed in " Capital." While carrying on his studies, and preparing to write books, Marx did not neglect his duty to the Communist League. In 1853, however, a split occurred in the camp, and after that decay set in and the League quietly disappeared from the scene. Marx came again prominently to the front in 1863 and 1864, when new endeavours were made to unite the working classes of various countries in a common movement, an object which he had for years had at heart. The result of the renewed agitation of the question was the formation, on May 28th, 1864, of the International Working Men's Association, whose history we shall need to follow more closely afterwards. Three years later Marx published the first volume of his great economic work, " Capital."[2] Upon this work, with whose theories we shall presently have to deal, rests the reputation of Marx as a political economist, and however its teaching may be viewed, no one[3] will venture to dispute

---

[1] " Zur Kritik der politischen Ökonomie " (Berlin, 1859).

[2] " Das Kapital : Kritik der politischen Ökonomie," Hamburg, 1867, (vol ii., 1885). An English translation, edited by Friedrich Engels, is published by Swan Sonnenschein & Co , and is already (1888) in a second edition.

[3] With the exception of Eugen Dühring, in whose " Kritische Geschichte der National-

the masterly ingenuity, the rare acumen, the close argumentation, and, let it be added, the incisive polemic which are displayed in its pages.

How far, however, Marx can claim absolute originality is a question which is still warmly debated in Germany. In writing "Capital," Marx took England for the illustration of his theories, because in England the capitalist mode of production has attained its greatest growth, and because exile from Germany led him to make this country a special study. At the same time, he warns his countrymen against imagining that the condition of the industrial and agricultural classes is better with them than with us. The very reverse is, he says, the fact, and the only reason of its not being known is that the truth is suppressed or not sought.[1] He allows England to be the only European country where a peaceful social revolution is possible. A word here as to a claim made on behalf of "Capital." Engels says in the preface to the third edition of the first volume that the work is often called on the Continent the "Bible of the working class." But if so it is a bible with which the working class can have little personal acquaintance. It is singular that although Marx prided himself on having written in a simple style,

ökonomie und des Socialismus" (2nd edition, Berlin, 1875) Marx is spoken of as "a disciple of Moses, Ricardo, and Hegel," who has had "a bastard and half-education." This is a sample of Dühring's utterances: "Affectation of superiority and dialectic mysticism will invite no one who possesses even a modicum of sound judgment to pay attention to the deformities of thought and style, the undignified mode of expression, and the vanity, dressed up in English measure, weight, and money, and thus in the narrower sense of the word Anglicised [which distinguish "Capital"]. With the extinction of the last remnant of dialectic folly this means of dupery will, even in its special radical applications, lose its delusive influence, and no one will any longer believe that he need put himself to trouble in order to reach deep wisdom when the pure kernel of the tangled business bears at best the aspect of ordinary theories, if not mere platitudes" (p. 497). This characteristic outburst, however, can only be appreciated properly in the original.

[1] It is impossible to resist the temptation to reproduce a passage from a small work by Julius Fröbel (Leipzig, 1871), entitled "Die Irrthümer des Sozialismus." "When one knows the extremes of misery in which a large part of the factory operatives and rural labourers of England live—a misery of which our poorest class has happily hardly a conception—it is only too intelligible that the consolation that the world is slowly improving should be of no value for these unfortunates, who have only the choice between resignation and the expectation of early deliverance" (p. 39). Unfortunately, it is the helpless classes which suffer from the existence of this wretched "God, I thank Thee that I am not as other men are" spirit. The same author writes: "Socialism did not originate in Germany, nor is Germany to any special degree threatened by its errors and extravagances." To-day there are a million Socialists in Germany—that is all.

G

"Capital" is in reality full of as cumbrous language and thought as a follower of Hegel could well choose. Even allowing for the necessities of a novel task—that of formulating theories requiring new expressions—Marx will never be pardoned for the offence of coining many words which sin as m_jch against philology as good taste. Engels once had to revise one of his own lectures, dropping words of foreign origin, so that it might serve for popular agitation ; how, then, comes he to suppose that the severely scientific "Capital" can become the "Bible of the working class?" A few sentences will chronicle the later work of the founder of the International. This organisation claimed to the last his undivided sympathies, and he placed it eventually in a position of such importance that it became a source of terror to most of the Governments of Europe, which vainly strove to dethrone it from its supremacy amongst the working classes. The great intellectual power, the tenacity and fixedness of purpose, the overpowering will, and above all the vehement hatred of monarchs and monarchies, capitalists and capitalism, which aided Marx in the prosecution of his ambitious aims, did not fail, and could not have failed, to give him pre-eminence amongst the friends of social and political revolution. So great became this pre-eminence that the name of the stern cynic at last grew to be a rallying cry, and his real fame was increased by fabulous attributes of influence and power. The second volume of "Capital" was published in 1885, with a long preface in which Engels endeavours to free the author's literary reputation from the aspersions cast upon it by Rodbertus and his friends. The only other important work which remains to be mentioned is "Der 18te Brumaire," [1] which was directed against Napoleon III. Marx died in London on March 14th, 1883. It is a fact worthy of notice that two of his daughters married French Socialists—one of whom has translated "Capital" into his native language—and another daughter became the wife of an English Socialist.

The monument by which the memory of Marx will be perpetuated is his great work "Capital." The problem he considers is that of value, and the discussion of this problem leads him to develop a new social and economic system. The first of the two bulky volumes deals with the production of capital and the second with its circulation. It is

[1] On the 18th of Brumaire (November 9th, 1799) Bonaparte deposed the Directory, an act followed by his election as Consul.

with the first that we shall chiefly have to do, the edition used being the third German edition of the year 1883. Distinguishing between value in use and exchange, Marx says that while the use-value of a commodity is determined by its utility—which quality is independent of the labour expended in imparting the utility—the value in exchange is the value as measured by other commodities. Apart from their use-value, commodities possess only one property in common, and it is that they are the products of labour. But when the use-value of labour is abstracted the material elements and forms that make the product a use-value are also abstracted, and there is nothing left but labour in the abstract or labour-power, a "social substance" as a crystal of which it is a value. Thus the only reason that causes a use-value or commodity to have value is that human labour in the abstract has been embodied or materialised in it.[1] Consequently, the only measure for the magnitude of the value is the amount of the value-creating substance, viz., labour, which has been expended upon it. As, however, the labour which forms the substance of value is "homogeneous human labour, the expenditure of the same human labour-power," this labour-time is the "socially necessary" quantity required to the production of a commodity. Marx defines "socially necessary" labour-time to be the time requisite to the production of a use-value under existing normal conditions of production, and with the average degree of skill and intensity of labour. Thus when power-looms began to compete with hand-looms, the "socially necessary" amount of labour needed to the weaving of yarn fell by one half, and as a consequence the value of the hand-weaver's labour was depreciated to the same extent. From what has been said it follows that commodities which embody equal amounts of normal labour possess equal value "As values in exchange, all commodities are only definite masses of congealed labour-time."[2] If there were no variation in the time required to the production of a commodity, the value of the same would not change, but the time varies with every variation in the productivity of labour. The value increases with the quantity of labour employed and decreases with the increase in productivity. In the use-value of a commodity there is contained a certain amount of useful labour, and if the useful character of the labour is left out of sight, there remains only the fact of an expenditure of human labour-power.

---

[1] "Capital," vol. i., p. 5.   [2] "Zur Kritik," p. 6.

Thus tailoring and weaving, though producing such different results, are merely two modes of expending this human labour-power. Even skilled labour and simple or unskilled labour are the same in character ; the former is only the latter multiplied, so that a small quantity of skilled is equal to a large quantity of unskilled labour. It is the fact that human labour is a common substance in all commodities which makes commodities commensurable. A bed and a house represent something which, when existing in proper proportions, may bring both into equality as to value, this something being labour. But though labour-power in an active state, in other words *labour*, is a creator of value, it is not itself value : it only becomes value when embodied in an object. Marx thus objects to the expression value of labour. Labour cannot be said to have value because it is itself the measure of value. "What," he asks, "is the value of a commodity? The objective form of the social labour expended in its production. And how do we measure the magnitude of its value? By the quantity of labour contained in it. How, for instance, would the value of a work-day of twelve hours be determined? By the twelve working hours contained in a work-day of twelve hours, which is absurd tautology." [1]

Marx shows that labour, like other commodities, has the two-fold character that it possesses both value in use and value in exchange, and this brings him to the consideration of capital and its origin. The gist of his theory is that the capitalist buys not labour, but labour-power, which exists in the personality of the labourer, but is as different from its functions as a machine from its work. The starting-point of capital is the circulation of commodities. A capitalist with £100 purchases, let us suppose, 2000 lb. of cotton with his money. He does not do this, however, in order that he may sell the cotton again and merely receive back his £100. If he only wished to receive back his original capital, the transactions of purchase and sale would have no meaning and serve no purpose. As a matter of fact, he receives for the cotton purchased for £100 the sum of £110. Here there is an increment of £10, an excess over the original value of the cotton, and thus the original capital of the money-owner, and this increment Marx calls surplus-value (*Mehrwerth*). The original value is not only preserved, but is increased by the addition of a surplus-value, and this movement converts it into capital. It is the prospect of gaining this

---

[1] "Capital," vol. i., p. 546.

surplus-value which causes the capitalist to circulate his capital. He does not seek merely the possession of commodities or use-values ; he only acquires these in order to dispose of them at a gain, and thus his aim is the ceaseless one of profit-making. " Considered abstractly, or independently of circumstances which do not proceed from the inherent laws of the simple circulation of commodities, the act of exchange is, apart from the substitution of one use-value by another, merely a metamorphosis, a change of form in the commodities. The same value—that is, the same quantity of incorporated social labour— remains in the hand of each owner of the commodity ; first in the form of his commodity, then in the form of money which it has assumed, and finally of the commodity to which the money is again changed. This change of form does not imply a change in the magnitude of the value. But the change which the value of the commodity itself undergoes in this process is confined to a change of its money-form. This form exists first as the price of the commodity offered for sale, then as a sum of money—expressed, however, in the price already—and finally as the price of an equivalent commodity. This change of form *per se* as little implies a change in the magnitude of the value as does the exchange of a five-pound note for sovereigns, half-sovereigns, and shillings. Thus, so far as the circulation of the commodity only implies a change in the form of its value, it implies, when the phenomenon takes place in a pure form, the exchange of equivalents." [1] If commodities, or commodities and money, of equal exchange-value— that is, equivalents—are exchanged, no one derives more value from circulation than he puts into circulation, and there is no formation of surplus-value. In reality, however, this is not the process that takes place. Let the value of a certain commodity be expressed by 100; the owner sells it, however, at 110, so that the price is nominally increased 10 per cent., and this surplus-value he appropriates. Now, however, he becomes buyer in turn, and the seller with whom he deals disposes of his own commodity in the same way, at a premium of 10 per cent. So the man only gains a surplus-value in order to lose it again. All owners of commodities, in fact, sell to one another 10 per cent. too dear, so that it is the same thing as if the commodities were sold at their proper value. If, instead of the price being 10 per cent. too high, the reverse process took place, the result would still be the same,

[1] " Capital," vol. i., p. 133.

for the seller, while losing in one way, would gain in another. "The formation of surplus-value, and therefore the conversion of money into capital, can thus be explained neither by the assumption that the sellers dispose of their commodities above their value nor that the buyers purchase them below their value." Whether equivalents or non-equivalents are exchanged, no surplus-value is created. The circulation or exchange of commodities does not create value. Consequently, in the formation of capital something must take place which is not visible in circulation. But, asks Marx, is it possible for surplus-value to originate elsewhere than in circulation, which is the sum of all the reciprocal relationships of the owners of commodities, for "apart from it the owner of commodities has only relationship to his own commodities?" He answers that the owner of commodities can by his labour form value, but not self-increasing value. He can increase the value of a commodity by adding new labour-value to the value existing—as by the conversion of a piece of leather into shoes—but no surplus-value arises here : the original value of the leather is the same, only a new value has been combined with it. "It is impossible for the producer of commodities to create value, and thus convert money or commodities into capital, beyond the sphere of circulation and without coming into contact with other owners of commodities. In other words, capital cannot originate in circulation, and similarly it cannot originate without circulation. It must at the same time have its origin in and not in circulation. . . . The change in the value of money which is to be converted into capital cannot take place in this money itself, since as a means of purchase and payment it only realises the price of the commodity which it buys or pays for, while, preserving its own form, it becomes the petrifaction of unchanging value. Nor can the change originate in the second act of circulation, the resale of the commodity, since this act merely changes the commodity from the natural form back into that of money. The change must therefore take piace in the commodity which is bought in the first act (the conversion of money into commodities), but not in its value, since equivalents are exchanged and the commodity is paid for at its proper value. The change can only spring from its use-value as such—that is, from its consumption. In order to be able to derive value from the consumption of a commodity, the capitalist must be fortunate enough to find within the sphere of circulation—in the market—a commodity whose use-value possesses the peculiar quality that it is the source of value, whose actual consumption is itself an embodiment of labour, and therefore a creation of value." [1] And this commodity is in reality found in the labour-faculty or labour-power.

" By labour-power or labour-faculty," says Marx, " we understand the sum of the physical and mental capacities which exist in the living personality of a man, and which he sets in motion as often as he produces a use-value of any kind." This commodity must, however, fulfil two indispensable conditions : first, it must be at the free disposal of the possessor, and secondly, the labourer must be compelled to sell this labour-power instead of commodities in which it is incorporated. As the labourer lacks the material in which to embody his labour-power, he is obliged to dispose of the power itself. Like all commodities, this labour-power possesses a value, but how is this value determined? " The value of labour-power, like that of every other commodity, is determined by the labour-time requisite to the production, and thus the reproduction of this specific article. So far as it possesses value, labour-power itself represents only a certain quantity of social normal-labour incorporated in it. Labour-power exists only as a faculty of the living individual, and its production presupposes his existence. Given the existence of the individual, the production of labour-power consists in his own reproduction or maintenance. The individual requires for his maintenance a certain quantity of means of subsistence. Thus the labour-time necessary to the production of labour-power resolves itself into the labour-time requisite to the production of these means of subsistence ; or, the value of the labour-power is the value of the means of subsistence necessary to the maintenance of its possessor." In the determination of the value of labour-power, however, the various historical and social facts which determine the standard of life must be taken into consideration. As, too, labour-power needs to be constantly renewed, owing to the mortality of the owner, provision has to be made for the production of fresh supplies, in the bringing up of the labourers' families. If, now, the mass of the commodities daily necessary to the production of a certain amount of labour-power be represented by six hours, or half-a-day of social labour, all the labour due beyond six hours is in excess of the cost of production. If the social labour of these six hours be

1 " Capital," vol. i., pp. 142, 143, 144.

represented by three shillings, this sum corresponds to the value of the labour-power of one day. "The minimum limit of the value of labour-power is formed by the value of the mass of commodities without the daily provision of which the labourer cannot renew his vital functions; therefore, by the value of the physically indispensable means of subsistence. If the price of labour-power falls to this minimum, it falls below its value, since it can only be maintained and developed in an inefficient state. But the value of every commodity is determined by the labour-time necessary to supply it in normal quality."[1] The capitalist having purchased labour-power, he buys at the full price all the material necessary to its use or consumption, and in the process of consumption there are at once produced commodities and surplus-value. The consumption of labour-power, like that of all commodities, is completed outside the market or sphere of circulation. It is only when we enter the sphere of production that we fully learn how capital produces and is produced: in other words, learn the secret of "plus-making" (*Plusmacherei*).[2] The use of labour-power is labour itself, and the buyer of this labour-power consumes it by making the seller work, the seller now becoming actually what he was formerly potentially, active labour-power: in a word a *labourer*. This labour-process, says Marx, exhibits the two peculiar phenomena that the labour is done under the control of the capitalist, and that the product of the labour belongs to him instead of its producer. As the capitalist has bought the day's labour, he can make what use of it he likes, just as he can employ as he wishes the day's labour of a hired horse. The product is a value in use—yarn, for instance, or boots—but the capitalist seeks to produce a use-value which is also an exchange-value or commodity, an article that he can sell, and more than that, an article by the sale of which he can obtain something more than the original cost, in fact, a surplus-value.

Let us follow the process of labour, supposing that the labour-power is used in the conversion of cotton into yarn. The raw material—suppose in this case 10 lb.—costs the capitalist ten shillings, and the wear and tear of the spindle and all instruments of labour employed

[1] *Ibid*, p. 150.

[2] For the consideration of surplus-value, see especially "Capital," vol. i., 2nd section, "Die Verwandlung von Geld in Kapital;" 3rd section, "Die Production des absoluten Mehrwerths;" 4th section, "Die Production des relativen Mehrwerths;" and 5th section, "Die Production des absoluten und relativen Mehrwerths," pp. 120—546.

may be placed at two shillings more. If a quantity of gold representing twelve shillings be the product of twenty-four working-hours or two working-days, it follows that the yarn already embodies two working-days. The question next arises, what value does the labour of the spinner give to the spun cotton? The addition of the value of the wear and tear of instruments has made the original ten shillings into twelve. Now we must find how the value of the cotton and spindle (or rather the use of the spindle) is increased when the labour is added. Let it be supposed that $1\frac{2}{3}$ lb. of cotton can be spun into $1\frac{2}{3}$ lb. of yarn in one hour, then 10 lb. of yarn will represent six hours of labour. If we assume the value of a day's labour-power to be three shillings, and this sum to embody six hours of social labour, it follows that the six hours consumed by the process of spinning give to the cotton an additional value of three shillings. The value of the yarn is therefore represented by the two-and-a-half days' labour it embodies: two days for the cotton and the use of the spindle = twelve shillings; and half-a-day for the spinning = three shillings; together fifteen shillings. But this is just the amount advanced by the money-owner, there is no surplus-value, and consequently the money has not been converted into capital. This does not satisfy the capitalist, who has made nothing by the labour-process. He gave his labourer a value of three shillings, and the labourer has returned him the same value. Soon, however, the capitalist recollects that the reason why he has paid this sum—which embodies half-a-day's labour—is that the production of the means of subsistence required daily by the labourer cost half-a-day's labour, and he reasons : " If half-a-day's labour be necessary in order to maintain the labourer twenty-four hours, there is nothing to prevent him from working a whole day." The capitalist sees that the labour-power which he has purchased may be made not only a source of value, but of more value than it possesses itself. Instead, therefore, of spinning only 10 lb. of cotton in the day, the labourer works double the time and spins 20 lb. Now the value of the yarn spun in a day is equal to five days or thirty shillings.

> 20 lb. of cotton and wear of spindle. = 4 days = 24 shill.
> Weaving.................................. = 1 day = 6 shill.

But the commodities which make up this value only cost the capitalist twenty-seven shillings, for the second half-day's labour (three shillings) cost nothing. Now, a surplus-value has been created, and money has been converted into capital. And yet, while the capitalist has secured a surplus-value, he has done it without violating the laws of exchange. Equivalents have been exchanged. The capitalist buys cotton, spindle, and labour at their proper value, and, like any other buyer of commodities, he consumes their use-value; yet, selling the commodities which are the result of the consumption of labour-power, he withdraws from circulation more than he put into it. This conversion of money into capital takes place both in and out of the sphere of circulation—in, because it is dependent on the purchase of labour-power in the market, and out because circulation only leads to the formation of surplus-value, which act in reality falls to the sphere of production. The creation of surplus-value is merely a continuation of the production of value, for surplus-value would not exist if the process of value-formation were to stop at the point where the labour-power yields its exact equivalent: all the value beyond that is *Mehrwerth*. In this process of production, however, it is necessary to assume average or normal labour—in which must be understood both exertion and skill—and also normal social conditions and technical circumstances.

Marx divides capital into constant and variable capital. Constant capital is that part of capital which takes the form of means of production, as raw material, auxiliary materials, and instruments of labour, and the value of which does not change during the process of production. Variable capital, on the other hand, is that part of capital which takes the form of labour-power, and this changes its value during production, for it reproduces a surplus-value beyond its own value. Still, the constituent parts of constant capital may vary in value. Cotton may sell at one price to-day and at twice the amount to-morrow; improved machinery may greatly depreciate the value of old machinery; but these changes of value do not spring from the process of production, and do not affect the surplus-value added to a raw product by the act of labour. Dealing with the exploitation of the purchased labour-power, Marx divides labour into necessary and surplus labour. Necessary labour is that which is requisite to the production of the means of subsistence upon which the labourer's existence depends, and the time it occupies he calls necessary labour-time (*nothwendige Arbeitszeit*). Surplus labour is that which the labourer performs for the capitalist after he has produced the necessaries for his own existence, and the time thus employed is surplus labour-time (*Surplusarbeitszeit*). If the value of the labourer's daily necessaries represent six hours' labour, this period constitutes the necessary labour-time, and all beyond it is occupied in creating for the capitalist a surplus-value. " Since the value of the variable capital is equal to the value of the labour-power it purchases, since the value of this labour-power determines the necessary part of the working-day, while the surplus-value is determined by the superfluous part of the working-day, it follows that the surplus-value bears the same ratio to the variable capital as the surplus to the necessary labour, or the rate of surplus-value $\frac{s}{v} = \frac{\text{surplus-labour}}{\text{necessary labour}}$. Both ratios express the same relationship though in different forms, in one case in the form of incorporated labour, and in the other case of fluent labour. The rate of surplus-value is therefore the exact expression of the degree of exploitation of labour-power by capital or of the labourer by the capitalist." [1] Thus if the money advanced by a capitalist be £500, made up of £410 constant capital, (raw material and instruments of labour), and £90 variable capital, (labour-power), and the surplus-value be £90, the exploitation of the labourer by the capitalist is 100 per cent., though according to the usual rate of calculation—in which surplus-value is confounded with rate of profit—it would only be 18 per cent. It is not in fact, $\frac{s}{c} = \frac{90}{410}$, or $\frac{s}{c v} = \frac{90}{410+90}$, but $\frac{s}{v} = \frac{90}{90}$. Marx calculates the rate of surplus-value as follows: " We take the entire value of the product (here £590) and equate the constant capital (£410) which merely reappears in it at 0. The value remaining over (£180) is the only value-product really created in the process of producing the commodity. Given the surplus-value (£90) we deduct it from this value in order to find the variable capital (£90). Conversely when the latter is given and we seek the surplus-value. If both are given the concluding operation has only to be performed—to calculate the ratio of the surplus-value to the variable capital, $\frac{s}{v}$. [2]

It may be well to illustrate the foregoing principles by an instance which Marx gives and which has the merit of being based on actual data. A spinning mill, with 10,000 spindles, spins yarn at the rate of 1 lb. per spindle weekly. The waste is 6 per cent., so that the weekly consumption of cotton in the production of 10,000 lb. of yarn is 10,600

---

[1] *Ibid*, pp. 199, 200.   [2] *Ibid*, pp. 200, 201.

lb. (of which 600 lb. go to waste). This cotton costs 7¾d. per lb., so that the value of the raw material is, roughly, £342. The cost of the spindles and all necessary machinery amounts to £1 per spindle, or £10,000 altogether, and the depreciation is 10 per cent., equal to £1000 yearly, or roughly, £20 weekly. Rent amounts to £6 per week, coal to £4 10s., gas to £1, and oil, &c., to £4 10s. So far constant capital. Wages cost £52 a week, the variable capital, and finally the yarn is sold at 12¼d. per lb. The result of this employment of capital will best be seen by a table :

10,600 lb. of cotton at 7¾d. (including 600 lb. as waste at 6 per cent.) - - - -			£342	0 0
10,000 spindles, with roving machinery and steam engine -	£10,000	0 0		
Wear at 10 per cent - -	1,000	0 0		
Or weekly (roughly) - -			20	0 0
Rent of building at £300 a year - - -			6	0 0
Coal consumed - - - - -			4	10 0
Gas „ - - - - -			1	0 0
Oil. &c. „ - - - - -			4	10 0
Making the constant capital			£378	0 0
Wages (=labour-power or variable capital) -			52	0 0
			£430	0 0
10,000 lb. of yarn sold at 12¼ d. - - -			510	0 0
Giving a surplus-value of -			£80	0 0

To find now the rate of surplus-value, we must, following the rule given, deduct from the value of the entire product, £510, the sum of the constant capital £378, as it takes no part in the formation of value. There remains £132, made up of variable capital £52 + surplus-value £80. Thus the rate of surplus-value is $\frac{80}{52} = 153\frac{11}{13}$ per cent. With a working-day of ten hours the result is found to be $3\frac{3}{13}$ hours of necessary and $6\frac{2}{13}$ hours of surplus-labour. In other words, after the labourer has returned to the capitalist in $3\frac{3}{13}$ hours of labour the value of the means of subsistence (wages) for which his labour-power has been bought, he is compelled to work $6\frac{2}{13}$ hours, or nearly twice as long, for the purpose of creating for the capitalist a surplus-value which is not paid for. The creation of this surplus-value is the end of capitalist production.

In an extended examination of the subject, Marx defends the normal workday. The capitalist buys the workman's labour-power for the cost of its production and reproduction, and if a labourer's daily subsistence can only be produced in six hours, he must work so long before the value he has received from the capitalist is returned. It is evident that when the necessary labour has been performed, the labourer will naturally seek to work as little, in addition, as possible. There is a clash of interests. The capitalist has bought the whole day's labour, and while he desires to make the most he can of the labour-power of a day, the labourer demands that his power shall not be prematurely exhausted by over-exertion. It is purely a question of money. Let the active life of a labourer be, with normal exertion, thirty years. then the value of a day's labour is $\frac{1}{365 \text{ x } 30}$ or $1/_{10950}$ of the entire value. But if the labour-power is exhausted in ten years, the capitalist is only paying daily $1/_{10950}$ instead of $1/_{3650}$ of the total value, that is a third, and the labourer is robbed of the remaining two-thirds.[1] The labourer, therefore, demands that a normal workday shall be fixed, and hence arises a struggle between the capitalist and labouring classes. But even if a normal (maximum) workday be fixed it is still possible for the capitalist to secure surplus-value. Suppose the normal day be ten hours long, and of these ten hours eight are needed to the production of the labourer's means of subsistence, in other words, are hours of necessary labour, while the remaining two are hours of surplus labour, the capitalist may increase the surplus labour at the expense of the necessary labour by reducing the price of the labour-power or the wages, and thus the proper reproduction of this power will be crippled. The more the necessary labour-time can be curtailed, the better for the capitalist's surplus labour-time and surplus-value. The invention of machinery has enabled the capitalist to appropriate more of the workman's labour, and to increase the surplus-value. As muscular power became less necessary, the labour of women and children was sought, and thus the workman's entire family passed into the service of the capitalist. Thus the man's labour-power was depreciate I, and though the labour of the whole family cost the capitalist more than that of the man formerly did, the increase in the surplus-value

---

[1] On this subject a very ingenious little work has been published by Dr. Engel, "Der Preis der Arbeit," (Berlin, 1866, one of the "Sammlung gemeinverständlicher wissenschaftlicher Vorträge.")

more than counterbalanced. Machinery has also led to a revolution in the relationships between labourer and capitalist. It will be remembered that the basis of the exchange of commodities which took place between the two was personal freedom as independent owners of commodities,—the one of money and means of production and the other of labour-power. But now capital buys the labour-power of children. " The labourer sold formerly his own labour-power, which was at his disposition as a nominally free agent. Now he sells his wife and child. He becomes a slave-dealer." The result of this capitalistic exploitation of the labour of women and children is physical and moral deterioration as well as social degradation. " Capital," says Marx, "is dead labour, which, vampire-like, becomes animate only by sucking living labour, and the more labour it sucks the more it lives."[1] It is no concern of capital that its excessive exploitation of labour-power prematurely exhausts the vital energies of the labourer. The capitalist seeks profit, and it is to his interest to make the purchased labour-power as remunerative as possible, let the labourer suffer as he may. *Après nous le déluge.*

From their very nature wages imply the performance by the labourer of labour which is not paid for. Wages are, in fact, a part of the labourer's own product, for though the capitalist pays him money, this money is merely the transmuted produce of labour. The labour of last week or last half-year pays for the labour of this week or the coming half-year. The money paid may be regarded as labour-orders on a part of the product produced by the labourer, but appropriated by the capitalist, and these orders the labourer returns to the capitalist for a share in his own product. With the capitalistic system all methods of increasing the productive power of labour are employed at the expense of the individual labourer, for all the means used to develop production are only expedients of the capitalist for the further exploitation of the producer. The labourer is made a mere appendage of the machine, he is subjected to a hateful despotism, he is perforce a life-long toiler, and his wife and children, too, are thrown beneath the Juggernaut of capital. But as all methods of producing surplus-value are at the same time methods of accumulation, and as every extension of accumulation becomes conversely a means of developing those methods, it follows that the condition of the labourer grows worse in the measure that capital accumulates, and that however high

[1] " Capital," vol. i., p. 216.

or low his wages. The law, too, which keeps the relative over-population or industrial reserve army proportionate to the extent and energy of accumulation, binds the labourer fast beyond liberation to capital. The accumulation of capital implies proportionate accumulation of distress. At one pole there are wealth and luxury, at the other there are want, the misery of toil, slavery, ignorance, brutalisation, and moral degradation. The conclusion to which Marx comes, is that the capitalist must be dispossessed, and the labourer be secured in the ownership of his product. The genesis of capital means, so far as it is not the immediate conversion of slaves and serfs into paid labourers, the expropriation of the direct producers, in that private property based on the producer's labour is abolished. Private property as opposed to social and collective property only exists where the means of labour and the external conditions of labour belong to private persons, but private property differs according as these private persons are labourers or non-labourers. Private property possessed by the labourer in his means of production—whether it be as land or tools—is the basis of the small industry. Naturally this mode of production necessitates the splitting up of the land and all the various means of production, and the consequence is that co-operation, the division of labour within each process of production, the social adaptation and application of the forces of nature, and the free development of social productive power, are all impossible. Such a mode of production is only compatible with an unprogressive state of society, and thus its rejection is only a question of time. The individual and divided means of production are concentrated and given a social character, and the small properties of the many become the large properties of the few. The bulk of the people must be dispossessed of the soil, of the instruments of labour, and the means of subsistence before the reign of capitalism can begin, and then capitalist private property subsists on the exploitation of the labour of the wage-earning class, labour which is nominally but not in reality free.[1] As soon as this transformation has sufficiently disintegrated society, and labourers have been made the *proletariat*,—their conditions of labour having been converted into capital, and the capitalist mode of production being supreme—then, says Marx, the further conversion of the soil and other means of production into socially-exploited or common means

[1] *Ibid*, pages 788 *et seq.*

of production takes place; in other words, private owners are further expropriated:

"There is now to be expropriated, not the independently working labourer, but the capitalist exploiting many labourers. This expropriation is effected by the working of the immanent laws of this very capitalist production, by the centralisation of capital. One capitalist ever kills many. Hand in hand with this centralisation, or the expropriation of many capitalists by few, are developed the co-operative form of the labour-process—and that on a constantly increasing scale—the intelligent application of science to technical purposes, the systematic exploitation of the soil, the transformation of the means of labour into means of labour only usable in common, the economising of all means of production by their use for production by combined, social labour, the entwining of all nations in the net of the world-market, and thus the international character of the capitalist *régime*. With the steady decrease of the capital-magnates, who usurp and monopolise all the advantages of this process of transformation, the mass of want, oppression, servitude, degradation, and spoliation grows; but the revolt of the labouring class—swelling ever in numbers, and disciplined, united and organised by the mechanism of the capitalist process of production itself—spreads at the same time. The capitalist monopoly becomes a fetter on the mode of production with and under which it has originated. The centralisation of the means of production and the socialisation of labour reach a point at which they become no longer compatible with their capitalist integument, and this is burst asunder. The last hour of capitalist private property strikes. The expropriators are expropriated." [1]

With Marx this change is a natural one, and is the certain result of historical development. The capitalist mode of appropriation, which proceeds from the capitalist mode of production, and thus also capitalist private property are the first negation of individual private property based on the owner's personal labour. "But capitalist production brings about its own negation with the necessity of a natural law. It is the negation of negation. This negation does not re-establish private property, but individual property based on the acquisition of the capitalist era, viz., co-operation and common possession of the soil and of the means of production which originate in labour. The

[1] *Ibid*, pp. 789, 790.

transformation of the scattered private property which is based on the labour of the individuals into capitalist property is naturally a process far more tedious, cruel, and difficult than the transformation of capitalist property, already based in reality on social production, into social property. In the first case there is the expropriation of the mass of the people by a few usurpers, but in the latter the expropriation of a few usurpers by the mass of the people." [1]

Thus Marx would not only make land, but all the instruments of production, collective and social property. He would go further: he would have all subjects of the State share equally in labour and the produce of labour. His future State is, in fact, to be a Labour State, in which labour will be compulsory on all who are capable, for unless men work they will not be allowed to eat. In "Capital" we find him developing the idea of uniting agriculture with industry which is advanced in the Communist Manifesto written in 1847. He would have great variety in the labour of the individual, so that he may be as many-sided as possible.

Throughout all his long public life Marx did not cease to proclaim the imperative necessity of coupling the political with the social question. We find him saying at the close of "The Misery of Philosophy":—"It cannot be said that the social movement excludes the political. There is no political movement that is not at the same time social. Only by so ordering things that there shall be no classes and no class distinctions will social evolutions cease to be political revolutions. Until then, on the eve of every general reorganisation of society the final word of social science will always run: 'Combat or death, bloody war or nothing. There is the question inexorably put.'" [2] Yet with all his advocacy of the subversion of society, he professed that the fall of the higher classes would not mean and should not entail the rise of the lower classes in their place. A new society is to be created in order that the oppressed may be emancipated, but this emancipation does not imply that the domination of one class will be followed by that of another. On the contrary, the condition of the freedom of the labouring class is the abolition of all class distinctions.

[1] "Capital:" chapter xxiv., "Die sogenannte ursprüngliche Akkumulation," sect. 7 "Geschichtliche Tendenz der kapitalistischen Akkumulation," pp. 789—791.
[2] George Sand.

H

CHAPTER V.

FERDINAND LASSALLE.

IT is one of the commonest aphorisms that the age always produces the men it requires. This is one of the many truths to which history, with its evolutions and revolutions, has given the character of irre-fragability. In the development of society it is not the man that makes the time, but the time that makes the man. The new era needs help at its birth, and those who give the required assistance are spoken of in later history as the inaugurators—it would be better, the proclaimers and heralds—of fresh epochs. Such a man of the time was Ferdinand Lassalle.[1] Lassalle was born at Breslau on April 11th, 1825. His parents were both of Jewish descent, and his father was a well-to-do tradesman ; a man not, indeed, possessing unusual in-tellectual gifts, but sagacious and upright. The family name was Lassal, the form it still preserves, but, like Isaac Disraeli, Ferdinand bore little love towards his race, and he took the name of Lassalle when quite young. This dislike of Judaism was a trait in Lassalle's character which became more prominent the older he grew, and we find him exclaiming at one time, "There are two classes of men especially which I cannot tolerate, the literary men and the Jews, and unfortunately I belong to both." It must not, however, be supposed that this prejudice was carried into domestic relationships. No more affectionate son ever lived than Ferdinand Lassalle, and though his sphere of activity lay far away from the Silesian home, from which he separated early in life, the ties that bound parents and child were never weakened. Especially cordial was the relationship which existed between Lassalle and his mother. The whole life of this devoted woman seemed to be bound up in that of her son, whose

---

[1] The best works dealing with Lassalle's life as a whole are " Ferdinand Lassalle, ein litera-risches Characterbild," by the Dane Georg Brandes (an excellent translation published in Berlin, 1877); "Die deutsche Socialdemokratie; ihre Geschichte und ihre Lehre," by Franz Mehring (3rd edition, Bremen, 1879): to which may be added an article by C. Plener in the " Allgemeine Deutsche Biographie " (vol. xvii., Leipzig, 1883). His correspondence with Rodbertus and Hans von Bülow is also very important. Works relating to his agitation and the closing period of his life will be mentioned later.

ambition she encouraged and whose achievements she was never weary of lauding.

Ferdinand, as a child, showed traces of the forwardness, the imperious bearing, and the unconscious arrogance which are often found to characterise Hebrew descent, traits which in his later life were to attain remarkable development. He seemed to have been born to rule, and long before ordinary youths dare trust as firm the ground beneath their feet, he had passed, and that quite naturally and unobserved, beyond parental control and guidance. He was a man in intelligence and will when still a boy in years. It is related that when he was fifteen or sixteen years old a perplexing difficulty arose in the domestic circle, and the peace was abruptly disturbed. Ferdinand assumed an uninvited dictatorship, stepped over the heads of father and mother, and in a short time restored matters to rights.[1] It was the characteristic which showed itself seven years later, when, a political prisoner, he ordered his warders about as though he were administering the affairs of his own house, and challenged their right to impose conditions upon his will. Brandes well says : " There was something of a Cæsar in this youth whom alarmed *bourgeois* were one day to regard as a Catilina. He was born for power, he bore the stamp of the ruler, and as he did not come into the world a prince or a nobleman, but the child of the middle-class, and of a disregarded race, he became a thinker, democrat, and agitator, in order to attain in this way the element for which he was created." [2] Even the poet Heine could write to Lassalle in 1846 :

" I have found in no one so much passion and clearness of intellect united in action. You have good right to be audacious—we others only usurp this divine right, this heavenly privilege." Never, perhaps, has the aphorism that the child is father of the man received a stronger confirmation than is furnished by the life of Lassalle.

The fact that Ferdinand should have been destined to follow a commercial career shows how little able one, at least, of the parents was to read the character of the precocious boy. The mother was, indeed, for making him a philologist, and then a professor, but the father wished his business to remain in the family, and for a time it seemed as though the wish would be gratified After receiving the

---

[1] Brandes' " Ferdinand Lassalle : ein literarisches Charakterbild," p. 15.
[2] Brandes, p. 15.

elements of education at home, he was sent to a Trade School at Leipzig, and here it was that his inclinations took a scientific direction. "You will never make a tradesman," is said to have been the remark made once to Lassalle by his schoolmaster. Nor did the young man desire or intend to become a tradesman. Leaving Leipzig he studied philology and philosophy at Breslau and Berlin, and passed his examinations with distinction. While yet a student he formed the resolution of unravelling the life and philosophy of Heracleitus the Ephesian, and largely in order to carry out this resolution he went in 1845 to Paris. Here, a youth of twenty years, he made the acquaintance of Heinrich Heine, who was then suffering acutely from the isolation which his own bitter pen had brought upon him, and who was thus all the more ready to take to one whose views and sympathies accorded in many respects with his own. Alexander von Humboldt [1] and August Boeckh [2] called Lassalle a prodigy (*Wunderkind*), but the sick poet did not hesitate to say that he was himself "only a humble fly," when compared with his new friend. Heine, however, found in the youth a devoted helper in legal and other difficulties, and when he thus spoke, gratitude as well as admiration and wonder influenced his judgment. He writes to Lassalle in February, 1846 :

"To-day I confine myself to thanking you ; never yet has anyone done so much for me."

And again :

"Farewell, and rest assured that I love you unspeakably. How glad I am that I am not mistaken in you ; though I have trusted no one so much—I, who am so distrustful from experience, not by nature. Since I received letters from you my spirits have risen and I feel better."

But Heine paid the highest compliment to his young friend's genius when he sent him to Varnhagen [3] with a letter of introduction, which ran: "My friend Herr Lassalle, who brings you this letter, is a young man of the most remarkable intellectual gifts. With the most

---

[1] Born September 14th, 1769, and died May 6th, 1859.

[2] August Boeckh, born November 24th, 1785, at Karlsruhe, renowned philologist and writer on classical antiquity. From 1810 until his death (August 3rd, 1867) he was professor of ancient literature at Berlin.

[3] Karl August Varnhagen von Ense, a prominent author, born February 21st, 1785, at Düsseldorf. He became first an Austrian and then a Russian officer, and from 1815 to 1819 was in the Prussian diplomatic service. He died October 10th, 1858, at Berlin. He is a master of German literary style.

thorough erudition, with the widest learning, with the greatest penetration which I have ever known, and with the richest gift of exposition, he combines an energy of will and a capacity for action which
astonish me, and unless his sympathy with me becomes extinguished
I shall expect from him the greatest stimulus. In any case, this
union of knowledge and capability, of talent and character, is for me
a very pleasing sight."[1]

Lassalle had no sooner made a beginning with his work on Heracleitus than events occurred which compelled him to lay his folios and
manuscripts aside. There lived at this time in Berlin a certain Countess Sophie von Hatzfeldt, a lady of forty years and of marked beauty,
and early in the year 1846 Lassalle made her acquaintance. Countess
Hatzfeldt was then engaged in a suit for divorce, and the story of her
wrongs enlisted the young man's sympathies. The lady's husband, a
noble of Silesia, a man of great wealth, but of brutal character, had
determined that his wife should be ruined if the law allowed him to
have his way. Lassalle came forward with an offer to champion the
aggrieved lady's cause, and the offer was readily accepted. This act
has been variously judged by biographers and critics, but Lassalle
was accustomed to say that there was no part of his life which gave
him greater pleasure. The first thing the young man did was to
challenge the count to a duel. The purse-proud noble, however, only
called him a "stupid young Jew" for his pains. The taunt was
bitterly felt, and it was enough to decide Lassalle to fight to the bitter
end, which, in fact, he did. Proceeding to Düsseldorf, in the train of
the countess, he at once opened the struggle. When defending himself, two years later, before a court of law, he told his judges the
reasons that first prompted him to interfere :

"The family was silent. But it is said : when men are silent the
stones will speak. When all human rights are outraged, when even
the voice of blood is mute, and the helpless mortal is deserted by his
born protectors—then rises up, and rightly, man's first and last
relation, man. You all know and have read with indignation the
frightful story of the unfortunate Duchess of Praslin.[2] Which of you
would not have hastened to succour her in her mortal struggle? Well,

---

[1] Letter of January 3rd, 1846.

[2] Murdered in 1847 by her husband, Count Theobald Choiseul, Duke of Praslin, who wa
arrested but poisoned himself in prison, August 24th, 1847.

gentlemen, I said to myself : here is Praslin ten times over.   For
what is the short death-struggle of an hour compared with the torment
of a mortal pain prolonged through twenty years?   What are the
wounds which a knife makes compared with the slow assassination
committed with refined cruelty throughout a human being's entire
existence, compared with the fearful misery of a woman, in whose
person every right of life had day after day for twenty years been
trampled underfoot, every human right outraged, and whom an attempt
had previously been made to bring into contempt, so that she might
be ill-used without punishment."

And further : "I saw embodied in this affair universal standpoints
and principles.   I said to myself that the countess was a sacrifice of
her class ; I said to myself that such misdeeds, such an outrage on
society in its moral depths, could only be hazarded without timidity
by one in the insolent position of a prince and a millionaire.   I did not
conceal from myself the difficulty of the enterprise.   I saw well how
hard the task of clearing up this wrong, already old and become
historical, would be ; and how, if it came to a process, my entire
activity would exclusively be required—and thus a long interruption
in my career be entailed—in order to carry the complicated business
to an issue.   I knew right well the difficulty of overcoming a false
appearance ; I did not conceal from myself what frightful antagonists
rank, influence, and wealth are, the fact that they alone can ever find
alliances in the ranks of the bureaucracy, and the danger that I might
myself run.   I knew all this without being restrained by it.   I resolved
to oppose false appearance with truth, rank with right, the power of
money with that of intellect.   The obstacles, the sacrifice, the
dangers did not frighten me ; but had I known what unworthy and
infamous slanders would be cast at me, how the purest motives would
be twisted and perverted into their exact opposite, and what ready
credence the most miserable lies would find : well, I hope my resolution would not have been changed, but it would have cost me a hard
and painful struggle."[1]

The struggle lasted eight years, but Lassalle won in the end.   He
fought in thirty-six courts and finally brought the count to his knees.
The result was a compromise which secured the wronged woman an

[1] Trial at Cologne, August 11th, 1848.   See " Meine Vertheidigungsrede wider die Anklage
der Verleitung zum Kassetten-Diebstahl," (Cologne, 1848).

ample fortune and her champion an income for life, the latter amounting, according to all accounts, to 5000 thalers or about £750 yearly.
The most noteworthy incident in the long legal dispute, an incident of
which the last was never heard during Lassalle's life, was the famous
casket robbery committed under his direction in 1846. It was known
that in the casket of Count Hatzfeldt's paramour, the Baroness von
Meyerdorff, there was the bond of a life annuity which had been
settled upon this lady by her lover. Lassalle determined to secure
the document, and he did so with the aid of two accomplices, who fell
into the hands of the law. Lassalle himself escaped punishment.
At the first trial, indeed, he was found guilty, but on appeal the
judgment was quashed. The character of the after relationship
between Lassalle and Countess Hatzfeldt was never truly known, but
it provided, and no wonder, ample material for scandal, and even
to-day it is regarded by many who wish to be charitable as a dark
blot upon a character which they would fain have seen free from
blemish. The two appear in later years—published letters show this
—to have considered the relationship as that of mother and son, and
it is unquestionable that the countess continued deeply devoted to
Lassalle up to the last hour of his life, as well as to his memory after
death. It is difficult to say how far Lassalle, in his zealous advocacy
of this lady's cause, was influenced by a strong sense of duty and how
far by a love of the romantic, but that both factors entered into play
can admit of no doubt. He was never tired of extolling the virtue
and honour of that intervention, which he appears to have regarded
as a religious act, and just before his death in 1864 he wrote to his
friend Huber :

" It is the most cherished recollection of my life, a recollection which,
in spite of the succession of years which have passed away, fills me
with the purest satisfaction. For eight years I carried on tha
struggle, not putting my weapons out of my hand, until I had won for
the countess right and victory. And I would have carried the struggle
on until to-day, had I not ended it victoriously in 1854. . . That intervention for the countess was nothing else than an insurrection, an insurrection upon my own account in a case which, like the purest
microcosm, contains within itself our entire social misery. My whole
man lies in that transaction."

Whatever Lassalle may himself have thought about an episode

which began with a casket robbery and ended with the reward of a life annuity, his character did not benefit by it in public estimation. His friends always preserved discreet silence on the subject, but his enemies found in it a fountain of poison into which they again and again dipped their keen lances.

While Lassalle was still engaged in the Hatzfeldt law-suit, events transpired which for a time caused him to devote attention to other things. In 1848, a revolutionary storm broke out once more, and though the waves of anarchy which swept from Paris broke long before they reached German soil, their effect was still very great. Lassalle had already identified himself with the German Republican party, and spite of his youth, he was a leader in the camp, and one, too, in whom high trust was reposed. He was at this time associated with men like Marx, Engels, and Wolff, who saw in the foment of that period an opportunity for furthering their long-cherished Communistic designs. As Lassalle was favourably known amongst the Düsseldorf working-men, he was charged with their organisation, and he did his duty with a zeal which brought him into trouble. Not only did he harangue meetings, but when the Prussian Government declared the National Assembly dissolved in November, he called on the citizens of Düsseldorf by placard to prepare for armed resistance to that step as being unconstitutional.[1] For this act Lassalle was apprehended, and

---

[1] On November 8th the king confirmed the nomination of a new Ministry, at the head of which was Count Brandenburg, and the following day a Cabinet ordinance was read in the Assembly, removing the seat of that body to Brandenburg, and adjourning further proceedings till the 27th, when the drawing up of a constitution was to be proceeded with. The President of the Assembly, Von Unruh, refused to close the sitting, whereupon Count Brandenburg declared that further deliberations would be illegal, and left the hall, being followed by the other Ministers. The Right also withdrew, but the Left and Centre remained, a body of 290 members. On the 10th, the Rump passed a resolution declaring that it would adhere to its liberties, but would not transgress the law. That day fifteen thousand guards entered Berlin, and when the National Assembly adjourned in the evening, Wrangel caused their meeting-place to be occupied by a company of soldiers. On the 12th, Berlin was placed in a state of siege ; the civic guard was ordered to surrender arms, all clubs and associations were closed, all open air meetings were prohibited, the carrying of weapons was forbidden, and newspapers and pamphlets were only allowed to be circulated with the permission of the police, while cases of illegality were to be adjudicated on by a court-martial. On the 13th the Rump issued a memorial, declaring the proceedings of the Ministry to be unconstitutional and an act of high treason, and this was sent to the Attorney-General with the request that he would act upon it, but this official could not, of course, move in the matter. On the evening of the 13th, troops occupied the Rump's provisional meeting-place, the Schützenhaus, and on the members assembling next day in the Cölln Rathhaus an officer appeared with thirty

indicted—as Marx and others were at Cologne—for exciting to armed opposition to the Executive Power. He was acquitted of this charge, but was kept in prison until he could be tried on the less serious count of inciting to resistance against officials, the result being a sentence of six months' imprisonment. Humboldt wished to intercede with the king on his behalf, but Lassalle would not hear of such a thing, and when he knew that his sister had done what he had refused to let Humboldt do, he wrote to the king to say that it was all a misunderstanding—he desired no free pardon.

The first speech made by Lassalle, a young man of twenty-three years, in defence of his conduct at Düsseldorf, is a marvellous performance, and historically is of great importance. Brandes contends that it is one of the most wonderful instances of manly courage and eloquence in a youth which the world's history furnishes. However this may be, it is impossible to disagree with the biographer's further remark that, "Were it not known, no one would believe that a young man of twenty-three had made this speech." More interesting than its excellence as a piece of oratory—its faultless construction, its logical sequence, its complete appositeness to the occasion, and above all its real eloquence—is, to the student of Lassalle and his work, the exposition which it contains of his political and social views. The speech bears evidence of most careful and elaborate preparation. It

soldiers. He called upon the president to close the proceedings, and on Von Unruh refusing, he summoned all members to quit the hall, another refusal being the only answer. He therefore decided to challenge the members individually, and beginning with the president, ordered him to leave. Von Unruh declining, he was carried out on his seat, and lodged in the street. This acted as a warning to the rest, and the room was soon empty.

Finally, the Rump, greatly reduced in numbers, resorted to an inn, and on the evening of the 15th it was there deliberating, when two officers with drawn swords entered, being followed by fifty soldiers. The meeting was called on to disperse, and the president requested the officers to withdraw with their men for a moment, on condition of immediate compliance with the summons. The request was granted, and no sooner had the last soldier withdrawn, than a resolution affirming the illegality of the levy of taxes by the Brandenburg Ministry was hastily put and carried with acclamation. Then the Assembly dispersed. On December 5th, the king dissolved the Assembly convened at Brandenburg, and a constitution was promulgated the same day. Herr Hans Victor von Unruh, mentioned above, was born March 28th, 1806, at Tilsit, and lived as engineer in Berlin and elsewhere. He sat in the National Assembly for Magdeburg in 1848, leading the Centre party, and became the president of the Chamber, in which capacity he opposed the reaction with might and main. For over ten years he remained in retirement, but in 1863 he entered the Prussian House of Deputies, and was its vice-president until 1867. In 1866, he joined the new National Liberal party, and supported it as a member of the Reichstag until he retired again into private life.

was evidently intended to be, not merely an address to a jury and a plea for acquittal, but a manifesto to Germany. It was a grand opportunity for letting the world, and above all the democracy, know that he was in existence, and he made the best use of it. The daring is sublime. He begins with the cool declaration : "I acknowledge to you with pleasure that from inmost conviction I take altogether a revolutionary standpoint, that from inmost conviction I am a pronounced adherent of the Social-Democratic Republic." By revolution, however, as we know from later works, Lassalle did not understand necessarily the violent overturn of a form of government. "A revolution," he says in one place, "takes place if—whether with or without force, for the question of means is of no importance—an entirely new principle is made to take the place of the existing state of things." He scorned the idea that it was impossible to conceive of a situation in which armed resistance against the Executive would be justifiable, and exclaimed :—

"Can the king tread the laws of the citizens under foot, confiscate their fortunes, murder their sons, dishonour their daughters,—can he destroy the constitution and restore the absolute State without you having the right to defend yourselves against his violence ? Who would be guilty of such antediluvian shame as to answer this question with Yes ? If the State Procurator dare affirm it ; if he says that no case would be imaginable in which a citizen would be justified in arming himself against the royal power, and if the Crown Solicitor says that this thought lies at the basis of his charge, then, gentlemen, their place is here (pointing to the prisoner's dock) since they say that Prussia is an absolute State as it was before March."

But if the right existed the question then arose, what would be sufficient justification for its exercise, and he answers :

"When the laws of the land are broken by the royal power—those first and holiest laws, those palladia of universal liberty which cannot be touched without shattering the State to its foundations, without giving a vital wound, as with an electric shock, to the rights of all citizens from the Oder to the Rhine—the laws respecting the civic guard, freedom of the Press, association, personal liberty, the rights and the inviolability of popular representation."

Such a case, Lassalle said, had occurred, and he held that he had done his duty as a good citizen and a good patriot. Quite logically he admitted that the National Assembly in inviting the nation to show passive resistance acted wrongly. Either the Crown was right in dissolving the Assembly, in which case opposition was illegal and criminal ; or it was wrong, and then there should be opposition—not, indeed, passive, but "active, with body and life"—in defence of the people's liberties. We find Lassalle preaching in this speech the doctrine of the ultimate supremacy of might which in later years he developed, when once again a constitutional crisis called him out of silence into the din of political controversy. One passage in which he refers prophetically to the mission which he felt sure he had to fulfil deserves to be borne in mind for the sake of later application :

" Yes, gentlemen, as the armour of a warrior is pierced by arrows, so am I by criminal prosecutions. The many dogs are at last to be the death of the game ; but, gentlemen, I feel something here which tells me that the many dogs will *not* be the death of the game." With Schiller's Maid of Orleans he believd, " Nicht heut, nicht hier ist mir bestimmt zu fallen." Finally, Lassalle in this speech struck the note of his entire public life, when he said :—

" Not to take sides, that means either to have little conviction or to disown conviction. Not to take sides, that means to prefer, in ignominious indifference to the highest interests which thrill the heart of mankind, one's own quiet and ease to the great questions upon which the weal and woe of the fatherland depend, and so to betray the duties which we owe to the fatherland. History can forgive all errors and all convictions, but not want of conviction." That was Lassalle as he stood upon the threshold of his career, and it was Lassalle when his work was completed.

The Hatzfeldt affair was settled in 1854, and Lassalle could now devote himself to the completion of his laborious work on Heracleitus of Ephesus, the preparations for which had been discontinued nearly ten years before. He revised the work already done, finished his researches, and by dint of close application he was able to write the preface in August, 1857, and publish the two bulky volumes early the following year.[1] The work has been variously judged by scholars, few of whom have awarded it a high place in philosophical literature. It is, however, easy to believe that the character and philosophy of the

---

1 " Die Philosophie Herakleitos des Dunklen von Ephesos : Nach einer neuen Sammlung Bruchstücke und der Zeugnisse der alten dargestellt," (Berlin, 1858).

moody Ephesian sage, who taught the doctrine of perpetual flux, and negativing the Being accepted only a Becoming, would have deep interest for Lassalle, the kernel of whose social teaching was that human institutions are without finality, and that the value and truth of all the economic creeds which have descended to the present age are relative rather than absolute. The next literary performance was a tragedy, "Franz von Sickingen."[1] This work was laid by a friend, as an anonymous production, before the director of the Royal Theatre in Berlin, as Lassalle desired to see it performed before it was published. As it was found unsuitable for the stage he at once had it printed. "Franz von Sickingen" is a work of mediocre ability now quite forgotten—if, indeed, it can be said to have ever attracted attention—and its only interest lies in the direct bearing which many passages have upon the author's career and the principles governing it. One involuntarily calls to mind Lassalle confronting his judges as a political prisoner in reading the words put into the mouth of Ulrich von Hütten :—[2]

> " Ich kann nicht schweigen, kann durch Schweigen nicht
> Mir Obdach und des Leibes Sicherheit erkaufen :
> Mich treibt der Geist ! Ich muss ihm Zeugniss legen,
> Kann nicht verschliessen, was so mächtig quillt."

And the following passage seems to portray a future agitator travelling from place to place, and followed everywhere by indictments and writs of commitment :

> " O, hätt' ich tausend Zungen—grade jetzt
> Mit allen tausenden wollt' ich zum Lande reden !
> Viel lieber will ich, elend wie ein Wild gehetzt,
> Von einem Dorfe mich zum andern tragen,
> Als an der Wahrheit schweigend zu verzagen !"

[1] "Franz von Sickingen : eine historische Tragödie" (Berlin, 1859). Brandes records how Lassalle was once found by a friend at work on this tragedy. He was astonished at Lassalle's hardihood, seeing that his nature was far from being poetic, but before he could speak Lassalle said : "I know what you are going to say : I know as well as you that I am no poet. But Lessing wrote dramas with the consciousness that he was no poet. Without comparing myself with Lessing I do not see why I should not," &c. (Brandes, p. 110).

[2] "Franz von Sickingen was one of the noblest men of the Reformation period. He defended Ulrich von Hütten, warred against perfidious Wurtemberg, was the terror of evil doers, the praise of whoso did well. Hütten and he read Luther together : light rising in darkness ! He also stood by Götz von Berlichingen, and now walks in poetry.' Carlyle in the Craigenputtock Journal 1829-1830 ("Thomas Carlyle : a History of the first forty years of his Life," by J. A. Froude, London, 1882).

Meanwhile, Lassalle had transferred his residence to Berlin. This he had long wished to do, but on account of his revolutionary exploits in 1848 the Government thought it desirable to keep the gates of the metropolis closed to him. It is said that the desire to see Berlin again grew at one time so strong that he entered the city by stealth, dressed as a waggoner. At last he begged Alexander von Humboldt to intercede, and Humboldt promised to do his best. The opportunity wished for came when Humboldt found himself one day the neighbour of Hinckeldey, the president of police, at the dinner-table of a friend. He seized a fitting moment, and asked if there were any difficulties in the way of Lassalle's return. The answer was altogether satisfactory : Hinckeldey had himself no objection whatever, but he did not know the king's views. Humboldt said he would ask the king, and he did, with the result that Lassalle was soon enrolled amongst the residents of Berlin, the Countess Hatzfeldt speedily following. It was, however, a long time before he dare venture into public life. That would have been taking liberties which the Government would not have quietly tolerated. For several years he had to be content with the rôle of a mere observer, and so he divided his time between study and amusement.

Lassalle was in the fullest sense of the word a man of the world, but he was not that alone. Had he been, the continual round of pleasure which he was able to follow during these early years of Berlin life would have satisfied his desires. For he became a central figure in society, and his conquests in the drawing-room were many and flattering. He was a man of fascinating appearance, and his keen eagle-eyes had a more than magnetic power. When tried before the Düsseldorf Assizes in 1848 the indictment described him as "five feet six inches high, with brown curly hair, open forehead, brown eye-brows, dark-blue eyes, well-proportioned nose and mouth, round chin, rather long face, and of slender build." But details of this kind give no idea of the living man, of the true personality, the commanding presence, the proud dignity, the intellectual bearing. One who saw him on a single occasion has recorded that " He looked like pure defiance ; but on his forehead was seen such an energy that one would not have wondered if he had won a throne." Add to all this the gift of brilliant conversational powers, and it is not surprising that Lassalle should have become a drawing-room hero, a lion of society. He was very fond of music, and for years Hans von

Bülow,[1] the pianist and composer, was counted amongst the closest of his friends. A man of cultivated tastes, his house was a model of elegance. He was never strong, and was compelled to travel a great deal. Thus two visits to the East, made while still young, afforded him the opportunity of acquiring many objects of art and virtu, which were afterwards used in the decoration of his rooms. His dinners and suppers are said to have been the choicest in Berlin, and certain it is that he outdid everybody in novelty, once serving his guests with hashish. So he lived, admired and petted by the ladies, and the life and soul of a small intellectual circle which gathered its inspiration from him : he was Byron and Alcibiades at the same time. Still he made enemies—men like Lassalle have invariably as many haters as lovers—and once he was challenged. Holding, however, that a member of the democratic party should be above appeal to barbarism, he declined to respond. Some time later his adversary, who was accompanied by a friend, met him near the Brandenburg Gate, and the two men attacked him with great violence. But Lassalle's democratic principles did not now forbid him to act in self-defence. He stood bravely up to his opponents, and soon compelled them to beat a hasty and undignified retreat. The affair became public, and for some days it was a topic of general conversation. Förster,[2] the historian, was so pleased with the part played by the victor that he presented him with Robespierre's walking-stick, and this was ever afterwards Lassalle's inseparable companion. Indeed, he fancied that he bore a certain resemblance to this hero of the "Terror," and in his own characteristic way he would tell intimate friends of the similarity. One day he accosted such a friend, at whose house he was visiting, with "See, here is Robespierre's walking-stick." Then transferring his hands to his head, "And here is Robespierre's head. I am like Robespierre!" Lassalle's hair was very thick and phenomenally strong. He used to say, "I am like Samson ; my strength lies in my hair."

The literary products attributable to this period include his principal

---

[1] Hans Guido von Bülow, born at Dresden, January 8th, 1830. Long after Lassalle's death a small volume of "Briefe an Hans von Bülow von Ferdinand Lassalle" (Dresden and Leipzig) appeared. The letters give an interesting picture of Lassalle's private life from 1862 to 1864.

[2] Friedrich Förster, born September 24th, 1791, at Münchengosserstädt, died November 8th, 1868. Author of many historical works.

work, "System of Acquired Rights," [1] to which it will be necessary to refer at length ; and a small anonymous work on the Italian war. [2] In 1862 he published a cutting satire [3] on Julian Schmidt's "History of German Literature," [4] a work, however, of purely ephemeral interest. The criticism of Lassalle and the "comments of the compositor and the compositor's wife" made the unlucky victim smart at the time, but the style of the work—a copy of which Lassalle sent to Hans von Bülow with the remark that he would "laugh himself to death" over it—is far below the author's reputation. Ten pages are taken up with an argument that Fichte [5] was to the last hostile to Christianity. This was the last literary work which Lassalle was able to do for a long time. Stirring events soon occurred causing him to relinquish the retirement of the study.

Lassalle's entrance into public life was accelerated by the constitutional struggle which began in Prussia in 1862. King William 1. came to the throne on January 2nd, 1861. At that time the Chamber of Deputies was strongly Liberal, and when the king endeavoured to force through his favourite scheme of army reorganisation he met with nothing but opposition. Repeated dissolutions of the Diet proved futile, for the Liberal majority always returned stronger than before. In September, 1862, Herr von Bismarck was called from the Paris Embassy to become Minister President, and the appointment was regarded as an intimation that the king had adopted the policy of "No surrender." As the Lower Chamber still refused to adopt the Army Bill, and went the length of declaring that in expending money without Parliamentary sanction the Government violated the constitution, the Diet was in October sent about its business, the king stating that as the estates had come to a deadlock he would act on his own responsibility for the good of the nation. Accordingly, the military reforms were proceeded with and completed, and the Government ruled for four years without budget.

1 "Das System der erworbenen Rechte" (Leipzig, 1861, 2 vols.)

2 "Der italienische Krieg und die Aufgabe Preussens : eine Stimme aus der Demokratie" (Berlin, 1859).

3 "Herr Julian Schmidt, der Literarhistoriker, mit Setzer-Scholien" (Berlin, 1862).

4 "Geschichte der deutschen Literatur" (Leipzig, 1858, 4th ed.)

5 In "Fichte's politisches Vermächtniss und die neueste Gegenwart" (a letter written January, 1860 : Leipzig, 1871), Lassalle speaks of Fichte as "the most glorious German patriot and one of the most powerful thinkers of all times." Fichte's grave is in one of the Berlin Cemeteries, and Hegel's is close at hand.

While the constitutional conflict was still in an early stage, Lassalle was invited to address, in the spring of 1862, one of the ratepayers' associations[1] of Berlin, and he chose for his subject the essence of the constitution. In this address,[2] which was several times repeated, he advanced the doctrine that constitutional questions are questions of power. The written constitution is merely the expression of the elements of power—as king, nobility, court influence, bankers, Stock Exchange, the great manufacturers, army, populace, &c.—which exist in a country and their relationship to each other, but these elements of power form themselves the real constitution.[3] Thus the proper constitution must correspond to this relationship of forces, and one consequence deducible from the argument is that so long as a king, nobility, and army constitute an undivided element of power, mere written guarantees cannot be binding upon a sovereign. The Progressists were furious at the impudence of one who was formerly an associate in propagating such doctrines, and their Press fulminated at him for becoming the tool of the unconstitutional party. The supporters of the Government, on the other hand, were delighted at receiving an accession of strength from so unexpected a quarter, and the *Kreuz-Zeitung* alluded to Lassalle as a "revolutionary Jew well known in his day, who has with right instinct hit the nail on the head, and has not by a long way said all he knows and thinks." Truer word was never spoken. Lassalle's tale was only half told, and he probably laughed heartily as he saw how short-sighted his critics all were. A second address soon followed with the sufficiently suggestive title "What now?" In this address he carried his argument further. As in Prussia the army stood behind the Government, what remedy had the Parliament against acts which it might deem to be illegal? Some said grants of money should be refused, but this experiment, though effective in England, where a preponderance of the organised power was on the side of the people, would be futile in Prussia. The only course

---

[1] Known then and now as *Bezirksvereine*. These associations exist for the purpose of allowing the citizens to deliberate together on municipal, industrial, political, and general questions. Berlin is divided into *Bezirke* or districts, and generally several *Bezirke* join together in the formation of a *Verein*, this being, however, quite voluntary, as the *Vereine* are not in reality official organisations.

[2] Published with the title "Ueber Verfassungswesen."

[3] Lorenz von Stein in the masterly essay on society and the State which forms an introduction to his "Geschichte der socialen Bewegung in Frankreich von 1789 bis auf unsere Tage" (Leipzig, 1850, 3 vols.) develops this idea in a more general way.

open was for the Chambers to refuse to meet. This would bring the Government face to face with the alternatives of absolutism or surrender, and as it was impossible for it to rule despotically and thus outrage the feelings of all civilised nations for any length of time, victory would eventually rest with the people. There was now no longer any justification for regarding Lassalle as a defender of unconstitutional government. The second lecture was published like the first and widely circulated, but beyond the confiscation of the work at Königsberg no harm was suffered by its daring author.

Less fortunate was Lassalle with his next lecture, delivered on April 12th, 1862, before an artisans' association in Berlin. On this occasion he dealt in a perfectly philosophical and historical way with the development of the State and society since the French Revolution, and he came to the conclusion that just as that Revolution gave to the third estate the leading place in the State, so the German Revolution of 1848 had elevated the fourth estate to that dignity. Doctrines like this were not to be tolerated, and when the lecture was published [1] the entire edition of three thousand copies was seized, while Lassalle was served with a writ by the Crown Solicitor requiring him to answer the charge of endangering the public peace by publicly exciting subjects of the State to hatred of each other. The trial took place at Berlin on January 16th, 1863, and the proceedings, as was to have been expected, were very memorable. The prosecution was conducted by a son of the philosopher Schelling,[2] and of this circumstance Lassalle, who regarded himself as a defender of science and freedom of philosophical inquiry against intolerance, did not omit to make good use. He endeavoured to justify himself on the ground of the twentieth article of the Prussian Constitution, which says "Science and its teaching are free," holding that this provision was to be understood absolutely, for if the qualification "free within the limits of the penal code" were to be added it became meaningless, since such an exemption and qualification would cover every expression of opinion. In reply to the allegation that the work was not scientific, Lassalle challenged the verdict of seven members of the Royal Academy of Sciences : August

[1] With the title "Arbeiterprogramm: über den besondern Zusammenhang der gegenwärtigen Geschichtsperiode mit der Idee des Arbeiterstandes." (April 12th, 1862.)

[2] Dr. H. von Schelling, born April 19th, 1824. Entered the Prussian Ministry of Justice as Under Secretary of State, and in 1879 made Secretary of State in the Imperial *Justizamt*.

I

Boeckh, Johannes Schulze,[1] Adolf Trendelenburg,[2] Leopold Ranke,[3] Theodor Mommsen,[4] Häusser,[5] and Dr. Pertz.[6] He declared: "The alliance of science and the working classes, of these opposite poles of society, which when they meet will crush all obstacles to civilisation in their iron arms, that is the end to which I have resolved to dedicate my life." He was in reality a benefactor and yet they prosecuted him as a criminal. He drew a picture of the state of Berlin in the frightful *Märztage* of 1848, when the barricades were red with blood, the power of the police broken down, the *bourgeoisie* trembling in fear, and Berlin in the hands of a mob, and he asked if his prosecutors desired a return of that reign of terror.

"If not, then thank the men who have devoted themselves to the work of filling up the abyss which divides scientific thought and language from the people, and so of breaking down the barrier which keeps *bourgeoisie* and people asunder. Thank these men, who at the expense of mental exertions have undertaken a work whose results will be to the benefit of each and all of you."

Then, with a Socratic air, he exclaimed: "Feast these men in the Prytaneion and do not arraign them!" The trial was a very stormy one, and time after time the judges, the Crown Solicitor, and the defendant engaged in angry and tumultuous argument. Lassalle in his defence was seen in all his various moods, as telling words of satire and raillery, indignation and fury, remonstrance and persuasion, entreaty and pathos left his lips by turn. He treated all the members of the Court like so many ninepins, but his handling of the Crown Solicitor was especially severe. This functionary had eventually to propose that Lassalle should no longer be heard, and that he should be removed from the hall in case of a further attempt to speak. An

[1] Johannes Schulze, famous authority on education, born January 15th, 1786, at Brühl, for many years active in the Prussian State service; died February 21st, 1869.
[2] Friedrich Adolf Trendelenburg, philosopher, born November 30th, 1802, at Eutin, and died professor at Berlin, January 24th, 1872.
[3] Leopold von Ranke, the honoured historian, whose long and active life came so recently to its end. Born December 21st, 1795, at Wiehe, in Thuringia.
[4] Theodor Mommsen, the Roman historian, born November 30th, 1817, at Garding, in Schleswig, and still living at Charlottenburg, Berlin.
[5] Ludwig Häusser, historian, born October 26th, 1818, at Cleeburg, Lower Alsace; professor at Heidelberg from 1845 until his death (March 17th, 1867).
[6] Georg Heinrich Pertz, historian, born March 28th, 1795, at Hanover, lived at Berlin from 1842 until close upon his death, which took place at Munich, October 7th, 1876. He was the originator of the "Monumenta Germaniae historica."

animated passage followed the President's intimation that right of further reply had been taken away.

"Lassalle : Herr President, I must extract a decision on the point from the entire Court. I move for it, and require to be allowed to establish this proposition.

"The Crown Solicitor : I must, on the other hand, protest against the accused speaking, since the President has refused him a hearing.

"Lassalle: This is a confusion of ideas. The opportunity of speaking has been taken from me *au fond*. I have now challenged a decision of the Court, and the Court cannot pronounce on so important a matter without first hearing me.

"The President : The accused may speak to the question whether or not he should be refused a hearing.

"The Crown Solicitor: Then I will, at least, remark that he cannot speak of anything else.

"Lassalle : Rest assured that I shall keep to the point." [1]

Having got his way, the accused, as may be imagined, was not very careful to observe the strict conditions which his prosecutor desired to impose. He went back to points previously closed, traversed ground to which he had been refused admission, and said all he wanted to say. All that the Court could do was to wonder and be silent. The dramatic scene was brought to a close by an appeal for acquittal in the name of the nation and its honour, of science and its dignity, the land and its judicial freedom, and of history's verdict upon the result of the trial. But the invocation fell on deaf ears, and Lassalle was sentenced to be imprisoned four months and to pay the costs of the trial. This sentence was, however, commuted on appeal into a fine.

The publication of the defence with the title "Science and the Working Men" [2] drew upon Lassalle the eyes of many persons who had hitherto given no heed to the democratic giant-killer who was making himself so much talked about in Berlin. In February, Lassalle published a small *brochure*, "Might and Right," [3] a sequel to the two addresses on the constitution. Herein he gives expression to the unmistakable doctrine, "With the democracy alone is all right, and with it alone will be might." The next publication was, "Indirect

---

1 See original edition of "Die Wissenschaft und die Arbeiter" for the defence and passages between the accused, the prosecution and the President. Later editions omit these passages.

2 "Die Wissenschaft und die Arbeiter."

3 "Macht und Recht."

Taxes and the Condition of the Working Classes," [1] which was a re-print of his defence on the rehearing of the trial of January on appeal. These legal proceedings must have given Lassalle annoyance in that they diverted him from political and scientific work, and, indeed, we find him writing to Rodbertus in February, 1863, that he is "over-burdened in consequence of a small series of indictments which the Crown Solicitor has opened against me, and which compels me to lay aside everything else in order to give fire from both broadsides." But annoying as they were, the prosecutions were not without a com-pensatory side, for they helped to prepare their victim for the career of agitation upon which he was shortly to enter.

[1] " Die indirecten Steuer und die Lag der arbeitenden Klassen."

CHAPTER VI.

ORGANISATION OF THE WORKING CLASSES.

THE Constitutional struggles of 1848-1850 were succeeded by a remarkable awakening in the political life of Germany. The admission of the working classes to a share in Parliamentary affairs aroused wider interest in politics. On many sides bids were made for the favour of the young and growing democracy, and Working Men's Associations of various kinds were established in all parts of the country. For some years, however, the force of the reaction continued to be strongly felt, and during this period little visible progress could be made by Socialistic or even advanced Liberal doctrines. One of the first associations formed in the interest of working-men was the "*Centralverein für das Wohl der arbeitenden Klassen in Preussen*," ("Central Association for the Welfare of the Working Classes in Prussia"), which was constituted in April, 1848. This organisation was reactionary, and was formed with the view of leading the popular classes in the path of moderation, and its programme was in every respect a worthy one, but it cannot be said to have at any time enlisted the sympathies of the masses. The membership was 344 in the first year, but this number fell to 155 in 1862, when Ferdinand Lassalle's agitation began. A far more important part was played in the political history of the time by the *Arbeiterbildungsvereine*, associations which were semi-political in character, though they professed to have for their object the intellectual advancement of the working classes. It became clear, however, that the Governments, now supported by the reaction, were not inclined to be lenient with any new tendencies towards disorder which might show themselves. In 1851, some of the States concluded treaties for the expulsion of political suspects, and not a few leaders of the Socialistic movement were compelled to withdraw from German soil. It was not long before the Working Men's Associations fell under suspicion, and measures were taken for their suppression. On April 14th, 1853, a report was presented to the German Diet which stated :—

"After various Federal Governments have in the ordinary way of diplomacy called attention to the dangers which threaten public safety, owing to the activity of the Working Men's Associations spread over a large part of Germany, the Governments of Austria and Prussia believe that they will be meeting the wishes of the Federal Governments when they bring forward the question of adopting means for counteracting the injurious influence exerted by these associations, especially on the labouring class. If it be beyond doubt that success can only be attained by common and identical measures on the part of all Federal Governments, the question still appears to require preliminary inquiry, what extent should be given to the resolutions to be adopted, in order, on the one hand, that associations of a revolutionary character may with safety be suppressed, and, on the other hand, that the existence of such associations as pursue useful purposes may not be prevented, and that no unnecessary interference with free intercourse may take place."[1]

On this occasion Herr von Bismarck spoke in favour of legislative measures, for he regarded the influence of the associations as injurious. The result of the proposal of the Prussian and Austrian Governments was the adoption by the Diet on July 13th, 1854, of a serious of resolutions intended to effectually check the agitation of political organisations. Clause 3 of the treaty ran :—"In regard especially to political associations, in so far as they are not prohibited by the law of the country, or require in each case the special sanction of the authorities, the Governments concerned are in a position to decree special and temporary restrictions and prohibitions in conformity with the existing circumstances." The final clause ran :—

"In the interest of the common safety all Federal Governments undertake further to dissolve, within two months, the working men's associations and fraternities existing in their territories which pursue political, Socialistic, or Communistic purposes, and to forbid the resuscitation of such organisations under penalty."

The next thing was to deal with the Press, and after long negociation and deliberation, a stringent Press Law was adopted by resolution of the Diet on July 6th, 1854. This law made "special personal licence" necessary to the carrying on of the callings of printer, lithographer, bookseller, art-dealer, second-hand-bookseller, owner of cir-

[1] See 12th and 15th Volumes of "Publicationen aus den Köning. Preussischen Staatsarchiven' (Leipzig, 1882), for diplomatic documents on the democratic movement.

culating library or reading-room, and newspaper or print seller. The publisher of a periodical was required to deposit bail ranging from 5000 thalers (as a rule) to 500 thalers (in exceptional cases), and if judicial proceedings were rendered necessary by any action of his, the costs were to be defrayed from this deposit, which must, however, be at once made up to the full amount. The hardest provision was one which made it dangerous for newspapers to criticise public men or to publish statements objectionable to the Governments or the authorities. An unhappy time followed for the Press, or at least for that section which had hitherto made show of advanced political tendencies. By means of this and other repressive measures, indirectly repressive but still very effective, most democratic journals were reduced to extremities. Many succumbed to the penalties for misdemeanour, and others to the burden of high bail, stamp duty, or as in Hamburg advertisement duty. Those that succeeded in eluding their persecutors were compelled, when discussing political and social questions, to exercise a moderation which was as distasteful and irksome as it was purposeless for agitation. The right of public meeting was also restricted. Obstacles were placed in the way of out-door assemblies, and indoor assemblies were subjected to surveillance. It seemed as though the working classes would have to cast politics away from them. The measures adopted appeared to succeed so well, that in May, 1857, a report could be presented to the Federal Diet, wherein it was stated that Frankfort, which had for years been a chief seat of the "revolutionary elements," had been delivered from the hands of the democracy, whose literature had no longer a sale.[1] After all, the democratic movement had not been killed, or even scotched : it had only disappeared from the surface, and this was before long seen to be the fact.

Another movement fared better, the co-operative movement, begun by Schulze-Delitzsch, an influential politician, and a political economist.[2] Although Schulze was known to hold Progressist opinions, his associations were allowed to exist on the understanding that they would be good and give the Governments no trouble, a condition readily complied with, and faithfully adhered to. The co-operative

[1] "Preussen im Bundestag," (vol. 15 of the " Publicationen aus den König. Preussischen Staatsarchiven," already mentioned), pp. 111, 112.

[2] An excellent biography of this notable man appeared a few years ago from the pen of Dr. A. Bernstein with the title "Schulze-Delitzsch : Leben und Wirken" (Berlin),

movement is important, not only because for a time it took great hold of the people, but because it was indirectly instrumental in bringing Lassalle to the front as a rival agitator and propagandist. Hermann Schulze was born at Delitzsch, in Prussian Saxony, August 29th, 1808. He studied jurisprudence at Leipzig and Halle, and afterwards occupied judicial posts under the Government, becoming District Judge at Delitzsch in 1841, a position which he held until 1850. In 1848, he was elected to the Prussian National Assembly, and the following year he became a member of the Second Chamber, in which he sat as Schulze-Delitzsch, a name which has since adhered to him. Being a member of the Progressist party, he proved a thorn in the Government's flesh, and he was made District Judge at Wreschen, but he returned later to the Prussian Diet, and became also a member of the North German and German Reichstags. For more than thirty years Schulze headed the co-operative movement in Germany, but his self-sacrifice impoverished him, and although his motto as a social reformer had always been " Self-help," as opposed to Lassalle's " State-help," he was compelled in his declining years to accept a gift of £7000 from his friends. Schulze died honoured if not famous on April 29th, 1883.

Schulze-Delitzsch is the father of the co-operative movement in Germany. He had watched the development of this movement in England, and as early as 1848 he had lifted up his voice in espousal of co-operative principles in his own country. Though a Radical, Schulze was no Socialist, and he believed co-operation to be a powerful weapon wherewith to withstand the steady advance of Socialistic doctrines in Germany. Besides carrying on agitation by means of platform-speaking, he published various works on the subject, the chief of which are : " Die arbeitenden Klassen und das Associationswesen in Deutschland, als Programm zu einem deutschen Congress," (Leipzig, 1858) ; " Kapitel zu einem deutschen Arbeitercatechismus," (Leipzig, 1863) ; " Die Abschaffung des geschäftlichen Risico durch Herrn Lassalle," (Berlin, 1865) ; " Die Entwickelung des Genossenschaftswesens in Deutschland," (Berlin, 1870); and "Die Genossenschaften in einzelnen Gewerbszweigen," (Leipzig, 1873). Schulze advocated the application of the co-operative principle to other organisations than the English stores, and especially to loan, raw material, and industrial associations. He made a practical beginning at his own home and the adjacent town of Eilenburg, where in 1849 he established two co-operative associations of shoemakers and joiners, the object of which was the purchase and supply to members of raw material at cost price.   In 1850 he formed a Loan Association (*Vorschussverein*) at Delitzsch on the principle of monthly payments, and in the following year a similar association on a larger scale at Eilenburg.   For a long time Schulze had the field of agitation to himself, and the consequence was that the more intelligent sections of the working classes took to his proposals readily.   Another reason for his success, however, was the fact that the movement was practical and entirely unpolitical.   It was a movement from which the Socialistic element was absent, and one in which, therefore, the moneyed classes could safely co-operate.   Schulze, in fact, sought to introduce reforms social rather than Socialistic.   The fault of his scheme as a regenerative agency was that it did not affect the masses of the people, and thus the roots of the social question were not touched.   Schulze could only look for any considerable support to small tradesmen and artisans, to those who were really able to help themselves if shown the way.   But his motto of " Self-help " was an unmeaning gospel to the vast class of people who were not in this happy position.   As we shall later see, Lassalle detected this vulnerable point in his rival's armour, and made the best of his advantage.   The movement neared a turning point in 1858. In that year Schulze identified himself with the capitalist party at a congress of German economists, held at Gotha, and he soon began to lose favour with the popular classes.   The high-water mark was reached in 1860, at which time the co-operative associations had a membership of 200,000, and the business done amounted to 40,000,000 thalers or about £6,000,000 ; the capital raised by contribution or loan approaching a third of this sum.   In the year 1864 no fewer than 800 Loan and Credit Associations had been established, while in 1861 the number of Raw Material and Productive Associations was 172, and that of Co-operative Stores 66.   Possibly the movement might have continued to prosper, even though Schulze was suspected of sympathy with the capitalists, had no rival appeared on the scene.   But a rival did appear, and he was none other than Lassalle.   Lassalle began by warmly acknowledging the beneficent services which Schulze had rendered to his fellow-men, and he ended by vilifying the philanthropist—for such Schulze undoubtedly was—in one of the most rancorous works ever penned.[1] Schulze might have known that he was no match for the brilliant intellect of a man like Lassalle, but he defied the lightning and suffered for his temerity.

We are now nearing the eventful inauguration of an association whose appearance heralded the birth of the German Social-Democratic movement. At the time already reached there were three great parties in Germany, the Conservative or Reactionary, the National Liberal, and the Democratic party. The Conservatives formed the Great German party, which desired the retention of Austria in the Federal union, while the Liberals constituted a Small German party, whose aims were the unity of Germany under Prussian hegemony and the exclusion of Austria. These parties rallied round associations known as the Grossdeutscher Verein,[2] and the Deutscher National-Verein.[3] The Democratic or working-men's party was alone without organisation. Of the existing associations it was naturally more in sympathy with the National than the Great German, but that body was under the influence of the middle and higher classes, and it refused to admit working-men save as honorary members. In 1861, however, the Progressist party was formed, and it drew into its ranks a large number of Democrats who had held aloof from the Liberal party. For a time Lassalle identified himself with the Progressists, but his claims to recognition were so completely ignored that he finally withdrew, and henceforth became a violent opponent of the party. The Progressists formed, however, in 1862, by far the strongest and most vigorous party in the country, and all the large towns were in their hands. There is no telling how long the working class party might have been without its desired organisation had not the Leipzig

[1] "Herr Bastlat-Schulze von Delitzsch : der ökonomische Julian, oder Kapital und Arbeit," (Berlin, 1864).

[2] The *Grossdeutsche Partei* existed from 1848 to 1866.

[3] The *Deutscher Nationalverein* was formed in 1859 with its seat at Coburg. It was dissolved in autumn 1867 at Frankfort. In 1861, during the Conflict Time in Prussia, the advanced wing of the Liberal Party seceded and formed the *Fortschrittspartei* or Progressists. A split occurred in the latter party in 1866, and the seceding members formed themselves into the moderate National Liberal party. Finally the *Fortschrittspartei* disappeared as to name, being merged into a new *Freisinnige Partei.* According to the official election returns for 1887 the parties now represented in the German Reichstag are the German Conservatives ; the German Imperial Party or Free Conservatives ; National Liberals ; Centre (Clerical and Ultramontane); Poles ; Social-Democrats ; Guelphs ; Alsacers; and Danes. The *Volkspartei* was swept out of existence during the last phenomenal elections.

Working Men's Association [1] resolved to take the lead. A Committee was appointed to take steps for the establishment of a Working Men's Association for all Germany. The first meeting was held in Berlin in October, 1862, but utter confusion existed in the minds of all the delegates as to the purposes and programme of the organisation to be formed. One party was in favour of a non-political platform, and another wished the association to be an appendage of the Progressist party.

At this juncture, when the Committee was sorely in need of advice, a man came forward—a very *deus ex machinâ*—who, better than any one else, was able to set it on the right path. This was Ferdinand Lassalle. Lassalle, as we have seen, had on April 12th, 1862—which has been called the birthday of German Social-Democracy—addressed a Trade Association in Berlin, and the address had been published with the title "Arbeiterprogramm." This *brochure* came to the notice of the Leipzig Committee, which in February, 1863, invited Lassalle to explain his views. He did not hesitate to comply with the request. He felt that the time for silence had passed, and that he must now speak out. Many friends advised him to keep quiet if he loved peace, and even those who saw the expediency of action refused to give encouragement out of regard for his happiness. Lassalle once referred to the importunities of his well-wishers as follows :

" I answered all this with old Luther. 'Here I stand, I can do no other : God help me, amen.' And if I had at that moment been morally dead and were to have been physically torn into seventy-seven pieces, I could not have done otherwise."

Theory, he felt, was of no value without practice, and his resolution was that he would enter the fray " even if it cost his head three and thirty times." This was early in February, at which time he was engaged with his friend Ziegler on the outlines of a workman's insurance scheme, which was at once thrown aside.

Lassalle placed his views before the Leipzig Committee in the form of an " Open Reply Letter."[2] In this letter, the doctrines propounded

---

1 This association was founded and for many years directed by Professor E. A. Rossmässler, a warm friend of the working classes. He was born March 3rd, 1806, and died April 8th, 1867, his last words, like those of Saint-Simon, breathing devotion to the cause of social reform. An interesting autobiography was posthumously published bearing the title " Mein Leben und Streben im Verkehr mit der Natur und dem Volke," (Hanover, 1874).

2 Published with the title " Offenes Antwortschreiben an das Central-Comité zur Berufung eines Allgemeinen Deutschen Arbeiter-Congresses zu Leipzig."

in which will call for notice later, he advanced a new programme as attractive as it was revolutionary. Hitherto the Committee had been floundering about in a bog of commonplace proposals for social reform, few of which could help in the construction of a popular platform for agitation. When Lassalle read in the newspapers that it had been discussing free migration and free choice of vocations he "smiled sadly," as he says, and he quotes a distich from Schiller for the benefit of these men who were debating questions "more than fifty years too late" :—

> " Jahre lang schon bedien' ich mich meine Nase zum Riechen,
> Aber hab' ich an sie auch ein *erweisliches Recht ?* " [1]

Why need they trouble their heads about free migration and free exercise of crafts? These were things which Legislatures now decreed in silence ; they no longer required debate. Then, again, a part of the Committee wished to establish savings banks, relief funds, and co-operative stores, but Lassalle answered that plans of this kind did not go below the surface of the social question. They were like the paddle of the steamship, agitating the face of the water but leaving the depths untouched. The kernel of the problem Lassalle saw in the "iron economic law," established by Ricardo, that "the average wages of labour always remain reduced to the necessary subsistence which is, conformably with the prevailing standard of life of a nation, requisite to the prolongation of existence and the propagation of the species." [2] Of what good, he asked, were Schulze's self-help associations to people who were barely able to live? Credit and raw material societies were all very well for small tradesmen, who were not without capital, but to the great bulk of the labouring class they were a mockery. Even the small industry would only be able for a time to compete with its great rival, capitalism. Similarly, the co-operative associations were inadequate, for it was not as consumers but producers that the working classes suffered. "As consumers we are in general all equal already. As before the gendarmes, so also before the sellers, all men are equal—if they only pay." There was only one solution of the difficulty : the labourer must be his own producer.

[1] " For years I have used my nose, true, for smelling,
But have I in it a demonstrable right ?"

[2] "Offenes Antwortschreiben," p. 13, and *passim* in Lassalle's works.

The working classes must be organised into Productive Associations and the State must provide the necessary capital. Thus alone would the produce of labour fall to its rightful owner, the producer. But how to bring the State over to such a p'an ? Easily done, answered Lassalle. "The working classes must constitute themselves an independent political party and must make universal, equal, and direct suffrage their watchword. The representation of the working classes in the legislative bodies of Germany—that alone can satisfy their legitimate interests in a political sense."[1] Let them acquire their rightful legislative power, and they would soon be able to give effect to their will.

The publication of the Letter produced a great sensation, and a majority of the Committee adopted it with enthusiasm. It was the first time any definite project had been laid before them, and light began to spring out of darkness. Although Lassalle had once predicted that his Letter would have the same effect as the publication of the theses by Luther, he had not been without grave anxiety as to its reception by the masses. "Perhaps," he said, "the working classes in general are not ready, and in that case I am certainly a dead man." The moderate leaders of the labour party were, it is true, shocked, and men like Rossmässler[2] threw themselves into the arms of the Progressist party, but on the whole Lassalle had good cause to be satisfied with the result of his hardihood. And now began a long and severe rivalry between two movements—that of Lassalle, based on the principle of State-help ; and that of Schulze, who adhered still to his motto of self-help. F. A. Lange[3] has well compared these remarkable men to two great millstones grinding one another. Apart from the inherent strength of the causes, every advantage appeared to be on the side of Schulze, who had at his back the entire Progressist party, in whose hands were nearly all the important newspapers in the country.

---

[1] "Offenes Antwortschreiben."

[2] Otto Dammer writes to Lassalle, March 26th : "Rossmässler is furious that you attack the Progressist party." Rossmässler had issued, during the time the Committee had been deliberating, an address to the working classes ("Ein Wort an die deutschen Arbeiter," Berlin, 1863, though the introduction is dated December 10, 1862), in which he sought to spur them to self-improvement.

[3] "Die Arbeiterfrage, ihre Bedeutung für Gegenwart und Zukunft" (2nd edition, Winterthur, 1870). Friedrich Albert Lange, philosopher and political economist, was born September 28th, 1828, near Solingen. Was professor at Zurich and Marburg. Died at the latter place, November 23rd, 1875

Both party and Press entered into a conspiracy of silence, and it was some time before Lassalle's agitation was openly recognised as a fact deserving of serious treatment. Schulze had further the inestimable advantage of priority. His name had already become a household word in a large part of Prussia, and it was also known in other States, while Lassalle was a comparative stranger to the working classes, save in the Rhine Province. At the outset of the struggle, Lassalle was generous in his treatment of his opponent, of whom he said :

" He is the only member of his party, the Progressist party—and this is therefore all the more to his praise—who has done anything for the people. Through his indefatigable energy he became, though standing alone and living in the most depressed times, the father and founder of the German co-operative system, and he has thus given an impulse to the cause of association having far-reaching results—a merit for which, though differing widely from him theoretically, I in spirit warmly shake his hand." Liberal praise like this only brings into more painful relief the abuse and undignified scoff which Lassalle at a later stage of his agitation heaped upon a rival who was earlier in the field than himself, and whose motives were certainly not less disinterested than his own.

The Leipzig Committee, meanwhile, found itself upon the horns of a dilemma. It had to choose whom it would serve : Lassalle or Schulze—Lassalle with his Productive Associations or Schulze with Co-operation. The former was invited to address a working-men's meeting at Leipzig, and this he did on April 16th, 1863, traversing again the ground covered in the " Open Letter."[1]   On this occasion he was able to announce that his State Socialism had won the approval of Professor Wuttke,[2] of Leipzig, and of Lothar Bucher.[3]   In order to bring matters to a climax, the Committee finally invited both Lassalle and Schulze to speak before a congress of working-men at

[1] The address was published with the title, " Zur Arbeiterfrage."

[2] Heinrich Wuttke, historian, born February 12th, 1818, at Brieg. Was a member of the Frankfort Parliament. Became professor at Leipzig, and as such died June 14th, 1876.

[3] Lothar Bucher, born October 25th, 1817, at Neustettin, jurist and author. Became in 1848 a member of the Prussian National Assembly, and in 1850 had to leave the country on account of his association with the no-taxation resolutions. He lived in London for some time as a journalist, and returned to Berlin in 1856. His great abilities caused Bismarck to call him to the Foreign Office in 1864, and he has since served the State. He used to be called " Bismarck's right hand."

Frankfort-on-Main on May 17th. They were to have publicly disputed, like Luther and Eck at Leipzig, but excusing himself on the plea of Parliamentary duties, Schulze did not respond to the invitation. Lassalle had thus to contend with opponents who were leaderless, and victory was easily won. Thirteen hundred delegates of Working Men's Associations were present, and the proceedings lasted two days. Lassalle delivered two addresses[1] and these were warmly debated. That he attributed great importance to the decision which was to be come to is shown by the concluding words of the second day's address. " If you vote against me," he said, " if the great majority of the German working class vote against me, then I shall say to Herr Schulze : ' You are right—these people are not yet advanced enough to be helped.' If I thought only of myself and my natural egoism, I should be compelled to desire ardently that you would decide against me ; for if you, and not only you, but the great majority of the German working class, were to do that, I should—justified in the eyes of science and certain of being justified by history—withdraw quietly to science ; I should, with a sad smile at your unreadiness, stretch myself out perhaps in the Gulf of Naples, and let the soft breezes of the South blow over me ; I should spare myself a life full of torment, exertion, vexation, and worry. Thus your decision would be exceedingly easy to bear. But you would lose one of the best friends of your class, and you would not only lose me, but perhaps for decades every one wishful to help you would be frightened. He would say to himself : ' This class is not ready ; let me be warned by the example of Lassalle.' Therefore I tell you, by all the love for the cause of the working classes which I bear in me, my whole soul hangs on your decision."

Lassalle conquered. On May 19th a vote was taken, and after forty delegates had left the hall with a cheer for Schulze-Delitzsch, the programme of Productive Associations and universal suffrage was adopted by four hundred votes to one. Lassalle had reached a turning-point in his life. Henceforth he was to stand out the head of the democratic movement in Germany. The task which he had undertaken—that of converting the working classes to views for the acceptance of which they had had little preparation—seemed, and indeed was, a formidable one, and a man not endowed with an indomitable

[1] Published with the title, " Arbeiterlesebuch."

will, and a confidence which no power could shake, would have contemplated the inevitable struggle with fear and trembling. In reality Lassalle's prospects of success seemed slight. A large part of the working class, won over to the Progressist party, was hostile to him, and all the forces of wealth and influence were ranged in antagonism. He was a Joshua whose way into the land of promise offered to his followers was blocked by the Canaanites, Amorites, Jebusites, Hittites, Hivites, Perizzites, and Girgashites of rank, capitalism, wealth, politics, science, the law, and the police. Could he overcome this great coalition? Lassalle believed he could, and said he would. How far his assurance was justified will appear later. The first step was the formation of a Working Men's Association which should act as a lever for agitation. His friends proposed to call it the "German" Association. Lassalle objected: it should be called the "Universal German," and so with the title, "Allgemeiner Deutscher Arbeiterverein," the organisation was founded. The statutes were adopted on May 23rd, 1863, the first section running as follows:—" With the name Universal German Working Men's Association the undersigned found for the German Federal States an association which, proceeding from the conviction that the adequate representation of the social interests of the German working classes and the real removal of class antagonism in society can alone be secured by universal, equal, and direct suffrage, has as its purpose the acquisition of such suffrage by peaceable and legal means, and particularly by gaining over public opinion." All German working-men were to be eligible for membership on a nominal payment. Agents were to be appointed in all important towns, and Lassalle was to be the president for five years. The duration of the Association was provisionally fixed at thirty years. The initial membership was six hundred, representing a dozen large towns.

CHAPTER VII.

THE PRODUCTIVE ASSOCIATION.

WHEN Lassalle entered the social and political arena as agitator and reformer, one of the first things he did was to seek the co-operation of Karl Rodbertus, who was his senior in years, and greatly his superior as a political economist.[1] That he had a very high opinion of the Pomeranian landowner and sage is shown by many passages in an extensive correspondence. From Rodbertus his mind, indeed, received important and beneficial stimulus, and he meant all he said when he wrote, " Intellectual intercourse with a man like you, is amongst the pleasantest things wherewith one can at present refresh himself." [2] He tells Rodbertus at another time, " You cannot form an adequate idea of the weight which I attach to your views,"[3] and even when differing from his friend on crucial principles, he says he will weigh all criticism " as carefully and painfully" as he thinks out his own writings. The two men had as economists very much in common and took naturally to each other. Lassalle goes so far as to say, " We appear in mind to have come into the world like Siamese twins," and this statement hardly involves an exaggeration.

Lassalle thought that with Rodbertus at his side his agitation would be sure to carry all before it. Unfortunately, however, for his hopes, it was impossible to induce Achilles to don his armour. For the attitude of reserve which Rodbertus, in spite of urgent entreaty and

---

[1] One of the best works bearing upon the Socialist movement in Germany is R. Meyer's "Der Emancipationskampf des vierten Standes," (2 vols., Berlin, 1874). This work contains a vast amount of information, but it suffers from bad arrangement. Meyer's economic studies have led him to introduce the principle of the division of labour into the writing of this history, for while he has collected an enormous quantity of facts his readers are expected to help him in the assortment of them. Still the work is very painstaking. There may also be mentioned F. Mehring's "Die deutsche Socialdemokratie," already spoken of; J. E. Joerg's "Geschichte der social-politischen Parteien in Deutschland," (Freiburg im Breisgau, 1867); Dr. G. Adler's "Geschichte der ersten sozialpolitischen Arbeiterbewegung in Deutschland" (Breslau, 1885); and Dr. Eugen Jäger's "Der moderne Socialismus," (Berlin, 1873). The fullest account of Lassalle's agitation is contained in Bernhard Becker's "Geschichte der Arbeiteragitation Ferdinand Lassalle's," (Brunswick, 1874).

[2] Letter of February 17th, 1863.   [3] Letter of June 26th, 1863.

K

of an importunity which at last becomes almost amusing, persisted in maintaining, there were two cogent reasons. In the first place, he was a man whose retiring disposition became a stronger trait in his character the older he grew. At the time of Lassalle's appearance as a popular leader he had long passed the prime of life. The attention which had in younger years been divided between politics and science, was now concentrated upon his favourite study, political economy. For public activity, he had no inclination whatever. He was essentially a student, and he rightly felt that his proper sphere was the study and not the platform. But even if Rodbertus had been willing to share in the bustle and tumult of agitation, there was another obstacle in the way of co-operation in the new movement, and this was insuperable He did not think Lassalle's programme was a practical one. He has referred to this disagreement as follows :—

" I had to decline participation in Lassalle's agitation since we could not agree on the two principal ends of the agitation. (1.) Lassalle wished to improve the condition of the working classes by means of a universal system of Productive Associations. I, on the other hand, wished to retain the wages principle, though, of course, to have it re-formed by the State. (2.) Lassalle wished to make the Socialist party at the same time a political party. I wished it to remain an entirely economic party. Lassalle made the formation of a political party a *sine qua non* of association with him. His reasons were the following. The working-men had already become under Schulze-Delitzsch a political party, but a party misguided economically. They could only be rescued from this economic misguidance by increased political agitation. Thence, the demand for universal suffrage, to which the Free Trade democracy had already become much inclined."[1]

When one considers the standpoints taken up by these two men, who, though holding views so similar in theory, differed radically in the practical application of them, it is impossible to come to any other conclusion than that both were right. It was manifestly too much to expect that Rodbertus would pin his faith to the Productive Associations, when that would mean the abandonment of projects of social reform which he had spent the best years of his life in perfecting. But putting this aspect of the question aside, Rodbertus was fully persuaded

---

[1] " Briefe von Ferdinand Lassalle an Karl Rodbertus-Jagetzow," (Berlin, 1878). See introduction by Adolph Wagner, pp. 2-4.

in his own mind that the Productive Associations would fail to do any good. Lassalle had, on the other hand, great, though not complete, confidence in his own plan, and when Rodbertus hints that the key of the difficulty is to adjust production to consumption, he triumphantly exclaims that this is just what the Productive Associations will do. "For," says he, "it can hardly be doubted that if they were established on a large scale with the aid of State credit, an entire branch of production would in a short time combine in one Association—or in very few. This branch Association would have, in its business books, the best statistical information as to consumption. The competition leading to over-production could only exert an effect—and that would be vastly diminished—from abroad. Eventually over-production would not in reality be over-production, but production in advance, since these Associations with their enormous credit would not be compelled to sell out, and it is this which alone converts excess of production, from production in advance into over-production."[1] While, however, Lassalle was so devoted to his Productive Associations he expressed willingness to abandon them in favour of a good substitute. "If you will show me an equally efficient remedy," he writes to Rodbertus, "I am quite ready to accept it. I have only proposed the Association provisionally, because I see at present no remedy which would be at once so comparatively easy and so efficient. Working-men must, however, have something quite definite, something that can be grasped, and not a general law, if they are to become interested." And again he writes, "Only because the working classes—and very properly—like to see somewhere a how and where, have I proposed the Association with State help."

It was this argument that influenced him when he resolved to give to his agitation a distinctly political character. Here, again, Rodbertus was obdurate. To use his own words, he could "tolerate no political agitation which would excite the working classes against the existing Executive Power," an expression which well shows how purely scientific his Socialistic standpoint was, and how far he was—however sweeping his proposals—from desiring to see social reform confounded with social confusion. Lassalle refused to divorce the political and social elements of his movement. "Both are,' he said, "as necessarily dependent as form and substance, and either isolated

[1] Letter of April 22nd, 1863.

would be powerless." When Rodbertus apprehended that if great
weight were attached to the political side of the question, the economic
side would be neglected, he only replied, "*L'homme a deux bras*, as
Victor Hugo says, and I think you will find that it is the right arm which
I have, in spite of all, reserved for economics." And, further, "Without
universal suffrage, that is, a practical handle by which to realise our
claims, we may be a philosophical school, or a religious sect, but never
a political party. Thus it appears to me that universal suffrage
belongs to our social demands as the handle to the axe."[1] Lassalle
knew, in fact, that abstract doctrines of political economy would fail
to touch the sympathies of the masses. They could furnish no efficient
basis for agitation, and he was an agitator. He saw that it would
be useless to attempt to rouse the working classes by the statement
of theories or even hard facts, as that they did not receive their proper
share of the produce of labour and that the capitalist appropriated
more than was by right his own. Some tangible proposal was necessary—a proposal simple yet all-sufficient and going to the root of the
matter—and with this proposal there must be shown the way of
realising it. Thus it was that he came to advocate the Productive
Association as an end and universal suffrage as a means to this end.
Yet he never pretended that even the Productive Associations would
of themselves solve the whole social problem. At the best they were
a transitional measure. Indeed, in the "Open Reply Letter" he
expressly omits reference to the social problem and its solution,
regarding his immediate proposals as calculated only to improve the
condition of the working class. The final solution, the supplanting of
the present form of personal property, might require for its accom-
plishment five hundred years.[2] Nevertheless, the Associations would
pave the way for further progress. There could be little hope of con-
ciliating views so divergent as were those of Lassalle and Rodbertus.
Even Lassalle's appeal to his friend's sense of duty produced no effect :
" It would not be right if I were left alone. I have only five fingers
on each hand and already everyone of them has too much to do. . .
Why should you not speak, who above all others are called on to do
so ? The negotiations were continued for a long time with forbearance and gallantry on both sides, but they ended as they began.

[1] Letter of April 30th, 1863.
[2] Letters to Rodbertus, April 28th and May 26th, 1863.

Rodbertus decided to stand aloof from the agitation,[1] and Lassalle had to take the field alone.

Lassalle well knew the importance of making a good beginning, and he at once threw the whole of his marvellous energy into the work of agitation and organisation. His hopes were built on an Association having a membership of more than a hundred thousand and an agitation fund of 450,000 marks (£22,500) yearly. "That," he wrote to a friend, "*would* be a power." The great opponent of the Universal was the National Association, which professed to have twenty thousand members, but Lassalle said frankly, "We must have seven times more members than the National Association or we shall have suffered a ridiculous shipwreck." Before the Universal was formally constituted, therefore, he was at work on the platform and in the study. He was a puzzle to many people—to friends who afterwards became enemies and to enemies who became friends. Faucher,[2] the Free Trade economist, said he knew nothing about political economy; Max Wirth[3] declared that his "iron law of wages" had long been controverted; and more than one Working Men's Association found him a mere tool of the reaction. In spite, however, of calumny on the one hand, and, what was far more damaging, mistrust on the other, he refused to be daunted, and by April 22nd he was able to inform Rodbertus that besides Leipzig, Hamburg, Düsseldorf, Solingen, and Elberfeld, the Provincial Assembly at Cologne had come over to his side. With pride and satisfaction he could write, "I knew that Rhineland would not leave me in the lurch." The tenacity with which he kept to his purpose is well shown in another letter to the same friend, written on April 28th. At that time the Press was closed to him, for he was still regarded as *une quantité négligeable* in public affairs. Lassalle greatly felt the need of publicity, and it was probably

[1] While the negotiations were going on Rodbertus consented to address an "Open Letter" to the Leipzig Committee and this was published. This was his only contribution to the agitation. Yet even up to the end of 1863 Lassalle refused to regard Rodbertus as lost to his cause. "Tell me especially," he writes to Rodbertus, "everything that can be of service to our cause; I call it such with right, although you continue to be a sleeping partner, not having entered the Association."

[2] Julius Faucher, born June 13th, 1820, in Berlin, was an ardent champion of Free Trade. He belonged to the Progressist party and sat in the Prussian Lower House. Died June 12th, 1878, in Rome.

[3] Max Wirth did a great deal to introduce Trade Unions into Germany. He studied the working of these organisations in England.

the shabby treatment received at this time which envenomed his later references to newspapers and their conductors. Now, as he stood at the threshold of his agitation, this attitude of indifference and silence angered him beyond measure, and he determined to adopt means which would break down the passive opposition. In the Frankfort meeting, called for May 17th, he saw the possibility of effecting his design. He writes to Rodbertus :

" You are quite right in saying that such disputes settle nothing. But this time I need one. After the way in which the Berlin Press has made use of the working-man comedy here, and in view of the fact that we have no organ in which to say a word, I require a great *éclat*, by which to compel the *bourgeois*[1] Press itself to serve me. For that reason I *must* go and win. I *need* to do it. The people there are all against me and have invited me out of mere courtesy. But I will leave no stone unturned ; I will shake my old revolutionary mane ; and it will go hard if I do not triumph." In the same letter he says that the correspondence which he is compelled to keep up with followers in all parts is enough to kill him. Everything has to be done in breathless haste, and he has not even time to think. Early in May he could report with jubilation, " The movement is

---

[1] It is here desirable to understand what Lassalle means by *bourgeois*. " In the German language the word *bourgeoisie* would be rendered *Bürgerthum*. But it has not this meaning with me. We are all *Bürger* (citizens), the working-man, the *Kleinbürger* (small citizen), the *Grossbürger* (great citizen), &c. The word *bourgeoisie* has in the course of history come to signify a definite political direction. The entire non-noble citizen class fell when the French Revolution took place, and falls to-day, into two under classes, viz., the class of those who draw their income wholly or principally from their labour, and are supported by no capital or a very moderate amount, which allows them to exercise a productive activity that maintains themselves and their families : to this class belong the labourers, the small citizens, the artisans, and on the whole the peasantry. There is then the class of those who have at disposal a large civil possession, who have a large capital and on the strength of it can either produce or draw income in *rente*. These may be called the *Grossbürger*. But a *Grossbürger* is by no means a *bourgeois*. . . When the *Grossbürger*, not satisfied with the actual pleasantness of a great possession, this civil possession capital, demands further, as a condition of its possession, that he shall be given a share in the ruling of the State, in the determining of the will and purpose of the State, then only does he become a *bourgeois*, for then he makes the fact of possession a legal condition of political authority, characterises himself as one of a new privileged class in the nation, which will impress the stamp of its privilege upon all social institutions just as much as the nobility with the privilege of land-ownership did in the Middle Ages." *Arbeiterprogramm* (Chicago edition of 1872), pp. 20, 21.

Liebknecht renders *bourgeoisie* by "middle-class," but the term is so distinctive that I have always adhered to it when taking it from the mouths or writings of others.

growing, growing, growing." Even the Press was beginning to break silence, and ten journals had declared for the cause, including the reactionary *Kreuz-Zeitung* and the *Norddeutsche Allgemeine Zeitung*. "All would be very beautiful if the burden of work did not oppress me." Then, too, he was badgered on all hands by his enemies. "I have the whole mob on my neck as a wild boar the hounds," he writes from Berlin on May 11th, "but at Frankfort I shall shake myself rather unpleasantly." He attended the Frankfort congress accordingly, and the formation of the Universal Association followed. "Frankfort is ours," he writes at the end of May, "Mayence as well, and Hanau will be ours very soon." At Frankfort, as we have seen, the voting was four hundred to one, and at Mayence it was eight hundred to two. On May 26th he writes to Rodbertus :

"The first act has been brought to a triumphant close. The second now begins, the numbering or rather the enlistment of members for the Association."

That Lassalle found it no light task to pilot the Association aright, and to keep its officials in order, will easily be imagined. He had himself a thorough knowledge of his mission, but this can hardly be said of those who worked alongside of him. The statutes of the Association had placed great power in the hands of the president, and it was not seldom that a mild form of despotism had to be resorted to, in order to prevent the disorder that always arises from the clash of different opinions. Oftentimes he found himself in the position of Johnson, and had to confess that although he could furnish his opponents with arguments, he could not supplement their intelligence; but now and then he had to take up a bolder attitude, as when he exclaimed, "If you are not convinced I shall simply call ' Discipline ;' there must only be one will." But his rare skill as an administrator none could question, and his assiduity and energy even his enemies did not hesitate to recognise. The president worked in Berlin, and the secretary in Leipzig, the seat of the Association, and for several months a torrent of pamphlets, circulars, and letters poured over Germany. Nor was literary help wanting from many men who were not able to take part in the agitation publicly. Thus Bernhard Becker[1] published a pamphlet justifying Lassalle against the attacks of

[1] Becker was the son of a Thuringian land-owner. He studied philosophy and political economy at more than one university, and is said to have been characterised as a student by extreme Radical tendencies. He lived some time in Switzerland, and visited England before

his detractors.[1]   Moses Hess, a tried Socialist, issued another on
" The right to work," and Jean Baptista von Schweitzer,[2] a Frankfort
advocate, wrote a social novel with the title " Lucinde," which he
dedicated to Lassalle.   The poet Herwegh also contributed a democratic song, which Hans von Bülow at Lassalle's request set to music.
Better than all, Rodbertus was persuaded to write an " Open Letter "
to the Leipzig Committee, which Lassalle published with amend-
ments.[3]   In this letter the Jagetzow Socialist commended the Association for standing aloof from Schulze's co-operative scheme, and
endorsed Lassalle's statement of the " iron law."   If the working
classes, he said, failed to participate in the increasing productivity, it
was clear that others must be benefiting at their expense, and thus
that the extremes of wealth and poverty must be widening.   It was
not the increase in the national wealth, or the possibility afforded to
the moneyed classes of the more liberal satisfaction of their wants, that
was a danger to the nation : the danger lay in the unequal distribution
of the produce, which led to discord in social relationships.   " Look
at our circumstances in general," he said ; "has the difference in the
incomes of the various classes of society become greater or less since
we have possessed machinery and railways, and since productivity
and production have increased so remarkably ?   The answer cannot
be doubtful.   Or look at things more particularly, and ask the older
ones among you whether wages—real wages—have in their native
countries or towns increased during the last forty years as rent, or
what is the same thing, the value of land, and the capital of the country have increased ? "   No, he answered, for wages were still pressed

participation in the democratic movements of 1848 converted him into a political refugee. He
returned to Germany about the year 1860. Becker has written a large number of works :
apart from those dealing with Lassalle and his agitation, the chief are " Die deutsche Bewegung von 1848 und die gegenwärtige " (Berlin, 1864); " Geschichte und Theorie der Pariser
revolutionären Kommune des Jahres 1871 " (Leipzig, 1879) ; " Die Reaktion in Deutschland
gegen die Revolution von 1848 " (Vienna, 1869) ; and " Der Missbrauch der Nationalitäts-
lehre " (Vienna, 1867).

[1] "Lassalle und seine Verkleinerer."

[2] Jean Baptista von Schweitzer, born July 12th, 1834, at Frankfort-on-Main. By profession an advocate, known better as a Socialist agitator and a writer of comedies. Sat in the
Reichstag. Died July 28th, 1875, at Giessbach.

[3] Rodbertus in this "Offener Brief an das Comité des Deutschen Arbeitervereins zu
Leipzig " said that he did not expect from the Productive Association even the slightest contribution to the solution of the social problem, but Lassalle struck this out, and then begged
for pardon.

down to the cost of living, and the labourer was kept from his due share in the produce. Rodbertus warned the Association against political agitation, which he prophesied would fail. The programme of universal suffrage would make all German Governments their enemies—and yet they relied on the State to help them! The "Open Letter," in spite of its encouraging words, contained some unpalatable truths, yet, coming from such an authority, Lassalle knew better than to ignore it, and so it was published at once.

At the end of June Lassalle was compelled to recruit his strength in Switzerland, and he remained absent from the scene of agitation until September. Bernhard Becker,[1] whom Lassalle, just before his death, nominated his successor in the presidency of the Association, and who made up for excess of adulation during his leader's life by a singular display of venom on his decease, sneers at Lassalle for going away at this time, and says he showed a "love of pleasure" which proved that "his person went before his cause." But letters written by Lassalle during the second quarter of the year show him to have been absolutely exhausted by work. He was ill even when the acclamation of the Frankfort congress proclaimed him the chosen democratic leader in May, and he speaks of himself more than once as being "weary to death." What he had already gone through that year would, indeed, have brought far stronger men to the ground. He had done a large amount of literary work, and had organised a great agitation, addressing numerous meetings—often stormy and always excited—attending conferences, carrying on an extensive correspondence, and managing the entire affairs of an organisation whose influence extended to all parts of Germany. In addition to this, he had been embroiled in police prosecutions, which, however indifferent he may have been to them on the score of personal consequences, caused him worry and vexation. During his absence from Berlin, however, he by no means abandoned his work as president. From his Swiss retreat he directed the movements of his subordinates, and that with as much decision and success as though he had been on the spot.

The Association did not make the progress which Lassalle had expected. In August, when it had existed a quarter of a year, the members only numbered between nine hundred and a thousand,

1 "Geschichte der Arbeiteragitation Ferdinand Lassalles. Nach authentischen Aktenstücken" (Brunswick, 1874)

Hamburg and Harburg having together 230, Elberfeld 223, and Leipzig 150, while Berlin had only 20. Lassalle had already shown that he was discouraged, but he urged his followers to fresh energy. We find him writing on July 18th

"Unless the agitation seizes hold of the masses of the working classes, do what we may all will be lost. If at the expiration of a year at the latest we are not able to secure large numbers, we shall be quite impotent, however many moral victories we may have won."

Nevertheless, he would not consent to a false representation of the position of the Association, and when an official hints at it he replies sharply:

"You must not allow our agents to tell untruths. You cannot ask them to speak of 10,000 members when we have perhaps only 1000. We can be silent on the point, but lying is not the thing for us."

In August he was so disheartened that he wrote to his secretary Vahlteich[1]:

"So there are about 1000 members in our entire Association! And this is at present the fruit of our work! This is the result for which I have worn my fingers through and talked my lungs out. This apathy of the masses is enough to drive one to despair, is it not? Such indifference towards a movement which is solely for them, solely in their interest!—and notwithstanding the enormous resources of agitation—in an intellectual respect—which have already been expended, and which with a nation like the French would already have produced vast results! When will this dull people shake off its lethargy?"

Still, he would not abandon hope, and when Vahlteich suggests the dissolution of the Association he replies: "Quite impossible! The shame for our nation and party would be too great." Whatever happened he would continue until spring or summer. "Only courage!" he adds.

Lassalle had promised to return in October, and then "reopen the campaign against the Progressists with redoubled energy."[2] He was, however, back in September full of a great plan upon which he relied for the creation of a new and intenser enthusiasm amongst the

[1] Karl Julius Vahlteich, born December 30th, 1839, at Leipzig. Originally a shoemaker, but later a journalist. He became a prominent Socialist member of the German Reichstag.
[2] Letter to Rodbertus, June 24th, 1863.

working classes. He would review his forces on the Rhine. To the Rhine he therefore went, and addressed great meetings at Barmen (September 20th), Solingen (27th), and Düsseldorf (28th). The address [1] was one of his greatest, if not his greatest, as an agitator. The rhetoric was enchanting, the fire and passion overwhelming, the pathos which appeared here and there irresistible. Lassalle seemed to grow in strength in proportion as the difficulty of his task increased. The Solingen meeting was broken up, it would appear, unjustifiably, by the Mayor of the town, and Lassalle, who was escorted to the post-office by a vast crowd of sympathisers, telegraphed at once to Minister von Bismarck in Berlin calling for satisfaction. So characteristic is the despatch that it would be a pity to omit it :

"Minister President von Bismarck, Berlin : Progressist Mayor, at the head of ten gendarmes armed with bayonetted rifles, and several policemen with drawn swords, has just dissolved without legal grounds a working-men's meeting called by me. Vainly protested, appealing to the law on coalition. The people—five thousand in the great hall of the Schützenhalle, several thousands more before the same—restrained with difficulty from acts of violence. Brought by gendarmes and tens of thousands of people, who believed me to have been arrested, to the telegraph office. Banner of the Elberfeld working-men confiscated. I beg for most severe and most speedy judicial satisfaction."

The appeal to Cæsar was without effect, but Lassalle was a gainer by the notoriety which the event gave him. The new ardour which he had gained during his retirement in Switzerland had told, and he returned to Berlin in a jubilant mood. He could write to Rodbertus :

"I am delighted and of good cheer, glad, as Plato sings, 'in the presentiment of mastery,' and full of inner assurance."

And again :

"I can hardly tell you how favourably matters stand on the Rhine, seven times better than I had hoped even in my boldest dreams. In all Saxony, too, in Hamburg and Frankfort, there is rapid progress. I will now concentrate my strength on Berlin."

The task of winning Berlin over seemed an impossible one, but Lassalle loved difficulties. "Berlin *must* be mine," he wrote, "before

---

[1] Published with the title "Die Feste, die Presse, und der Frankfurter Abgeordnetentag : drei Symptome des öffentlichen Geistes."

six months are passed. I will invest it. Let me only have 200 working-men and I shall have 2000, and soon the whole of them."
Already he had prepared the way for operations by the circulation of
sixteen thousand copies of an "Address to the Working-men of
Berlin," in which he endeavoured to show that the Progressists were
unmanning the artisan, and also sought support for his Productive
Associations.   Two principal factors played against Lassalle's prospects
of success in Berlin.   The one, with which we have already become
acquainted, was the predominance of the Progressist party, which
controlled the Press, and the other was the hostility of the police.   It
is not a little singular that Lassalle was perpetually being denounced
as a tool of the reaction, while at the same time the emissaries of
the law were ever dogging his steps and serving him with indictments for high treason.   Probably Lassalle, with his fondness for
comparison with Luther, thought of Worms and the devils which the
Reformer dared to molest him, as he began the work of subjugating
Berlin.   His friends had said that he could "do absolutely nothing
there," but his answer was that the conquest of Berlin was now "the
most important thing" for him and the cause.   All the hostility which
had been predicted was shown.   The Progressist Press did its best to
stifle the movement, and the police, by compelling the owners of
assembly-rooms to refuse him admittance, by molesting members of
the Association, and by confiscating the agitator's published writings,
ably seconded the endeavours of the opposition party.   On November
22nd, the police forced their way into a room in which Lassalle was
speaking and arrested him on a charge of high treason, based on the
publication of the "Address."   He was, however, bailed out in three
days on providing sureties of £450.[1]   The "investment" of Berlin did
not succeed to the extent that was hoped, but good headway was
made, and at the end of December Lassalle was able to address not
only indulgent but enthusiastic audiences of working-men in the strong-
hold of the enemy.

It was now that Wilhelm Liebknecht, one of the principal leaders
of the German Social-Democratic party of to-day, joined the Universal Association, and the president congratulated himself on the

[1] Becker in his "Geschichte" thinks it necessary to say in a footnote that Lassalle is *said*
to have given the prison warders orders, on which account he is also *said* to have been
threatened with the straight-jacket. The spitefulness of this man and his work is almost
incredible.

acquisition of a valuable recruit. Thus ended the year 1863. The agitation had only partially prospered, so far as its immediate purpose was concerned, but it had given an incalculable impetus to the democratic cause, and its author and only evangelist, Ferdinand Lassalle, had become for the time the most famous public man in Germany.

CHAPTER VIII.

FAILURE OF LASSALLE'S AGITATION.

DURING the winter of 1863-1864 Lassalle's time was divided between the work of his Association and an extensive series of disputes with law courts and official bodies. Bernhard Becker enumerates no fewer than fifty-five documents of all kinds which were exchanged between Lassalle and various legal and municipal authorities during this time. Twice he was arrested in Berlin on account of the publication of writings deemed to be treasonable, and his followers in that city had hardly less unpleasant experience than himself, for the police were determined to put a stop to their propagandism. The wonderful energy of the man is shown by the fact that, in spite of a thousand and one occurrences which would have rendered the average mind incapable of the concentration necessary to thoughtful literary work, he produced in January, 1864, a volume of nearly three hundred pages, criticising the doctrines of Schulze-Delitzsch,[1] which he wrote in four months. The work is not, however, one that helps Lassalle's reputation greatly. It is a work, it is true, of great ability; it shows a marvellous mental grasp, and a rare power of penetration; but from the æsthetic point of view, it leaves everything to be desired. The tone is undignified, and at times coarse, as when Lassalle, in a vulgar simile, vulgarly expressed in the original, likens his antagonist to an eviscerated deer. The work has not undeservedly earned the title of *Schimpfwerk*, for it teems with abuse where, above all things, the soberest argument is desirable.

Pressure of work and the provocation of innumerable enemies told on his health at this time, and he writes on February 14th:

"I am dead-beat. . . . My excitement is so great that I can no longer sleep at night. I roll about on my bed till five o'clock, and then get up with headache and thoroughly exhausted. I am over-worked, over-exerted, over-wearied to the most frightful degree. The mad exertion of writing 'Bastiat-Schulze,' in addition to all my other work; the deep and painful disillusion, the gnawing inner vexation,

---

[1] "Herr Bastiat-Schulze von Delitzsch, der ökonomische Julian, oder Kapital und Arbeit," (dated January 16th, 1864).

which the indifference and apathy of the working classes, taken in the mass, cause me—all this has been too much even for me. I am carrying on a *métier de dupe*, and inwardly I am vexed to death, and that the more as I cannot give vent to this vexation and overcome it." And again, the same month :

"I am so brought down by inordinate exertion and excessive nervous excitement through work, that my nerves hang loose like cords about my body. There is for every nature, what I did not wish to believe, a *Ne nimis*, and I have this time sadly violated it. Adieu, your wretched F. Lassalle."[1]

Still, he would not despair, dark as the outlook appeared. The motto which Carlyle wrote in his journal, round the sketch of a flickering candle, was his as well—"*Terar dum prosim*," "Let me be wasted so I am but useful." "I will not let the banner fall," he writes, "so long as even a small flame of hope gleams on the horizon." The difficulties and sufferings must have been great when they proved "too much even for me," but like a "brave man struggling with the storms of fate," he determined still to press onward. Lassalle's enfeebled condition was not the only misfortune with which the Universal Association had to contend. Another was the lack of funds. On February 14th, the president writes to one of his agents :

"I can furnish absolutely no more money, and it is equally impossible to let the Association fall to the ground, so long as there is hope in the political heavens. I have not only reached the limits of the financial sacrifice which I am able to make, but I have really far exceeded what I could reasonably sacrifice. You know what financial sacrifices I made up to last September : what a capital there !"

Before it is supposed that he here exaggerates the help which came from his own purse, it should be remembered that the revenues of the Association were insignificant, for not only were the contributions required of members very small, but the secretaries of the branches often neglected to collect them, or when collected to forward them to the head treasury, while, on the other hand, the expense of the agitation—in organisation, in the publication of pamphlets, the subsidising of poor democratic newspapers, and a hundred other ways—must have been enormous, and Lassalle was responsible for all.[2]

[1] Letter to Rodbertus.
[2] The secretary writes to Lassalle, August 27th, when the Association had existed three months that only three persons have sent money.

The first trial of 1864 arose out of the publication of the "Address to the Working-men of Berlin," which appeared on October 14th, 1863. In this address Lassalle said the primary object of the Universal Association was the attainment of universal suffrage. When this had been gained the Prussian State would be remoulded into a "democratic State," the object of which would be the improvement of the social condition of the working classes by legislation, funds being granted for the formation of Productive Associations. The Prussian State, he said, had never been founded on justice, "and everyone who agitates for the maintenance of the constitution must be regarded as an enemy of the popular party." This language was bad enough, but when Lassalle declared that the folly of the Government had brought Prussia to the eve of a great social revolution, and finally sneered at the "sceptre, crown, star, and other toys," he manifestly established himself, in the eyes of the authorities, as a man whose freedom it would be dangerous to tolerate. He was, therefore, summoned to answer the threefold charge of inciting to the alteration of the Prussian constitution by violence, of publicly ridiculing State institutions, and of insulting the Ministry of State. The trial took place on March 12th, and the Crown Solicitor proposed as punishment three years' imprisonment, a fine of a hundred thalers (£15), and five years' police surveillance. Lassalle spoke for four hours amid storm and wild wave-rolling. He began by deriding the high-treason scare which had taken possession of the people in high places, but which gave him no alarm, and quoted the satire :

> " Es ist ein rechtes Elend mit dem Hochverrath !
> Es ist so schlimm, ja schlimmer selbst als Flöhe !
> Allüberall zudringlich knüpft er einem an,
> Schneutz' ich die Nase—aber mein ! 's ist Hochverrath ;
> Kratz' ich am Kopfe—wehe mir ! 's ist Hochverrath ;
> Ja, selbst ins Bett leg' ich mich des Nachts mit Angst,
> Dass mir ein hochverrätherischer—Traum entführt ! "

Lassalle sought to refute the Crown's interpretation of his utterances and of the constitution, and he drew a comparison between himself and Sir Robert Peel.

"When Peel repealed the Corn Laws, and many voices in the House of Commons thanked him for it, he said, ' These thanks belong not to me but to Richard Cobden.' But instead of following that example (added Lassalle) the Crown Solicitor charges me with high treason. A truly melancholy difference between the circumstances of England and those here."

The President of the Court objected to the comparison as untenable and Lassalle rejoined :

"The agitation which causes me to appear here and that of Cobden are on exactly the same lines, and the comparison of the two is a justifiable part of my defence. . . (and elsewhere) The corn duties were based on the law. In regard to their obligation there is no difference between law and constitution."

From beginning to end the proceedings were tempestuous. Lassalle demanded to be allowed to conduct his defence in his own way, and to say what he pleased. The consequence was that he was repeatedly called to order, treatment which raised his indignation to a high pitch. When he quoted a poet the President asked that such "effusions" might be omitted, and the same interruption taking place again as he was about to strengthen his case by a passage from "Wallenstein's Death," Lassalle exclaimed in fury : "Are then our great poets—is Schiller proscribed in these halls?" on which he continued the quotation without further molestation. Fortune favoured the brave, for Lassalle was acquitted of the charge of high treason, though the Court found that the address to the working-men of Berlin was "eccentric." It was decided, however, to proceed against him on less serious charges. The singular collapse of the prosecution, which began with a proposal for three years' imprisonment and ended in an acquittal, greatly enhanced Lassalle's reputation and encouraged his supporters. It is not improbable that his personal relationships with Minister von Bismarck at this time had something to do with the fortunate issue of the trial.

The next trial of this year was a result of the Rhenish address of the preceding September. The address was first published at Düsseldorf.[1] An edition of ten thousand copies was printed, and on October 21st the unsold remnant of the work, about a thousand copies, was confiscated at Düsseldorf and Berlin. Proceedings were at once instituted against Lassalle on the strength of several passages in which reflection was thrown on the Prussian Government and an endeavour made, as was alleged, to excite the working classes. The Provincial Court at Düs-

---

1 "Die Feste, die Presse, und der Frankfurter Abgeordnetentag.'

L

seldorf gave authority for his arrest, and on January 29th he was apprehended in the streets of Berlin by three police officers while in the company of Countess Hatzfeldt. The officers accompanied him home, and refused to leave until he should be ready to travel to Düsseldorf the same evening. Lassalle was physically broken down and was unable to bear any such exertion, yet it was only late at night that the revocation of the order for his removal could be obtained and his house be relieved of the presence of the policemen. The Düsseldorf Court sentenced him *in contumaciam* to a year's imprisonment, though the Crown Solicitor had demanded two years. Both Lassalle and his prosecutors appealed, and the second trial took place on June 27th. The Court found the accused guilty, but this time the sentence was reduced to six months' imprisonment. The publication of the defence led to a new prosecution,[1] as was the case with the defence in the trial of March 12th in Berlin.

But Lassalle grew to like prosecutions and trials. The prisoners' dock was a tribune whence he could address an entire nation. There at least he counted on free speech and had it, even if against the will of his prosecutors, and perhaps of his judges as well. It may be that his vanity was fed by law-court fame, but the success of his agitation always weighed most with him, and that benefited incalculably by the notoriety which prosecution gave to his person and principles. But, above all, the atmosphere of the Courthouse was congenial to his stormy spirit. Never, perhaps, was he more in his element than when badgering judges, browbeating Crown Solicitors, and bringing *bourgeois* juries to their wits' end. He was never in perplexity. If the prosecution advanced one argument against him, he had immediately ten ready wherewith to answer it. He might not always succeed in overcoming his enemies, but he would content himself with the thought that if he failed it was not owing to his fault or the weakness of his cause, but to the obtuseness or injustice of the law's administrators. Yet the battle was worth fighting for itself, and brave defence was its own reward. No wonder that Lassalle attributed so much importance to the trials in which he was the central figure. He always appeared in Court dressed as for the dancing-room. His speeches were prepared with the utmost care, and he ostentatiously ranged round him all the legal works to which it might be necessary to refer in support

---

[1] He died before his prosecutors could bring him to the prisoners' dock.

of his own arguments or in opposition to those of others. Never once did he show the white flag even when his chances of success were the faintest. On one occasion the bench had withdrawn for deliberation, and his friends, in view of the certainty of conviction, besought him in tears from the spectators' benches to leave the Court and if necessary to take flight. Lassalle turned round and answered with dignity: "That is not becoming." However annoying his legal disputes were, however, he could nevertheless joke at them. At the end of a long letter written to Rodbertus in reply to his indictment against "Acquired Rights," Lassalle finds time to add, "And now I must return to the Crown Solicitor and the Court of First Instance, who have both an 'acquired right' to very attentive service on my part."[1]

What progress was the agitation meanwhile making? The Association camp had never been a very amiable one, and early in 1864 the animosities and jealousies which existed between subordinate officials threatened to produce serious consequences. In April, Lassalle wrote to Dammer, the vice-president :—

"Should frictions, trivialities, intrigues and disputes spread in our Association as amongst the Progressists, I would—for without them I am full of disgust, very full—resign my office at once and let the gentlemen quarrel amongst themselves."

The first serious symptom of disaffection amongst the officials was seen in the hostility and resignation of the secretary Vahlteich in February. A young Solingen sword-cutler, by name Willms, was appointed his successor, and it was hoped that all danger had been removed. It was, however, soon found that the late secretary was organising opposition against Lassalle, whose absolute power he wished to disturb by the introduction of a measure of decentralisation. Thus internal disaffection was fed by intrigue without, and it seemed to Lassalle that only such a great triumph as rewarded his Rhenish review would arrest decline.

His birthday was celebrated by the Berlin members of the Association on April 5th, and two days later he formed the intention of proceeding early in May to the Rhine, there to commemorate the founding of the Universal. He accordingly left Berlin on May 8th, travelling by way of Leipzig, with the object, as the official announce-

[1] February 12th, 1862.

ment ran, of holding another "review"—this time a "glorious review"—of his Rhenish followers. On the 14th he spoke at Solingen, on the 15th at Barmen, on the 16th at Cologne, and on the 18th at Wermelskirchen. The enthusiasm he aroused was intense, and on the 20th he wrote to Countess Hatzfeldt :

"I have never seen anything like it. Involuntarily one thought of the scenes in *Faust :* both that in the first part ('Zufrieden jauchzet Gross und Klein ; hier bin ich Mensch, hier darf ich's sein ?'[1]) and that at the end of the second part, where Faust stands still, contented.[2] The entire population indulged in indescribable jubilation. The impression made upon me was that such scenes must have attended the founding of new religions."

Lassalle may be pardoned for the vanity which shows itself in this letter. He had, indeed, been received everywhere like a warrior returned victorious from the din and danger of battle. At Wermelskirchen the people gave themselves over to festivity on the day of his arrival. Deputations of working-men met their trusted leader at the station with carriages covered with wreaths of flowers. The roads were spanned by triumphal arches, and as the procession advanced slowly to the town the air was filled with the acclamations of a countless crowd, which greeted Lassalle with a song of welcome. Such ovations would have turned far less giddy heads than Lassalle's.

Then came, on May 22nd, the festival of the foundation of the Association. This took place at Ronsdorf, near Elberfeld. The reception of the great agitator was a repetition of the scene at Wermelskirchen, and on the evening of the commemoration, Lassalle could telegraph to the " Berlin brethren " the congratulations of an assembly of two thousand Rhinelanders. At Ronsdorf he did what

---

[1] *Faust*, 1st part : Scene, Before the Gate.

[2] Lassalle evidently refers to the passage wherein Faust says :

> " Solch ein Gewimmel möcht' ich sehn,
> Auf freiem Grund mit freiem Volke stehn.
> Zum Augenblicke dürft' ich sagen :
> Verweile doch, du bist so schön !
> Es kann die Spur von meinen Erdetagen
> Nicht in Aeonen untergehn.—
> Im Vorgefühl von solchem hohen Glück
> Geniess' ich jetzt den höchsten Augenblick."

Faust, 2nd part : scene in the Great Forecourt of Palace.

was expected of him : he made a great speech, [1] a speech at once his most sanguine and his most extravagant. He did not hesitate to remind his followers that he had alone—" one man against all "—raised the banner of the Association. He told the legend of the Middle Ages according to which the lion's whelp is born dead and is only wakened into life by the roaring of its sire. It almost seemed, at first, as if the Association had been still born, " but we roared so frightfully that the cry found an echo in all German States, and the child awoke to gladdest life and has proved itself a genuine lion." What, however, had been the result of the Association's work and of its author's agitation ? Lassalle claimed that he had converted both the King of Prussia and the Bishop of Mayence. [2] A short time before this a deputation of Silesian weavers had been received by the king, to whom they had presented a petition in which it was said that the weekly wages of a weaver, working twelve hours a day, varied from three to eight shillings. The published accounts of the interview stated that the king not only expressed sympathy with the supplicants but promised speedy legislation on the labour question. [3] Lassalle, with more boldness than justification, accepted as correct the reports in circulation, and claimed the so-called royal promise as a victory for the Association. He pointed his hearers to "the acknowledgment by the king that a settlement of the working-men's question by legislation is necessary ; in other words, the acknowledgment of the principal proposition in favour of which we began our agitation, and the acknowledgment of the necessity and justice of that which I have everywhere—in my ' Reply Letter ' as well as in my 'Working Man's Reading Book'—developed as the quintessence of our demands ; the acknowledgment of the principle which lies at the basis of the entire agitation of the Universal German Working Men's Association and of our most radical proposal—as opposed to the proposition of Liberal political economy, which is that the work-

[1] Published as " Die Agitation des allgemeinen Deutschen Arbeitervereins und das Versprechen des Königs von Preussen."

[2] Baron Wilhelm Emmanuel von Ketteler was born December 25th, 1811, at Münster, Westphalia. He became a priest of the Catholic Church in 1839, and in 1850 was made Bishop of Mayence. In 1871 he was elected to the Reichstag. He died July 13th, 1877. Ketteler wrote " Die Arbeiterfrage und das Christenthum " (Mayence, 1864), " Die Katholiken und das deutsche Reich " (Mayence, 1873), and "Die grossen socialen Fragen der Gegenwart " (Mayence, 1878).

[3] The subject came up during a debate in the Reichstag on the Socialist Bill on September 16th, 1878, and in the Prussian Lower House on February 11th and 15th, 1865.

ing classes should be left defenceless to the play of free competition, and to the domination of supply and demand :—the acknowledgment, I say, of its irrefragable justice and of its unassailable truth."

Then, coming to the alleged promise, he said : " While in 1844 the bayonet was the only answer given to the want of the Silesian weavers,[1] the king now promises that their condition shall be altered by means of legislation. You see, friends, that this promise is our work." But as the legislative settlement of the labour question could not take place unless there were a Parliament elected by universal suffrage to give approval to it, Lassalle saw in the royal promise another concession, implied if not expressed ; the king had, in fact, been won round to the demand for universal franchise which the Association had placed at the beginning of its programme. And all this was the result of the agitation ! The meeting is reported to have broken out at this point into indescribable jubilation, and it was some minutes before Lassalle could resume his speech. Whatever may be thought of the logic and honesty which Lassalle displays here—Mehring speaks of the whole speech as "a shameful tissue of falsehoods from beginning to end," [2] but this is going too far—he undoubtedly had right on his side in claiming Bishop von Ketteler as a convert.[3]

The conclusion of the speech almost reads like a prophecy. He said :

" I have not grasped this banner, as you might think, without knowing quite clearly that I myself might fall. The feelings which fill me at the thought that I may be removed cannot better be expressed than in the words of the Roman poet · '*Exoriare aliquis nostris ex ossibus ultor* !' or in German, '*Möge wenn ich beseitigt werde, irgend ein*

[1] Referring to the hand weavers' riots of 1844 alluded to in Chapter I.

[2] " Die Deutsche Socialdemokratie," p. 54.

[3] The views of Baron von Ketteler are set forth in his work "Die Arbeiterfrage und das Christenthum " (Mayence, 1864). Lassalle's influence may be recognised in various passages and amongst them the following : "This is the condition of our working classes ; they are dependent upon wages ; the wages of labour are a commodity whose price is daily determined by supply and demand ; the axle upon which the price moves are the necessaries of life, and if the demand be larger than the supply it rises a little upon this axle. while it falls if the supply be larger than the demand. But the general tendency is, as with other commodities, towards cheapness of production, and cheapness of production means here the curtailment of the necessaries of life, and so with this entirely mechanical-mathematical movement it is sure to happen at times that even the most essential necessaries can no longer be covered by the price of labour, and that entire labouring families and classes will pine away and slowly starve." (p. 19).

Rächer und Nachfolger aus meinen Gebeinen auferstehen.'[1] May this great and national movement of civilisation not fall with my person, but may the conflagration which I have kindled spread farther and farther so long as one of you still breathes. Promise me that, and in token raise your right hands."

The scene was an impressive one as the grave tones of the orator's voice ceased, and the hands were raised in silence. But the silence only lasted for a moment, and the storm of acclamation which followed showed that a responsive chord had been touched in the hearts of those two thousand men, few of whom were to see their leader again. The Ronsdorf address was all hope and cheer, but there were many people who likened it to the song of the dying swan.

To this period must be attributed the formation of an intimate acquaintance between Lassalle and the Prussian Minister President, then Count von Bismarck, now Prince Bismarck, the Imperial Chancellor of Germany, a circumstance which may rightly be regarded as historic on account of its political results. The interest shown by the Prussian Minister in the social movement was so great that he invited Lassalle on various occasions to meet him, nor has he ever sought to deny the admiration in which he held the talented agitator, the "revolutionary Jew, well known in his day." When Deputy Richter[2] once laid it to his charge that he had taken counsel with Socialist leaders, Prince Bismarck could only express impatient astonishment that distinction should not be drawn between men who honestly strove to improve the lot of the working classes and those whose only gospel was violence.[3] But Prince Bismarck has never cared much about what the world has said of him, and least of all has he been frightened of mere names. "Call it Socialism or what you will," he declared once, when speaking of the insurance of workpeople, "it is all the same to

---

[1] "If I should be removed, may some avenger (and follower) rise up out of my bones. It is worthy of note that the idea of revenge for Lassalle's death continued for years to be a source of inspiration to his disciples. Thus at a great *Todtenfeier* once held at Hamburg, a song was sung amidst enthusiasm, the last lines of which ran :

      "Lassalle, Lassalle, erweck' Dir einen Rächer,
      Wo um Dein Grab der Leichenrabe kreist."

This incident had of itself no importance, but it was full of significance.

[2] The eloquent leader of the *Freisinnige Partei*. Eugen Richter was born July 30th, 1838, at Düsseldorf, and studied at Bonn, Heidelberg, and Berlin. Formerly in the service of the State in a judicial capacity, but since 1864 resident in Berlin as author and publicist.

[3] Debate in the German Reichstag, September 17th, 1878.

me."[1]   There was much in Lassalle which could not but attract Prince Bismarck, and the character of the latter was certainly one after Lassalle's own heart.   The respect and admiration entertained on both sides were very great.   The Prussian Minister found the agitator "a great man with whom one might be glad to converse ;" and the agitator once said of the Minister, " If we exchanged musket shots with Herr von Bismarck, justice would require us to allow, even amid the volleys, that he was a man, while the Progressists are only old women."   Little is known respecting the relationships which existed between these two remarkable men.   Lassalle has left no account of the interviews which he had with the statesman, and so far as he is concerned the only information on the subject which is extant consists of odd references found amongst the documents of the Universal Association, after its founder's death, showing that Lassalle was accustomed to send reprints of his speeches to the Minister President.   Thus a letter of June 15th, 1864, to the secretary contains the direction : " The things sent to Bismarck should go in an envelope."   At another time two copies of the Ronsdorf speech are to be sent to the Count with the superscription " Personally."   More important than evidence of this kind are the reminiscences of the historical interviews which Prince Bismarck narrated during a debate in the Reichstag on September 16th, 1878. On that occasion the Socialist Bebel compelled the Chancellor to break silence.   Bebel's account was that Lassalle was approached indirectly long before the Prussian Minister President addressed him in person.   Prince Bismarck said :

" Lassalle himself wanted urgently to enter into negotiations with me, and if I could find time to search amongst old papers, I believe I could yet find the letter in which the wish is expressed, and in which reasons are given why I should allow the wish to be fulfilled.   Nor did I make it difficult for Lassalle to meet me.   I saw him, and from the time that I first spoke an hour with him I have not regretted it. I did not see him three or four times a week, but only three or four times altogether.   Our relations could not have had the nature of political negotiations.   For what could Lassalle offer or give me ? He had nothing behind him, and in all political negotiations *Do ut des* lies in the background, even though for the sake of decorum one may not say so.   If I were to have said to myself, 'What hast thou, poor

---

[1] Debate in the German Reichstag, April 2nd, 1881.

devil, to give?'[1] he had nothing which he could have given me as Minister; but what he had was something which attracted me extraordinarily as a private man. He was one of the most intellectual and gifted men with whom I have ever had intercourse, a man who was ambitious in high style, but who was by no means a Republican : he had very decided national and monarchical sympathies, and the idea which he strove to realise was the German Empire, and therein we had a point of contact.[2] Lassalle was extremely ambitious, and it was perhaps a matter of doubt to him whether the German Empire would close with the Hohenzollern dynasty or the Lassalle dynasty ; but he was monarchical through and through. Lassalle was an energetic and very intellectual man, to talk with whom was very instructive. Our conversations lasted hours, and I was always sorry when they came to an end. There was no talk of negotiations, for in our conversation I could scarcely get a word in. He bore the costs of the conversation alone, but he did so in a pleasant and amiable manner; everyone who knew him will allow that my description is correct. I would have been glad to have had a man of his genius and of such an intellectual nature as neighbouring landlord in the country."

Prince Bismarck has put it on record that the conversations ranged over a wide field of political and social questions, but Lassalle endeavoured especially to convert the Prussian Minister to his proposals of universal franchise and Productive Associations. That the scheme of Associations worked by the aid of State funds was thoughtfully weighed by Prince Bismarck, both at that time and afterwards, he himself has admitted, though he was never able clearly to recognise its wisdom or utility. At the same time he did not shrink from the idea of an expenditure of 100,000,000 thalers, Lassalle's estimated capital. Nay, the Government even experimented in co-operative production. When in England in 1862, Prince Bismarck inquired into the working of the Productive Associations, and on his return he persuaded the Prussian king to devote a considerable sum out of his private purse to experiments.

---

1 Faust to Mephistopheles : "Was willst du armer Teufel geben?" (1st part : scene in the Study).

2 Lassalle writes to Rodbertus, May 2nd, 1863, "If I have hated anything in my life, it is the Small Germany party. A year and a half ago, I once held a meeting of my friends here, and I formulated the matter so : we must all desire Great Germany *moins les dynasties.*" That was evidently Lassalle's attitude in current politics, with which his ulterior social aims had nothing to do.

These experiments were not, however, continued long enough to allow of a fair trial, for war broke out, and the Government had to give attention to other and more urgent questions. Prince Bismarck, though never won over to productive partnerships, has always kept an open mind on the subject. This he showed during the debate already referred to. He then said :

" In the Ministry of Agriculture we carry on experiments respecting agricultural systems, and we also experiment in our manufactures : would it not be useful to make experiments similarly in the employment of the people and in the endeavour to solve the so-called Social-Democratic—or, I would rather say, social question, by improving the lot of working-men ? On a great scale it might not be possible to carry out [the co-operative principle]. Such establishments, for instance, as that of Krupp would not be possible under a constitution other than monarchical ;—for example, they would be impossible under a Republican constitution. But in ordinary manufactures I do not regard this way of helping working-men to a better existence as out of the question, and I do not think it a crime for a statesman to grant State funds for the formation of an association on behalf of working-men, and especially for experiments in that direction."

But to resume the narrative of Lassalle's movements during 1864. According to the plan drawn up in April he intended to leave the Rhine towards the end of the following month for the baths and to return to Berlin late in the year. He now needed rest more than ever. Ill as he was on undertaking the " glorious review," his physical condition was now worse. Two days before the Ronsdorf meeting he wrote to Countess Hatzfeldt from Düsseldorf :

" Though quite ill—indeed, reduced to extremities—I am writing to you again. At last, at last the greater part of the fatigue is behind me. If I had been quite well on leaving Berlin it would have been a trifle for me. . . To-day I am again voiceless, and besides I look exhausted, shaken, feeble, and very ill."

There was only too much truth in all this, and it was no doubt with a sigh of real relief that he bid good-bye to his Rhenish friends, whose fidelity had done much to cheer him. There was, however, another reason besides ill-health which made it expedient to increase the distance between himself and Berlin. The day before the Ronsdorf gathering he received information thence that the Court had again sentenced him *in contumaciam* to four months' imprisonment, having, in spite of medical evidence of Lassalle's wrecked condition, refused to adjourn the proceedings. The first place visited was Ems, where he stayed from May 26th to June 25th. Now, however, his rest was broken, for it was necessary to hasten to Düsseldorf in order to defend himself before the Correctional Court of Appeal on a charge of high treason, the trial resulting in a sentence of six months' imprisonment.[1] This prosecution over, he went to Cologne, where he remained till July 6th," then travelled in the Palatinate ten days, reaching Karlsruhe on the 16th and proceeding without delay to Rigi-Kaltbad, where he hoped to recruit his strength.

During this time the affairs of the Association never once ceased to occupy his attention. At Ems he negotiated with Herren von Schweitzer and von Hofstetten, the latter a Bavarian ex-lieutenant, for the establishment of a newspaper to advocate the principles of the movement.[2] At Frankfort he addressed meetings and was in return serenaded by a party of his admirers, a token of regard which afforded him great pleasure. Arrived at Rigi-Kaltbad, he put himself in regular correspondence with the officials of the Association. There was, indeed, need for correspondence and plenty of it, for during Lassalle's absence from headquarters his enemies in the camp had been making good use of their opportunities. Vahlteich had been advocating his decentralisation scheme with renewed persistence, and with growing success. His plan was more than one of decentralisation, which alone was objectionable in the present weak condition of the affiliated organisations ; he desired to pave the way for union with the Progressist party, so heartily hated by Lassalle. In a long circular issued from Kaltbad, and dated July 27th, the president of the Association demanded the expulsion of Vahlteich, and again threatened as in April that unless concord were preserved he would resign.

" If such frictions are repeated, and unless the directorate protect me energetically against their repetition, I shall simply resign the presidency and return to my old *rôle* as defender of the interests of the working classes. Only unwillingly and after long refusal did I finally determine at Leipzig to take the presidency of the Association,

---

[1] The trial of June 27th, already referred to.
[2] The *Social-Democrat*, which first appeared January 1st, 1865.

in order to be able to carry on the struggle for the interests of the working classes with greater energy. But frictions within the Association—between working-men and members of the Association, and even members of the directorate, who, above all, should present a bright example of unanimity, and who have, in fact, done so as yet, with one exception—I do not regard as belonging to my office. '

It has been maintained that Lassalle did not intend to return to Germany, but that, fearing the accumulation of commitment orders which had gathered over his head, he had come to the determination to remain abroad. After weighing all the evidence carefully, it is not possible to doubt that some such plan was favourably thought of. Not, however, that Lassalle intended to sever connection with the Universal Association, whose affairs he may have believed it practicable to direct from a neighbouring country. Countess Hatzfeldt repeatedly urged him to leave Germany, but his letters to that lady only show him to have been revolving the idea in his mind, and nowhere to have come to a decision. Paul Lindau,[1] in an interesting description which he has written of Lassalle's appearance at the Düsseldorf Court on June 27th throws some light upon this question. Lindau took leave of Lassalle at the railway station on the 29th, and he writes respecting the parting :

"Though I had never in my life had presentiments, still I had at this moment a distinct feeling that I should not see that man again. In order to get rid of it I said to him—he had entered the carriage, the door was closed, and he had put his head out of the window—'*Auf Wiedersehen* [*Au revoir*] Herr Lassalle !' He answered : 'Who knows?' and as I looked at him astonished, he added : 'I can no longer allow myself to be deprived of freedom a year or even half a year. I simply cannot bear it. I will rather expatriate myself. I am nervous and quite knocked-up. Rigi-Kaltbad will, I hope, make me fit for work again.'"

Lassalle knew that his constitution, broken down by two years of intense excitement and superhuman labour, would not hold out much longer unless he were able to secure rest and quiet in salubrious parts. No doubt he intended that his future movements should be influenced by the results of his Swiss travels. At this time there were two Lassalles in the same person, one the hopeful and confident orator of

---

[1] Article in the *Deutsche Bücherei* (Breslau), No. 4, 1882.

Ronsdorf, to whom the future was bright with the promise of great things, and the other the moody, discouraged invalid of the Rigi, who was temporarily broken in spirits and heartily weary of agitation. Let this be remembered when judgment is passed on the last events in Lassalle's life. We have seen the one Lassalle : we may now look upon the other as he painted himself in a letter to Countess Hatzfeldt. The countess had asked him if he could not be content for a time with " science, friendship, and beautiful nature." He writes from his Swiss retreat on July 28th :

" You think I must have politics ? Ah, how little you know me ! I wish nothing more ardently than to be free from politics altogether and to retire to science and nature. I am tired, and have had enough of politics. True, I would rouse up as passionately as ever for politics if serious occurrences took place, or if I had power or saw means of gaining pre-eminence—such means as were suited to me—for without the highest power nothing can be done. I am, however, too old and too big for child's play. That is why I undertook the presidency so very unwillingly. I only gave in to you. That is why it oppresses me so greatly."

It is difficult to reconcile the contradictions furnished by the Ronsdorf speech and letters of this kind. Reconciliation is, indeed, impossible save on the supposition that Lassalle feared to tell the world all he thought and felt, believing that the result would be disaster to his cherished but unsuccessful schemes. He clung to hope in public long after he had abandoned it in private. When, however, immaculate critics speak of " glaring dissonance, flagrant contradiction, and deep falsehood," [1] one is reminded forcibly of the stern fact that there is yet plenty of room for charity in the world.

[1] Mehring, " Deutsche Socialdemokratie," p. 56.

CHAPTER IX.

LASSALLE'S DEATH.

THE concluding passage in Lassalle's career it is impossible to approach with satisfaction. It cannot, indeed, be omitted from a faithful account of his eventful life, and yet there is in the story so much that is disagreeable and even revolting that the wish to pass it over is only natural.[1] We last saw Lassalle as he had arrived at Rigi-Kaltbad—it would seem as though a mysterious fatalism had taken him thither—wrecked in body and suffering from the mental torture of aggravation and disappointment. One day, while he was writing, a visitor was announced, and he went out to find that the comer who sought to speak with him was a young lady, by name Helene von Dönniges. About the personality of this friend of Lassalle's it is necessary that we should know more. Fräulein von Dönniges was the daughter of a Bavarian diplomat, holding an appointment at this time in Switzerland. Beauty appears to have been hereditary in the family,

[1] A vast amount of literature—for the most part not of an edifying character—has accumulated respecting the episode in Lassalle's life which is here dealt with as shortly as may be. The chief works on the subject are :

"Enthüllungen über das tragische Lebensende Ferdinand Lassalles. Auf Grunde authentischer Belege dargestellt von Bernhard Becker, dem testamentarischen Nachfolger Lassalles." (Schleiz, 1868).

"Meine Beziehungen zu Ferdinand Lassalle, von Helene von Racowitza geb. v. Dönniges." (Breslau and Leipzig.) In this work Helene claims that "tout comprendre, c'est tout pardonner." How far, however, she writes fact and how far fiction, it is hard to say ; in any case there is plenty of fiction in the narrative.

"Lassalle's Tod : Im Anschluss an die Memoire der Helene von Racowitza, 'Meine Beziehungen zu Ferdinand Lassalle,' zur Ergänzung derselben," by A. Kutschbach. (Chemnitz, 1880.)

Other works are, as a whole, mere hashes of the foregoing. In 1878 there was published at Leipzig "Eine Liebesepisode aus dem Leben Ferdinand Lassalles," said to be a reprint of letters which appeared in November, 1877, in the *European Messenger* in the Russian language. The work professes to give the contents of a diary kept by a Russian lady who corresponded with Lassalle. The inane production is probably a forgery.

Just recently another contribution to the already superabundant literature on this subject has appeared with the title "Lassalle's Leiden," (Berlin, 1887), a work containing several hitherto unpublished letters by Lassalle, but otherwise worthless.

and Helene was both beautiful and vain. She was a talented girl— from her Jewish mother she had inherited a lively imagination and an imperious spirit—but she had been spoiled as a child. She tells us herself that she was at the age of twelve years engaged by her mother to an Italian of forty or forty-two, for she then looked quite nineteen years old. The unwholesome atmosphere in which her youth was passed exerted the natural effect of destroying maidenly innocence and reserve, and she grew up a vain coquette whose head was full of romantic notions. Lassalle made the acquaintance of Helene in 1862, when the girl was visiting her mother's relations in Berlin. Helene had already been betrothed two or three times, and was then pledged to a young Walachian nobleman, a student, by name Racowitz, de- scribed as a "small, dark, ugly man," but possessing the redeeming quality that he was rich. The girl lost her head, as many others of her sex did, when fastened by Lassalle's glittering eye and enchanted by his gallant ways and fair speech. Racowitz was thrown overboard, and Helene became attached to his more gifted rival. She was proud to have attracted the attention of one whose name was on everybody's tongue, and Lassalle was hardly less pleased with his new conquest. The acquaintance continued more than a year without an actual en- gagement taking place.

Knowledge of Lassalle's journey to Rigi-Kaltbad was soon gained by Helene, who was living in Geneva, and she organised an excursion thither with several friends. On July 25th the girl presented herself before her lover. It is evident that tender passages passed between the two before the time of separation came on the following day, and Helene and her friends—an English lady, an American lady, and a Frenchman—descended the Rigi in "the most frightful mist and rain."[1] For not only had Lassalle promised to be in Geneva between the 15th and 25th of August, but we find Helene writing to him the day after the romantic interview : "When I left you, and your lips touched my hand for the last time, I said to myself that my decision for life should be taken before I left Weggis. *Eh bien, c'est fait !* And now know, you with your fine, magnificent intellect and your great but to me so pleasant vanity, how my decision runs. I wish to be and will be your wife. You said to me yesterday evening : 'Give me only a sensible and independent yes, *et je me charge du reste.'*

[1] Letter of Lassalle to Countess Hatzfeldt, July 27th, 1864.

Well, here is my yes—and now, *chargez-vous donc du reste.* Only I impose two very small conditions, and they are these. I will—only think, the child *wills*—that we shall do all that lies in our power (and in your power, my fine Satanic friend, there lies so very much) to attain our ends in a seemly and sensible way : in other words, you must come to us, and we will try to prepossess both my parents and ———— in your favour, and so win their consent. But if not, if they are and remain inexorable, even when we have done everything—*eh bien, alors tant pis*—then there is always Egypt.[1] That is one condition, and the second is this : I *will* and desire that the whole affair may proceed as speedily as possible. I know that the obstacles which we have to overcome are very great, yes, gigantic, but then we have a great end in view, and you have a gigantic intellect, which will with God's help grind the rocks to sand and dust, so that even my weak breath would be able to blow it away. The hardest part falls to me, for I must with cold hand kill a faithful heart [2] which is devoted with true love to me ; I must destroy with crass selfishness a fond, youthful dream, the realisation of which was to have been the happiness, the life's happiness, of a noble man. Believe me, it will be fearfully hard, but I will do it now, and for your sake will be bad."

The companionship of his lover and the tender words which came from her worked a great change in Lassalle, and we find him exclaiming in a moment of bright hopefulness, "All my ills are as good as disappeared—how quickly one forgets what has troubled him !—and I am cheerful and full of energy !" So he no doubt was when he wrote, for a sunbeam had fallen upon the darkness. Yet the anticipation of visiting Helene in Geneva in August for the purpose of finally claiming her from her parents was coupled in Lassalle's mind with the fear that the prize might after all be lost. He writes to Countess Hatzfeldt from Bern on July 30th :

"Her single but gigantic defect is that she has no will—not the least trace of it. In itself this is certainly a great defect, though if we were man and wife it would perhaps not be so, for I have will enough for her as well, and she would be as a flute in the hand of the artist. But the union itself might thereby be made difficult. To-day, it is true, she is firmly resolved, but how long will ɪ creature without will

[1] Lassalle had proposed to take Helene after marriage to Egypt or Italy.
[2] This refers to Racowitz.

be able to resist shock?" The countess advises him to reflect before going farther and reminds him that he has just been "desperately in love" (*sterblich verliebt*) with another.[1] Lassalle, after explaining away his "desperate love," says Helene is absolutely suited to him; indeed, he had never expected to find anyone so well suited. Moreover, "it is really no small piece of fortune to find, at the age of 39½ years, a woman so beautiful and of so free and suitable a personality, who loves me so much and who—what with me is an absolute necessity—is quite absorbed in my will." The countess again urges her "dear child" to be prudent, and tells him that he has "no sense and no judgment in women's affairs." Lassalle answers that he intends to persist in his plan, and fearing that the countess may appear on the scene he advises her, twice in the same letter, to recruit her health at the baths. At the end of July the lover was at Bern, his betrothed was with friends at the adjacent Wabern, and frequent interviews took place between them. On August 3rd Helene left for Geneva and it was agreed that Lassalle should follow at once. The arrangement was carried out, and he took rooms not far from the villa of Herr von Dönniges.

Meanwhile, stormy scene had been enacted in Helene's home. The girl on returning had found her mother alone, and to her she made known the attachment. The mother cried and endeavoured to dissuade her, but in vain, and a warm disputation ended by Frau von Dönniges declaring that she would tell the father all. "God only knows what he will do when he comes back," wrote Helene to her Siegfried[2] the same day; "in any case I am as firm as a rock." Herr von Dönniges returned home in the evening and a scene more painful than before took place. The father refused to hear of a marriage and threatened to disown his daughter unless she at once disowned Lassalle. Just before this Helene's sister had been betrothed to a count; how, then, could it be expected that an alliance

---

[1] In a letter, dated April 16th, 1864, which has hitherto escaped the inquisitive eyes of Lassallian scandal-mongers, he writes to the lady here referred to :—"My sister can tell you how often I think of you. Far more often than is really proper for a man of my understanding." In this letter he says his intention is to leave Berlin in May and not return till October, though "perhaps not even then. Who knows what will become of me when I am once on my travels?"

[2] Lassalle called Helene, and the girl signed herself, Brunhild, and he was in return addressed as Siegfried. So far did the sentimental courtship go.

would be contracted with a tradesman's family? It looked like the story of Rousseau's Baron d'Étange, Julie, and *le petit bourgeois*, over again. Yet, after all, Herr von Dönniges was not without justification. He called to mind that Lassalle had once been implicated in a robbery and that he had for years maintained questionable relationships with an elderly noblewoman. In any case a *bourgeois* son-in-law would, perhaps, have been unwelcome, but one with such antecedents was not to be thought of. Driven at last to despair, Helene fled from the house and sought the abode of her lover, whom she besought in tears to carry her away, for that was now the only course open. What Lassalle did was not Lassalle-like. He coolly offered the girl his arm and led her back to her father's door, wishing to receive her free from reproach from her parents. Dühring sneers at Lassalle for his "inconceivable stupidity,"[1] but everyone must judge the act according to his individual views of gallantry and honour. It is true Lassalle himself afterwards regretted his unromantic step, but the merits of the dealing must be weighed according to the motives which prompted it. This aspect of the question aside, it is certain that Helene was herself surprised at her lover's unexpected proceeding, and from this moment her passion began to cool down. The parents were not, however, more favourably disposed towards Lassalle, and they refused him admittance to their house. Difficulties began to thicken around him, and he grew desperate when information came that Helene had been locked up and subjected to ill treatment. He wrote to the Countess Hatzfeldt and to his friend Rüstow, begging them to come to his assistance. To the countess he unburdened his heart : " I cannot help it, although I have striven against it for twenty-four hours—I must weep myself out on the breast of my best and only friend. I am so unhappy that I am weeping, the first time for fifteen years."

Helene's parents had meantime sent for young Racowitz from Berlin ; and, yielding partly to entreaty but more to menace, the girl was persuaded to write a letter to Lassalle notifying her reconciliation to her former lover and renouncing for ever him to whom she had just sworn eternal faith. The correspondence which followed between Lassalle, his beloved, the Countess, Herr von Dönniges, Rüstow, and other

---

[1] " Kritische Geschichte der Nationalökonomie und des Socialismus," p 515, (Leipzig, 1875).

persons drawn into the painful affair, may be passed over ; for the most part it is not edifying reading. A fortnight was spent in fruitless endeavours to remove the obstacles against a union, and the interposition of no less important personages than the Bishop of Mayence, Richard Wagner, and a Bavarian Minister of State, not to speak of noblemen, generals, and scholars, was sought. All was in vain, and Rüstow, who had before telegraphed with grim humour to Lassalle—whom he had persuaded to leave Switzerland—that his "shares stood very low," withdrew on August 24th from the thankless position of mediator, and the game was given up as lost. Before, however, Lassalle ceased to address his beloved, he upbraided her in bitter language for her treachery and invoked his own fate as her punishment. "Helene," he wrote, "my destiny is in thy hands. But if thou shatterest me by this villainous treachery, which I cannot overcome, may my fate recoil upon thee and my curse follow thee to the grave. It is the curse of the truest heart—maliciously broken by thee—with which thou hast shamefully trifled. It will hit its mark ! " [1]

When Lassalle could not obtain the satisfaction he desired, he sought satisfaction of another kind. He challenged Herr von Dönniges, who, however, was in no hurry to accept the arbitration of the duel, and imposed upon his prospective son-in-law, young Racowitz, the duty of representing him. [2] That the jilted lover bore no malice —as, indeed, he had no ground for doing—against Racowitz is proved by the altogether respectful letter which he addressed to him along with a copy of the challenge served upon Dönniges. Only a deep sense of wrongs suffered could have allowed the democratic enemy of duelling to override the principles to which he stood firm when provoked in Berlin some years before. But Lassalle was beside himself with passion at the thought, not only of slighted honour, but of the delight with which his enemies would gaze upon his misfortunes. He was disgusted with everybody and everything, himself and life included. "Adieu, dear friend," he writes to Hans von Bülow about this time—the farewell might have been intended as a final one, for it was the last he spoke to this companion of his happier days—" adieu, dear friend ; life is a wretched dog-and-ape-comedy . . . Everything is tattered and greasy, it is a true *dégoût*. Adieu, adieu ! "

---

[1] Written from Munich, August 20th. Becker's " Enthüllungen," p. 85.
[2] Old Dönniges, in fact, fled to Bern when the challenge reached him.

Lassalle's seconds were Herr von Hofstetten and General Bethlen, and the weapons were pistols. Although no shot, Lassalle refused to practice beforehand, while Racowitz used his time diligently. The duel was fought on the morning of August 28th near Geneva. Rüstow tried in vain to have the meeting deferred on the ground that Dönniges, who was the one with whom Lassalle had alone to do, had quitted the scene, but his friend was past persuasion, and would suffer no delay. In a Geneva hotel Lassalle made his will, bequeathing Countess Hatzfeldt, who meanwhile had arrived in Switzerland, 90,000 marks, and assigning liberal legacies to Rüstow, Lothar Bucher, and Holthoff, a legal friend who had helped him in the difficulty. The morning came. Rüstow, who has left a long account of this affair, tells us how he rose at three and went to the gunsmith who had been ordered to prepare pistols. He chose a weapon and returned with it to the hotel. At five o'clock he woke Lassalle from a sound sleep, and he, seeing the pistol, seized it, and falling on his friend's neck, said, "Now I have just what suits me." By seven o'clock the party was ready to start for the place of meeting. Lassalle, who had drunk a cup of tea, was perfectly calm. At the appointed time the duellists were on the ground. Just before Lassalle had remarked, "My star is still in the ascendant." Undiscerning astrologer! The order was given to fire. Young Racowitz got his ball away first and Lassalle followed five seconds later—but too late : he missed, for he had received his antagonist's shot in the abdomen. To the question "Are you wounded?" Lassalle merely answered "Yes." He was removed, suffering terribly, to his hotel, and he lay there two days, though he scarcely ever spoke. During the night of August 30th-31st he died, his hand resting in that of Countess Hatzfeldt, who sat weeping at his bedside.[1] August 31st is thus regarded as the day of his death. Heine said of Lassalle, when he first knew him as a young man of nineteen years, that he appeared to have been born to die like a gladiator with a smile upon his lips. But his end was, unhappily, far less proud and majestic. The democrat who from principle would not fight a duel to satisfy a political enemy, sacrificed his life in an affray with a man with whom he had had no quarrel.[2]

[1] Just before his death Lassalle wrote : "I hereby declare that I myself took my life."

[2] A few words may be added regarding the leading characters who figured in this sad tragedy. Herr von Dönniges died in Rome on January 5th, 1872, of small-pox. Young Ra-

The first thought that occurred to Countess Hatzfeldt was that of punishment for the murderer of her "dear child." She wrote to Hans von Bülow, "I have sworn an oath on Lassalle's dead body that he shall be avenged, and I must keep it." Endeavours were made to move the police, but they had no result. The countess proposed, moreover, to carry the body round Germany in triumph, and had the family of the dead not interfered the morbid idea would have been realised. But at Cologne the police took possession of the coffin on behalf of Lassalle's relatives, and it was at once taken to Breslau, and there interred on September 14th in the Jewish Cemetery, where a grave-stone bears the following inscription, written by Boeckh: "Here rests what was mortal of Ferdinand Lassalle, the Thinker and the Fighter."[1]

Lassalle's death created great consternation throughout the democratic camp, and meetings in honour of the dead agitator and leader were held wherever branches of the Universal Association existed. A bullet wound was the cause of the calamity, but Lassalle's physician declared that he could not in any case have lived much longer, for bronchitis had laid firm hold upon his system. "To die in strife is the law of life," says Goethe. The agitation, with its severe strain upon his physical as well as mental powers, had undoubtedly been slowly killing him, and the ball of his rival in love only accelerated the impending end. And now the old story was repeated: yes-

cowitz married Helene and died within a year of consumption. On becoming a widow Helene settled in Berlin, being disowned by her relations. Without adequate means, she studied for the stage, relying principally upon her remarkable beauty as a recommendation, and eventually she married a gifted German actor, who is still living in Berlin. A writer tells how when Helene went upon the stage all eyes were rivetted upon her, and persons whispered to each other with something of awe, "That is Lassalle!" Persons who saw the actress have described to the author the strange effect always produced by her appearance. There seemed to be something of the supernatural about her, and as she gazed upon the audience with brilliant eyes—her rich golden-red hair falling in heavy masses upon her well-proportioned figure—all faces were turned upon her as if drawn by magnetic power. The later history of Helene von Dönniges almost seems to suggest the visitation of the Nemesis whose vengeance Lassalle invoked. She was separated from her husband, and since the divorce she had passed a checkered life as an actress in America. Lenbach has painted a striking portrait of this singular woman.

[1] "Hier ruht, was sterblich war von Ferdinand Lassalle, dem Denker und dem Kämpfer." A "Working Men's Song" contains the verse:

> " Zu Breslau ein Kirchhof,
> Ein Todter im Grab ;
> Dort schlummert der Eine,
> Der Schwerter uns gab."

terday's preacher became the text for to-day's sermon.   Lassalle's
melancholy death excited a flood of comments, as wells as estimates
of his character, in the German Press.   The *Allgemeine Zeitung* of
Augsburg wrote : " In any case Germany has lost in Lassalle a great
power, and it can only be deplored that it was a *vis intemperata* . . .
Many thorns but also laurels will grow upon his grave."   Heine once
said, with the cynicism characteristic of him, that the most agreeable
of all tasks is that of following the funeral of an enemy.   There may
thus be some slight excuse for the studied strictures which were
passed upon the dead by a part of the opposition Press.   Strange to
say, a great number of Lassalle's followers refused to believe that he
was dead.   Heine had called him the Messiah of the nineteenth century, and many people were convinced then and for years later that
he had only disappeared for a time in order one day to return to the
scene of his labours and conquests with enhanced glory, a singular
belief which only proves further the vast influence of the man.

Immediately after Lassalle's decease the documents relating to the
duel and the events which led up to it were collected with a view to
the publication of an authenic narrative.   In this work Wilhelm Lieb·
knecht, Schweitzer, Hofstetten, and Bernhard Becker were associated,
and Countess Hatzfeldt first entrusted Lothar Bucher with the duty of
chronicling his friend's last days.   But the choice was soon recalled,
and Karl Marx, then in London, was next addressed on the subject
Marx excused himself on account of want of time, though in truth the
work would not in any case have been congenial.   Finally Becker
was asked to edit the collected documents.   He undertook the task,
and the result of his labours was a volume bearing the title of " Revelations concerning the tragic end of Ferdinand Lassalle," which
appeared in 1868, a work containing about as much unwholesome
reading as could well be packed into 137 pages of small print.   Becker
says in his preface that he acted independently of the countess and
thus drew upon himself her " deep rancour and ire."   But Becker's
work was not in the proper sense of the word official, for before its
completion Countess Hatzfeldt demanded the return of all letters.
The editor gave up the originals but retained copies.   From the original documents Liebknecht was then asked to prepare the desired
narrative.   Working alone with the countess he finished a part of the
story, but he, too, in the end quarrelled with the lady, and the ultimate re·

sult of this succession of interrupted plans was that the countess refused to allow the work to be published, although many sheets had been printed. The compiler of the "Revelations" tells us that two generals, a knight of the Military Order of Savoy, a colonel of the Baden Insurrection, two notaries, a bishop, a Bavarian Minister, a Bavarian *chargé d'affaires*, a Berlin advocate, a count, a baron, a contributor to *Monumenta Germaniæ Historica*, as well as persons of less note, took part in one way or another in the final scene in Lassalle's life-tragedy.

Lassalle seemed to disappear just when his powerful help was most needful to the democratic cause. But although the mission which he undertook to perform remained incomplete he had accomplished a great work. It is often said that Lassalle was the founder of Socialism in Germany. If by that it be meant that he was the cause, such credit cannot be bestowed upon him. Though, however, not the cause, he was certainly the occasion of modern Socialistic developments, and to him may fairly be attributed the introduction of Social-Democracy into German politics. Until Lassalle entered public life the working classes had been without organisation, and had wandered about like sheep without a shepherd. He it was who drew the masses together and formed for the first time a true working-men's party. Thus the more advanced organisations which have followed the Universal Association owe their existence and success largely to his almost unaided exertions. Where later associations have often departed from the ideal which he always held before him has been in their taking an international character. This is, indeed, the fundamental difference between Lassalle and Karl Marx. The former was national in sympathies and aims—a German of the Germans—whereas the latter was in the fullest sense of the word cosmopolitan, for his home was the wide world and his countrymen were all mankind.

CHAPTER X.

CHARACTERISTICS OF LASSALLE, THE MAN AND THE AGITATOR.

To analyse the character of a man like Ferdinand Lassalle is by no means the easiest of tasks. It is a character which seems full of inconsistencies and contradictions. We see in it some of the noblest virtues existing side by side with some of the greatest faults. In his own day Lassalle was to most people an inexplicable riddle, and even now, nearly a quarter of a century after his death, it cannot be said that all mystery has disappeared from his singular personality. Very probably Lassalle did not thoroughly understand himself, and in any case he was a man whom it was and is difficult for others to understand. We have already seen enough of him to be sure that his was no ordinary intellect. Precocious as a child, he developed powers of mind which were capable of achieving far more than they did. Leaving out of the question his premature death—when he fell to an adversary's bullet he was not yet forty years old—it is impossible to say to how high a position he might have climbed in science and literature had he lived in the quiet of the study instead of in the din of political warfare. And yet speculation like this is vain, for Lassalle was no more born for the study than the eagle is born for the prairie-land. He was a thinker, but he was also, and this above all things, a fighter ; and thus no epitaph more truthfully describes the dead than does the simple line which may be read upon Lassalle's gravestone. He threw himself into the wild conflict of parties because he could not help it. The man who could say, " I have been a Republican from childhood," who, urged on by irresistible conviction, defied the crown and the law at the age of three-and-twenty and for his pains was sent to prison—whither he went, as he says, " with the indifference with which another would go to a ball "—such a man could not have kept out of politics if he had wished. And living at a time when constitutional struggles were fierce and frequent, he necessarily threw his whole soul into controversial warfare : he could not have done otherwise. " My spirit drives me on," Lassalle makes one of his characters say in, fortunately, the only drama which he ever wrote. Therein we have a key to the whole public life of the man.

But before considering Lassalle as an agitator, let us inquire into his character as a man. Was he quite human, human in his sympathies and passions, in his aspirations and strivings ? It must be answered that both in strength and weakness he was like as other men. His was a proud spirit, and a spirit fearless as it was proud. He seldom knew a difficulty and he never acknowledged an impossibility. He had a confidence and a will which time after time removed mountains of obstacles such as would have taken the heart out of most men ; and even if the obstacles could not be cleared away, he always saw a way through or over them. Brave men and cataracts, we are told, channel their own paths. That is what Lassalle did and had to do, for he struck out in a direction which no one had hitherto taken. The difficulties with which he had to contend were enormous, but he never feared them. Indeed, his true manhood asserted itself most when he was wrestling with perplexities and " grappling with his evil star." True, there were moments when he felt that the measure of his success did not come up to the extent of his exertions, but these times of discouragement were also times of severe physical weakness and suffering, against which the stoutest courage would have vainly striven ; and when annoyance and vexation disappeared hope shone forth again bright as before. Lassalle was a man of powerful passions, and in this fact we have the explanation both of much that was good and much that was bad in his life and acts. Only strong passions would have enabled him to become the great power he was as an orator, an agitator, and a ruler of men ; and only strong and uncurbed passions would have allowed him to fall into the mistakes which sullied his private character and were the indirect cause of his unhappy death. He was, indeed, essentially a man of extremes. He went to extremes in nearly everything he did and said. He could be an ardent friend and he could be a rancorous enemy. As an orator he could speak words of deepest pathos or rain down anathemas pointed with poison and winged with fire. Lassalle had no sooner entered the political arena with his gospel of salvation for the working classes than he saw the meaning of that saying of his friend Heine, that " Wherever a great soul gives utterance

to its thoughts, there also is Golgotha." He was pursued with relentless violence by his old associates of the all-powerful Progressist party,
but he answered hate with hate—an eye for an eye, a tooth for a tooth.
With the bellicose warrior in Wallenstein's Camp he said, "Do they seek
quarrels? I am ready." Thus in his denunciations of this party we
see Lassalle's passionate nature in its fiercest mood. A man like this
was hardly likely to win the love of others. Fair women courted him,
friends eagerly sought his society, and the working classes followed
him with blind devotion, but in all this there was little real affection.
His grand individuality and his brilliant parts fascinated, dazzled,
magnetised. There was something in him—that proverbial "inexplicable something"—which attracted people and held them as by a spell.
The lady [1] who most of all fell a victim to this wonderful power called
him a Satan, and spoke of his "daimonic presence."[2] There was,
indeed, besides a Faustian similarity, a certain Mephistophelian trait
in his character : not that the trait was acquired, for it formed part of
his being from the beginning. And so we find that throughout all his
agitation he never got right to the hearts of the great masses of the
people. He was a sort of political Mahomet, the attachment of whose
followers was not without a fanatical side. Genuine affection implies not
only lovingness in the subject but lovableness in the object, and let us
be as indulgent as we may, Lassalle's was not a very lovable nature. In
private life none had so many admirers with so few true friends, and in
public life no one, perhaps, received so much adulation and caressing
and so little real love. The homage paid to him in his own social
circle was unbounded. There he ruled alone, king by divine right.
Even Prince Bismarck found the society of Lassalle agreeable and
stimulating, was content when in his presence to listen without himself
speaking, and was always sorry when conversations which lasted hours
came to an end.[3] As a debater and a conversationalist, indeed, Lassalle was approached by none who came in contact with him. Quick
of perception, he saw through an argument before his opponent had
well begun to develop it. Questions which to ordinary people only

[1] Helene von Dönniges.

[2] In the sense in which Bayard Taylor speaks of Lord Beaconsfield : " He is what Goethe
calls a daimonic (not demoniac !) nature . . . possessed with a strange, weird spirit.' —
Letter to a friend, September 10th, 1878, " Life and Letters of Bayard Taylor." (London,
1884), vol. ii., p. 757.

[3] Speech in the German Reichstag, September 17th, 1878.

had two sides, he would at once show to have as many as a tetrahexa-
hedron.   No wonder that he could not bear to be misunderstood,
who himself understood others so easily.   Once he wrote to Rodbertus
—it was the only time he showed ruffled feathers during a long controversial correspondence with this valued friend—that one of his
criticisms had "nearly made him angry" because it proved that he
had not been comprehended.   Like Lord Palmerston he was very im-
petuous, and was wont to regard slowness of perception as equivalent
to downright stupidity.

It is often said that a clear dividing line should be drawn between
the public and the private life of great men, and that it is nothing less
than impious curiosity to penetrate beyond the sphere of public conduct.   Whatever be the ethics of such a doctrine, it is impossible to
regard it as applicable to the case of one like Lassalle.   To cloak his
frailties would be to approve them, to conceal his mistakes would be
to share in their guilt.   For Lassalle was a social reformer ; his life
was professedly devoted to the regeneration of society.   Again and
again he preached, as from the housetops, the gravity of life's mission,
and the responsibilities resting upon the favoured portion of mankind.
Thus, for instance, he once addressed his judges in Berlin : "If I may
give you the quintessence of long and painful studies, the universal
result of my researches in the most various historical sciences, in a
single sentence, this sentence runs : One of two things.   Either let us
drink Cyprian wine and kiss beautiful maidens,—in other words, indulge in the most common selfishness of pleasure—or, if we are to
speak of the State and morality, let us dedicate all our powers to the improvement of the dark lot of the vast majority of mankind, out of whose
night-covered floods we, the propertied class, only rise like solitary
pillars as if to show how dark are those floods, how deep is their
abyss."   That is noble, that is sublime.   Surely the man who spoke thus
should be held to his principles.   It cannot be said that his private affairs
have no concern for the world.   But *De mortuis* is a cry that is always
raised when much that is disagreeable might be said.   Rodbertus once
wrote that Lassalle had politically both an exoteric and an esoteric
character, and the same may be said of Lassalle the everyday man.
There was the exoteric Lassalle, the eloquent orator, the skilful
writer of books, the evangelist of the working classes, the reformer of
society, the crusader against class abuses, the castigator of the rich

man's selfishness, the pleader of the poor man's wrongs. This was the Lassalle who spent his money freely in a cause that was dear to his heart and his ambition, who devoted to that cause his great intellectual powers and his profound learning, who, for that cause, " scorned delights and lived laborious days," toiling like a galley-slave, sacrificing his health, daring the judge and the gaol. How pleasant if the veil had never been drawn—or, better still, if there had been no veil to draw. But there was the esoteric Lassalle, whom one would rather not have known. During his life the truth was only half revealed, but after his death his enemies and even some of his former friends emulated each other in the unwholesome task of dragging the whole dismal history to the light of day. Had Lassalle been as ready to practise private morality as he was to preach public morality, he might have left behind him an influence which would have lived on through generations, blessing and edifying. The man who could say in public, "My friends, I do not belong to the pious," was frank and straightforward, but if he had left questions of morality alone, he would have been more than that—he would have been honest. This is the blot on the escutcheon. After all, it is true what Imlac says in "Rasselas," that preachers of morality often discourse like angels, and live like ordinary men.

But here we have one of those strange inconsistencies in Lassalle's character which are observable in whatever direction we turn. Though his private conduct was so unworthy of him, he could be a very saint when enunciating public and political principles, and a very martyr in defending them. What could be finer than this :

"With truth there can be no arguing. You might as well wish to argue with the pillar of fire which went before the Children of Israel."

Or read his denunciation of the scribblers, whose opinions were dependent on the amount of their hire :

"I hate the prostitution of the pen ; I would never debase myself to it. I regard it as contemptible and more degrading to a man than the prostitution of the body, since my mind is holier to me than that which envelops it."

Lassalle's contradictory character must be borne in mind when endeavours are made, as they yet are, to prove that he was after all only an actor. If his early life had not been reconcilable with his later, it might have been difficult to show that the zeal and devotion which he threw into his political agitation were the outcome of deep conviction. But no man has ever shown more steadfast fidelity to principles espoused in early youth. A touch of vanity may be traced in the words which he once addressed to a Berlin Court of Law, but the words are indisputable truth for all that :—

" What makes me," he asked, " direct public opinion to the unjust and crying condition of the lower classes? Alone I go my way through society, persecuted by Crown Solicitors, condemned by the Courts, and, believe me, regarded by the Liberal Press with even greater horror than by Crown Solicitors and Courts. What, I say, constrains me to all this? I will tell you. It is because—I can say it, and on this occasion I must say it—it is because my studies are deeper, my knowledge more extensive, and my horizon wider than theirs : therefore it is impossible for me to appease myself with the shibboleths of the day."

It was not love of fame but the conviction formed by long study, thought, and observation, which caused him to take to arms and dare all opposition. A man who divided two years pretty equally between the prisoners' dock, the public platform, and his own home should be the last man in the world to charge with insincerity.

Bernhard Becker says that Lassalle wished to be a German Garibaldi, and he seeks to show that he purposed gaining the highest power in the State by means of a Social-Democratic revolution.[1] These are, however, the idle speculations of a friend turned enemy and they do not deserve to be treated seriously. Lassalle was at heart Republican, but he knew as well as any one that the monarchical principle was firmly established in Prussia, and he even went so far as to say at one time that monarchy with a reformed society would be a beneficent form of government. If, however, Lassalle was not so inordinately ambitious as some people try to make out, he was inordinately vain. This was one of the most striking, though at the same time most harmless traits in his character. His vanity was of the kind that neither hurts nor offends. Vanity seemed natural to him as it is to the peacock, and if he had been less vain he would have been less interesting. Even in his manhood, when at the head of a popular agitation, he was excessively fond of dressing well. He appeared both on the platform and in the Court of Law attired like a fop. He was in

[1] The palpable fiction which Helene von Racowitza writes on this subject in " Meine Beziehungen zu Ferdinand Lassalle ' is on a par with most of the contents of that work.

the habit, too, of comparing himself with great men. Now it was Socrates, now Luther, or Robespierre, or Cobden, or Sir Robert Peel, and
once he found his parallel by going to Faust. Heine told him that he
had good reason to be proud of his attainments, and Lassalle took Heine
at his word. He would often assume a tone of lofty superiority when
addressing even judges on the bench. "Ask friends and foes alike
about me," he once exclaimed, "and if they are men who have themselves learned something, both will agree unanimously that I write
every line armed with the entire culture of my century,"[1] and in the
same breath he added that his great political antagonist, Schulze—a
man of no mean parts, and nearly twenty years his senior—had only
" the education of a barber."

Nor would he hesitate to point publicly to the "remarkable spectacle
of an agitation which has laid hold on the masses, which agitates an
entire nation *pro* and *contra*, and which has, without the aid of events
which throw the people into the street, proceeded from the conscience
of *one* man," or to claim not only scholars, but a bishop, and even a
king as his disciples. After all, it was hard for one like Lassalle to
tolerate quietly all the ignorance, and what was worse, the science
falsely so called which he found rife, and it is not strange that he
should have entertained the liveliest contempt for the men, neither by
nature nor nurture wise—"ridiculous people," as he called them, "who
think themselves political economists, fill all the columns of our daily
Press, and sing to the misguided a Hosannah on the perfection and
excellence of our economic conditions"—who, without having devoted
a hundredth part of his toil to the study of political and social questions, presumed to answer his arguments with mere affirmations and
contradictions. Nowhere do we see the spirit of haughtiness and the
feeling of superiority which were so characteristic of Lassalle better
displayed than in an incident that occurred during the speech made at
Frankfort on May 17th, 1863. Lassalle had been interrupted, and the
chairman pleaded for fair play since he was "on his defence." The re-
joinder was, perhaps, unexpected.

"I must protest," said Lassalle, "against the word which has

Adolf Held remarks (" Sozialismus, Sozialdemokratie und Sozialpolitik," p. 8. Leipzig,
1878): " When Lassalle says of himself that he writes every line armed with the entire culture
of the century, there is undoubtedly contained in this bold phrase the truth that the leaders of
the Social-Democracy of to-day do not in any way come behind their literary opponents in
philosophical, historical, and economic training."

escaped the chairman, and which he himself will not desire to adhere to. I do not stand here in the position of an accused person who has to defend himself. I stand entirely in the position of a man who wishes to instruct and inform you, and not to defend himself." At the same time he did not scruple to say upon another occasion that "In order to lecture to working-men a far higher degree of education is necessary than would be requisite for lectures to students in the lecture-room."

Like many great men before him, Lassalle was also superstitious. He would never be one of a company of thirteen at dinner, and he used to comment upon the fact that he had always lived in houses bearing the number thirteen. Conversing once, long before the end of his life, with a friend, now living, to whom he was greatly attached, he referred to a certain augury and added, "I shall not live to be forty years old." As a matter of fact, his age fell seven months short of that term.

But it is especially as an agitator that Lassalle has interest for us. Brandes says aptly that the word agitator might have been invented for him. In this capacity it was that he achieved his greatest triumphs, for in agitation his genius found a fitting sphere for exercise. When in 1862 he came forward in Berlin as a platform lecturer the city was taken by storm. Even the reactionary Press saw there was more in the "revolutionary Jew well known in his day" than appeared on the surface, and predicted that the last had not been heard of him. The Progressists were wild that this maker of books should dare to claim the platform as his battle ground, and yet they were puzzled with it all, just as Miles Standish was after reading his Cæsar :

> "A wonderful man was this Cæsar :
> You are a writer and I am a fighter, but here is a fellow
> Who could both write and fight, and in both was equally skilful."

What was it, then, that gave Lassalle his marvellous power as a demagogue ? Let it be remembered that the subjects on which he spoke were for the most part scientific and technical. His addresses dealt largely with dry theories of political economy, which often have little interest for the educated and might be expected to have less still for the uneducated. Eloquence, enthusiasm, and deep earnestness account for a good deal of Lassalle's success, but all these advantages in his favour would have failed to win the masses had he not joined to them a great qualification which distinguished him from all popular orators of the day. This was his rare capacity for presenting scientific truths and theories in such a form that they could be "understanded of the people." His speeches never presumed prior knowledge. He took up a subject at the beginning, discussed and examined it thoroughly, and only left it when he had reached the logical end. The momentous address which he delivered in Berlin in the spring of 1862, and which he afterwards published with the title "Über Verfassungswesen," is a model composition of the kind. Step by step—and only one step at a time—he follows his complicated theme, until when the conclusions of the argument are reached, it is easy to anticipate them. Necessarily this thorough method of treating a question made his speeches at times long. He hardly ever spoke for a shorter time than two hours, but he once reached four hours. This was at Frankfort on May 17th, 1863, and the opposition Press spoke of his loquacity as unconscionable. Lassalle in his next speech would not allow that he had exceeded the bounds of moderation. "The time a speaker takes," he said, " does not depend upon the speaker but the subject." Luthei disputed with Eck for three whole weeks : might he not speak for four hours when the question at issue was not less important ? But Lassalle could be abstruse, and he often was when engaged in wordy contests with his opponents. Then all the pugnacity of his nature showed itself, as he confused his antagonists with irony and demolished them with subtle logic or dialectic. On such occasions he was to be seen at his best, as, with proud mien and eye "in a fine frenzy rolling," he watched the torture of the enemy who had dared to rouse him.

Lassalle strove after effect : of course he did, as orators have always done, in spite of the sublime principles of Socrates. He admitted as much, when he apologised to Rodbertus for the roughness of his speeches as delivered on the ground of "the exciting rather than theoretically contemplative effect which I must seek after." But one thing he did not do, and that is, flatter the vanity and play to the caprice of his hearers. Of this kind of thing we find no trace in his published speeches. On the other hand this is what we do find :

"You German working-men are curious people. French and English working-men have to be shown how their miserable condition may be improved ; but *you* have first to be shown that you *are* in a miserable condition. So long as you have a piece of bad sausage and a glass of beer, you do not observe that you want anything. That is a result of your accursed absence of needs. What, you will say, is this, then, not a virtue? Yes, in the eyes of the Christian preacher of morality it is certainly a virtue. Absence of needs is the virtue of the Indian pillar saint and of the Christian monk, but in the eyes of the student of history and the political economist it is not. Ask all political economists what is the greatest misfortune for a nation? The absence of wants. For these are the spurs of its development and of civilisation. The Neapolitan lazaroni are so far behind in civilisation, because they have no wants, because they stretch themselves out contentedly and warm themselves in the sun when they have secured a handful of maccaroni. Why is the Russian Cossack so backward in civilisation? Because he eats tallow candles and is happy when he can fuddle himself on bad liquor. To have as many needs as possible, but to satisfy them in a respectable way, that is the virtue of the present, of the economic age! And so long as you do not understand and follow that truth I shall preach in vain."[1]

He also quoted Ludwig Börne's [2] words : " Other nations may be slaves ; they may be put in chains and be held down by force, but the Germans are flunkies—it is not necessary to lay chains on them, they may be allowed to wander free about the house." Outspoken words like these may not have flattered ; but it was no object of Lassalle to flatter. The motto of his public life was "*Aussprechen Das was ist,*" and to this motto he was always faithful. Lassalle spoke extempore. At the most he used a few notes, unless indeed his subject required statistical treatment, and then he would carry with him written and printed statements even to superfluity.[3] If he had to deliver an important speech he would generally draw out a rough draft, and this he would carefully peruse, a strong memory enabling him to retain all that was necessary of the scheme. Still, even if he committed a speech entirely to memory, he was never put out if unexpected incidents occurred in the course of its delivery, for his self-

---

[1] "Arbeiterlesebuch," pp. 31, 32.

[2] Ludwig Börne, the famous German publicist, was born May 18th, 1786, at Frankfort-on Main. Like Lassalle he was a Jew and changed his name, the original form being Löb Baruch. He died February 12th, 1837.

[3] He writes to Rodbertus April 28th, 1863 : "At Frankfort I shall speak four hours and still I shall not have time to go into detail as I should like. I shall have to refer to everything briefly. I shall attack them with all sorts of things, mortality lists, statistics on the duration of life amongst various classes, but in everything I shall be very brief." This was the speech whose length caused the Opposition Press so much vexation.

N

control was complete.   Gifted though he was, it was with him no light
matter to speak, and he always looked back upon the finished task
with feelings of intense relief.   A tribute paid to Lassalle on his death
by a leading German newspaper [1] deserves to be quoted : " Lassalle
was amongst the greatest orators whom Germany has produced.   We
do not say this thoughtlessly or without authority, for we have heard
nearly all the celebrated orators who have come forward in this
country during the last generation."

Le style c'est l'homme.   The words are very true in the case of
Lassalle.   Who could be mistaken in the character of a man whose
favourite metaphors are derived from the army, and whose commonest
expressions breathe the spirit of force and resolution.   He speaks of
his followers as his " troops " or his " battalions," he talks of fighting
" battles," of defeating the " enemy," of holding " reviews," and of
surrounding his arguments with " coats of mail."   Ricardo's law of
wages becomes in his hand an " iron law," and he is never tired of
using phrases like " iron fate," " iron hand," and " iron grasp."   For
iron he had an especial affection ; he terms it the " God of man," the
" magic rod," man's " last retreat in despair," and " the highest pledge
of his liberty."   When Lassalle speaks of the old system of absolutism
he declares that it must be met with " firm grip and the knee on its
breast."   He has not originated a social movement, but " kindled a
conflagration."   Similes of this kind and figures like that of Revolution
advancing " with wild, flowing hair and with iron sandals on its feet "
are not uncommon in Lassalle's speeches.   We should expect the
orator who employed this forceful style of speech to be himself a man
of force and iron will, and such Lassalle was.   His language but expressed the stern mould of his character.   He loved to speak of iron
and fire, for his nature was full of both.   He went to the battlefield for
his similes, because to him life was a battle, an endless, truceless
struggle in which no quarter could be given or expected.   And if he
personified violent changes by weird and dreadful forms, it was because the problems which agitated society and the State had for him
a terrible importance.   He speaks somewhere of his " glowing soul "
(*meine glühende Seele*).   That was no idle or exaggerated form of
speech.   His soul did indeed glow, and it seemed at times to be
heated by a hundred fires.   It is worthy of notice that although

[1] *Allgemeine Zeitung* of Augsburg, September 6th, 1864

Lassalle looked favourably upon the use of metaphorical language when he wished to bring a great thought home to the minds of his hearers, his speeches were strikingly poor in illustration, a common expedient with so many orators. Not that he was lacking in resource. The explanation rather is that he preferred to keep attention centred upon the regular course of his argument, and this would scarcely have been possible had distracting elements been introduced into his discourse.

Very fortunately we have preserved an excellent description of Lassalle as an orator, and it has the twofold merit that it is from a very careful observer, and from a friend of the agitator. Paul Lindau[1] relates that one day in June, 1864—at which time he was the editor of a Düsseldorf newspaper—an agent of the Social-Democratic Working Men's Party came to tell him that Lassalle was expected at Düsseldorf shortly, as he had to defend himself in a trial to be reheard there on appeal, and the publicity of his journal was desired. Lindau gave the assistance sought, and the result was that on Lassalle's arrival an introduction took place. The following account is given of the first interview :

" The conversation was almost one-sided, for I was satisfied with playing the *rôle* of hearer. A word discreetly interpolated was enough to prompt Lassalle immediately to a long and always interesting and well-connected reply. He accompanied his words with very expressive though at times too uneasy gestures. He would often stop, and he frequently changed the tone of his voice. He had the habit of beginning his sentences in a high tenor voice and of ending them in a euphonious baritone. He articulated very distinctly, and spoke with precision, but he could not disown the Silesian. On separating, Lassalle pressed my hand as though I had been a close friend."

When Lindau called upon Lassalle the following morning, he found him stretched upon the sofa with his legs reared up against a table. In this position he was drawing up an outline of the speech he intended to make. What follows is amusing. Lindau had been invited to dine at one o'clock.

" Shortly before one I appeared in his room. He rehearsed his speech before me while making his toilette—I had found him in an unusually elegant, almost foppishly fashionable morning undress— but two o'clock struck in the meantime. By three I had risen at least

---

1 See article " Ferdinand Lassalle's letzte Rede : eine persönliche Errinerung von Paul Lindau " in the *Deutsche Bucherei*, No. 4, 1882 (Breslau).

ten times as a hint that we should go, but while he was speaking
Lassalle appeared to have entirely lost interest in all secondary things,
such as time and the stomach.   He grew more and more animated as
he spoke, though I did little to excite this vivacity.   All the time he
was walking to and fro in the tolerably large room, pacing probably
several hundred times from the door to the window and from the
window to the door, gesticulating the while and oscillating his head
peculiarly, now right and now left, now lowering it and now raising it.
All he had said was fulmination ; but although the remarkable man so
enthralled me, I could not forget that I had for two hours been vainly
striving to get to dinner.   It was a quarter past three, and now I finally
braced myself up for a long speech : ' Herr Lassalle,' I said, ' I'm
frightfully hungry !'   'Then why 'didn't you say so *long* ago ?' he
replied, speaking the first part of the sentence in his ordinary tone,
but rising to an unusually high falsetto at the words ' long ago,' and
ending in the deepest baritone."

The day of the trial came—it was June 27th—and all Düsseldorf
was astir.   As usual Lassalle appeared in Court in full dress, with
polished shoes, dress coat, and white cravat, but he carried with him
so many books that the Public Prosecutor involuntarily exclaimed,
" Um Gotteswillen !" and a buzz of hilarity passed through the
spectators.   A special table had to be allotted to the accused, for he
had brought a whole library—a library of books, pamphlets, newspapers, and documents.   Of the speech Lindau says :—

" Lassalle's speech gave throughout the impression of a free oration,
which certainly had been previously well thought out and had been
consolidated by concise arrangement on paper.   He held in his right
hand an octavo sheet at which he would every now and then cast a
hurried glance, and then he appeared to extemporise for a long time.
He spoke with exemplary clearness and with great rhetorical force.
The peculiarity which I had observed in private conversation, the
modulation of his flexible voice in all keys, showed itself here and in
still greater measure.   His speech was effective in the highest degree,
though it was not entirely free from the theatrical.   For every humour
which he wished to produce he could find the right tone of voice ; but
everything gave one the impression—as with Gambetta—that it had
been predesigned, had been previously studied, or at least rehearsed.
Whether he became scornful and ironical over the deficient knowledge

of his judges, whether he employed the pathos of his own consciousness and struck the natural tone of conviction, or sought to produce
an effect by the scornful recital of his martyrdom :—notwithstanding
admiration for the acuteness of his thoughts, for his conciseness and
power of expression, and for his great eloquence, one could not get rid
of the feeling that he was an actor. This was increased by the panto-
mime and the gestures with which Lassalle accompanied the speech.

" The expression of his countenance continually changed. Now a
scornful smile played upon his mouth and he half closed his eyes—
half pitifully, half contemptuously ; but he soon opened them wide,
and threatening looks shot up to the raised seats of the judges. Now
he moved his head carelessly to and fro—as, for instance, when he
alluded to a most weighty and most abstruse scientific statement as
something quite secondary, and as a matter of course known to every
judge—but he soon raised his head haughtily and defiantly as a
Roman Emperor.

" His spoken thoughts were mostly illustrated by movements of the
hands. Hands and arms were in almost uninterrupted activity. He
was only quiet when drawing keen, purely legal deductions, for which
he wished to gain the full attention of the judges ; then he supported
himself lightly with his left hand upon the table, and hid the right, in
which there was always one of the octavo sheets, behind the fold of
his wide-cut waistcoat. If he wished to produce a rhetorical effect, he
gesticulated in a most remarkable manner with his right hand. First
he jerked his arm forward as if boxing, then he hacked the air with
the crumpled sheets of paper as though he were beating two-four time
prestissimo; then he raised his hand threateningly and lashed about
with it so passionately that several times the written sheets slipped
from his fingers and fell fluttering slowly to the ground. . .

" During the long speech Lassalle often changed his position. He
walked to and fro behind the book-covered table, anon remaining
stationary for a few moments as if rooted to the ground, but only to
advance again several steps and slowly approach the judges. This
pacing movement was especially noticeable at the close of the speech.
During the very effective sentences with which he ended, he moved
gradually and quite imperceptibly forward, so that in uttering the last
words he had nearly reached the steps leading to the podium of the
judges' bench. The peroration he addressed to the judges in so elevated

a voice and with such violent gestures that the President involuntarily drew back somewhat. The speech produced the deepest effect."

Let us form what opinions we will of Lassalle's doctrines, and judge as we will of his faults, the fact remains that we have to do with a remarkable man, with one who on many grounds deserves to rank amongst the representative men of the century. In Germany his work is commemorated by one of the most momentous movements of the age. Let Social-Democracy be what it may, it is a great power in German politics, a power which cannot be ignored, and Ferdinand Lassalle must be regarded as its originator. It is now nearly a quarter of a century since Lassalle died, yet his memory is kept fresh by the thought of what he did and wrote and said and suffered for the popular cause when democratic tribunes were not so plentiful as now. Every year his birthday and the day of his unhappy death are religiously observed by Socialist organisations,[1] and so far as can be judged at present, there seems every likelihood that the prediction which the agitator made in the ears of his prosecutors more than twenty years ago will be fulfilled :

" Oh, gentlemen," he said, " fifty years after my death people will think otherwise than do the Düsseldorf Judges of First Instance of the powerful and remarkable movement of civilisation which I am accomplishing under your eyes ; and a grateful posterity—of that I am certain—will apologise to my shades for the affronts which this judgment and this Crown Solicitor have offered to me."

Lassalle would have been a very Savonarola of social reform had he only possessed the holy inspiration of the wild Florentine. That, however, he lacked conspicuously, and his work suffered for the deficiency. As it is, his figure stands forth upon the canvas of modern history clear and prominent with its light and shade, its attractive and its repellent features. "He is great," says Emerson, "who is what he is from nature, and who never reminds us of others." Tried by that test Lassalle must clearly be awarded the laurels of greatness.

---

[1] On September 4th, 1887, a very remarkable *Lassalle-Feier* took place at Basel, in whose Burgvogtei Hall a great assembly of German and Swiss Socialists met to commemorate the death of the father of Social-Democracy. Liebknecht lectured on the position of Lassalle in modern history and claimed it as Lassalle's special merit that he had placed the labourers' question upon a ground both scientific and practical by the organisation of the working classes and the proclamation of a Social-Democratic programme.

CHAPTER XI.

LASSALLE'S SOCIALISM.

LASSALLE attributes the modern growth of the working class in importance to the doctrines proclaimed by the French Revolution. From the Middle Ages downward the supreme element in the State and society had been land-ownership. Landed proprietors, favoured by both political and economic conditions, were able for centuries to retain predominant power, and thus the classes excluded from ownership of the soil were kept in a condition of impotence or servitude. The Reformation came, and during the following two centuries a gradual revolution took place, whose culmination was the epoch-making event of 1789. Before this time the position of the nobility, as of the clergy, had vastly altered in fact if not in law, owing largely to the development of industry, the accumulation of capital, and the growth of personal estate. What the French Revolution did, therefore, was to proclaim rather than create a new order of things. It struck the hour, telling how far mankind had got in the onward march of time. In the new order the third estate or the *bourgeoisie* came to ascendency in the State, the rights of man were proclaimed, and the abolition of privilege and prerogative was decreed. But it was not long before a new oligarchy usurped the powers of that which had been dethroned from supremacy, and the last state became worse than the first. Where the nobility had ruled with the ownership of land, the *bourgeoisie* ruled with the ownership of capital. The nobility, on the strength of their privileged position, escaped taxation, and imposed the burden on the third estate ; and in the same way the *bourgeoisie*, by means of the system of indirect taxation, transferred the weight from their own shoulders to those of the working classes.

Lassalle holds that a new historical era began with February 24th, 1848, for then the predominance of the fourth estate was proclaimed. Now, however, we have reached the last stage of social development. As the fourth estate cannot lay claim to new privileges, it is equivalent to the entire human race, its cause is that of all humanity, its liberty is the liberty of mankind, and its supremacy is the supremacy of all. The supremacy of all, because the principle of the working class will henceforth be the ruling principle of society, and all members of the human family will be workers in so far as they have the will to make themselves useful to society. Holding these views regarding the development of society, it is not surprising to find Lassalle making constant use of the idea of revolution. But revolution with him does not mean necessarily a violent organic change in the institutions of the State. " Revolution," he once told his judges, " is an overturning, and a revolution always takes place—whether it be with or without force is a matter of no importance—when an entirely new principle is introduced in the place of the existing order. Reform, on the other hand, takes place when the principle of the existing order is retained, but is developed to more liberal or more consequent and just con- clusions. Here, again, the question of means is of no importance. A reform may be effected by insurrection and bloodshed, and a revolution may take place in the deepest peace."[1] Thus he regarded the development of princely power in Germany as a revolutionary phenomenon, but the Peasant War of 1525, bloody as it was, as merely a reactionary movement ; the progress made by industry in the same century was likewise revolutionary, and the invention of the spinning jenny in the eighteenth was essentially such. Revolution is, therefore, the handmaid of progress, but there can be no such thing as creating or even hastening revolution. " To wish to *make* a revolution," he says in the *Arbeiterprogramm*, " is the foolishness of immature men, who have no knowledge of the laws of history." In the same way it is equally childish to think of stemming a revolution for which society is prepared. " If the revolution be in society, in its actual condition, then it must come out—there is no help for it—and pass into legisla- tion." Lassalle felt that in his day revolution was approaching. History told him of its approach, and told him, too, that its advance could not be impeded. It was Lassalle's master, Hegel, who once wrote, " We learn from history that no one ever learns anything from history." This apothegm may be taken as the sum and substance of more than one speech delivered by Lassalle before the Law Courts. " You do not believe in revolution," he said once to his judges, " but my studies have taught me to believe in revolution." Come it would,

---

[1] " Die Wissenschaft und die Arbeiter," p. 34, defence of 1863.

and nothing could stay it. " It will either come in complete legality
and with all the blessings of peace—if people are only wise enough to
resolve that it shall be introduced in time and from above—or it will
one day break in amid all the convulsions of violence, with wild, flowing
hair, and iron sandals upon its feet. In one way or the other it will
come, and when, shutting myself from the noise of the day, I lose
myself in history—then I hear its tread. But do you not see, then,
that in spite of this difference in what we believe, our endeavours go
hand in hand? You do not believe in revolution, and therefore you
want to prevent it. Good, do that which is your duty. But I do
believe in revolution, and because I believe in it I wish—not to
precipitate it, for I have already told you that according to my view of
history the efforts of a tribune are in this respect necessarily as
impotent as the breath of my mouth would be to unfetter the storm
upon the sea—but in case it should come and from below, I will
humanise it, civilise it beforehand."[1]

We shall be prepared to find a man of this kind extolling, too, the
idea of might. Lassalle's standpoint is a thoroughly practical one.
His ethical view is that right goes before might, but he cannot deny
that in a world where things are to a large extent turned upside-down,
might is necessarily if wrongly supreme, and will continue to be so
until justice shall become the law of human dealings. He recognises
might as the predominant force in society. The constitution of a
country is merely the expression of the relationship which the various
elements of power bear to each other. So long as the king has on
his side a nobility and an army, the nation is impotent, and must take
what its ruler chooses to offer ; and, on the other hand, when that
power is on the side of the people, the king must submit to the
dictatorship of those who are nominally his subjects. This is the
whole secret of constitutions. "Constitutional questions," he says,
" are primarily not questions of law but of power."[2] Nevertheless,
he does not apotheosise might to the disparagement of right. On
the contrary, he says that " the sword is certainly the sword, but it is
never right." He will have the two go hand in hand, for then alone
can might reach its highest dignity, and right assert its true claims.
Nowhere does Lassalle express himself better upon this point than in

[1] " Die indirecte Steuer."
[2] " Über Verfassungswesen," p. 25.

the words which are placed in the mouth of Ulrich von Hutten in the drama "Franz von Sickingen.

> " Es ist die Macht das höchste Gut des Himmels,
> Wenn man sie nützt für einen grossen Zweck ;
> Ein elend Spielzug, wenn zum Flitterstaate
> Sie nur die Hand beschwert, in der sie ruht." [1]

His ultimate conclusion is that right and might can only be properly combined when the democracy attains full supremacy, for "with the democracy alone is right, and with it will be the might." [2]

To turn now to Lassalle's strictly economic views. His standpoint is that of advanced Socialism, a Socialism which in his day counted for more than mere heresy, though it is only right to acknowledge that the many prosecutions which were instituted against him during two and a half years of public agitation were not based upon economic but political utterances. Lassalle, who on his second appearance upon the platform in Berlin proclaimed that he belonged to "the party of pure and decided democracy," regards labour as a ladder by means of which mankind has climbed to the heights f civilisation, and a favoured portion of mankind to the heights of wealth and luxury. The labourer has been a victim from the beginning. At the dawn of civilisation and down to the Christian era, slavery prevailed universally, and the labourers and all they produced were the property of a master-class. Then came Christianity, but it was slow to bring the labourer emancipation. Instead of the ancient slavery, the system of serfage and bond service was established, and still the labourers were in a greater or less degree the property of their employers. The guilds followed the abolition of serfage in the towns, and the same principle of dependence continued. Finally, amid the thunders and lightnings of the French Revolution, free competition was proclaimed, and labour was declared to be legally free. Yet the freedom was only partial, for labour was not economically emancipated, nor is it to-day. The working classes form now, indeed, a powerful fourth estate, but the power possessed is yet only potential. No greater story of fraud, thinks Lassalle, can be told than that which recounts the dealings of capital with labour during this century. The

---

[1] "Franz von Sickingen," p 92.
[2] "Macht und Recht," (1863).

entire history of European industry since the century began is a record of wild speculation, blind and ignorant trading, overstraining of credit, unbridled over-production, commercial crises, and misfortune to the labourers, who are the scapegoats of the capitalists. Even to-day, " The back of the labourer is the green table on which under-takers and speculators play the game of fortune which production has become. It is the green table on which they receive the heaps of money thrown to them by the lucky *coup* of the *roulette*, and which they smite as they console themselves for an unlucky throw with the hope of better chances soon. The labourer it is who pays, with diminished work, with hard-earned savings, with entire loss of em-ployment, and thus of the means of subsistence, for the failures en-tailed in this gambling of employers and speculators, whose false speculations and reckonings he has not caused, of whose greed he is not guilty, and whose good fortune he does not share."[1] Legally the labourers are perfectly free, but the freedom is only apparent, and not real. There is one serious difficulty in the way of actual freedom, and it consists in the labourer's want of capital, without which he can-not begin work. Had he this he might be independent, might be his own master, but he has not, and so he is not independent, but is the servant of someone else. In reality, free competition is a sad misnomer. How can there be free competition, when there is free-dom for only one of the contracting parties? What we have now is a system of unfree, unequal competition, a competition between the armed and the unarmed. And yet, Lassalle points out, this so-called free competition has wonderfully increased the wealth of countries. He calls it the most powerful machine for the increase of social wealth that has ever been invented.

How comes it, then, that the labourer is so badly off? When all around there is abundance, why should he alone live in want? This brings Lassalle to the statement of that "iron economic law" which played such a great part in his agitation, and which receives such prominence in his works, the law of wages, according to which " the average wages of labour always remain reduced to the subsistence necessary, conformably with a nation's standard of life, to the pro-longation of existence, and to the propagation of the species." The labourer is compelled to sell his labour, and meagre wages are all the

---

[1] " Herr Bastiat-Schulze von Delitzsch," (Berlin, 1864).

return he receives for it. Wages which only allow him to live admit of no saving, and thus his condition of dependence is irremediable so long as he is subject to this "iron law." "What," asked Lassalle once of a meeting of working-men, "what is the result of this law, which is unanimously acknowledged by men of science? Perhaps you believe that you are men? But economically considered you are only commodities. You are increased by higher wages like stockings when there is a lack; and you are again got rid of, you are by means of lower wages—by what Malthus, the English economist, calls preventive and destructive checks—decreased, like vermin against which society wages war." What, however, makes the labourer's hardship worse is the fact that he is all the time of his servitude making his employer richer; he is placing himself more and more completely in the hands of his master; he is forging heavier and yet heavier fetters for his own arms. It is true that wages may for a short time rise slightly beyond the level of absolute necessaries, but directly the number of labourers increases, there is a fall to the old mark, or else below it, in which case emigration, want, disease, and abstention from marriage and procreation take place. This is the blessing of a competition legally free, but economically the reverse. The labourer has not escaped slavery; he has only exchanged masters. Where formerly the surplus produce left over and above the support of the labourer went to the serf-owner, it now goes to the capitalist, who, strengthened in his supreme position by every further addition of wealth which the labourer's exertions bring him, can look unconcernedly upon his bondsman's struggles to be free.[1] "The produce of his labour strangles the labourer; his labour of yesterday rises against him, strikes him to the ground, and robs him of the produce of to-day." Labour is a commodity, but the labourer does not stand in the favourable position of other owners of commodities. When the merchant finds on frequenting the market that prices are too low to allow of the profitable sale of his goods, he reserves them. The labourer, however, has no option: he must sell his commodity labour or starve with all his family.

Lassalle asks how the labourer is to be helped out of this condition of dependence and want. The evil is that a portion of the produce is retained by the capitalist or undertaker. Clearly, then, the proper

---

[1] Lassalle intended to write a work which should contain the "Outlines of a scientific political economy," and in this work the theory of value would have been fully considered.

remedy is that which will secure to the producer all he produces. This is, therefore, the panacea which Lassalle proposes. It is a medicine which will not only cure but prevent. The labourer will be doubly bene-fited, for he will be secured his produce now, and he will receive all the advantage that will accrue as labour becomes more productive. Hitherto the capitalist has alone received the fruits of greater produc-tivity, but henceforth the sower will be at the same time the reaper. The plan which he proposes is, as we have seen, the association of the working classes in productive undertakings worked with capital ad-vanced by the State. With this co-operation the labourer will become his own undertaker, and the distinction between wages and profit will disappear, and the produce will go to the producer. Lassalle thought that if this scheme could be realised a good step would be taken to-wards the settlement of the social problem. In order, then, to bring the change about in a simple, legal, and peaceful way, he recommended the establishment of Productive Associations on the basis of voluntary coalition. There was to be no compulsion ; but the working classes were to be attracted by the offer of State help, without which, indeed, the project would be incapable of realisation. He proposed the ad-vance of capital by the State—first at low interest, and eventually free —because he regarded the working classes as the greatest power in the State, and as having a peculiar claim upon its resources. Lassalle could not tolerate the "let alone" argument which was always advanced when mention was made of the State. He not only held it to be allowable for the State to come forward with help for such a purpose, but he regarded it as a duty of the State to give this help, and it is worth notice that no less important a man than Prince Bismarck has, as we shall see, adopted the same standpoint. The *bourgeois* econo-mists objected that monetary aid was unjustifiable, and yet the State had helped the *bourgeois* and the capitalist again and again in the construction or maintenance of railways, canals, roads, telegraphs, posts, banks, and in the introduction of agricultural improvements and of inventions. If State help had been justifiable in the past for the capitalist, why not now for the labourer? It was said that with such aid the incentive to self-help would be entirely taken away, but to this objection Lassalle answered : "It is not true that I prevent a man from climbing a tower by his own strength, because I reach him a ladder or a rope. It is not true that the State prevents a youth from educating himself by his own power, because it offers teachers, schools, and libraries. It is not true that I prevent a man from ploughing a field by his own strength when I reach him a plough. It is not true that I prevent a man from defeating a hostile enemy with his own strength when I place a weapon in his hand."[1] Towers may be climbed without ladders or ropes; persons may be educated without teachers, schools, and libraries; fields ploughed without machines, and enemies worsted without weapons, but in every case the task may be far more easily accomplished with the help of suitable auxiliary means.

Nor was Lassalle frightened because his proposal was denounced as a piece of pure Socialism. "As often as a great man of science has thought it proper to find ways and means for improving the condition of the labouring class, an attempt has been made to cry him down with the catchword 'Socialist!' Now, if it is Socialism to try to improve the position of the working classes and to relieve their want, then in the name of thirty-three thousand devils we are Socialists! Does any one think I am frightened of a name?—not I, indeed."[2] But would not State control be dangerous; would not personal liberty be threatened if, after providing capital, the State required to exercise supervision over the financial affairs of its debtors? No, there could be no question of endangering personal liberty, for the State would only have the rights of a creditor. It would have a right to demand that the machinery which its money provided should not be destroyed but employed, and to inquire into the way in which business was carried on; but every day the books and affairs of public companies are subjected to the same supervision, and yet no one ever talks of the loss of liberty or independence. The Associations would be formed according to statutes, and so long as the conditions of these statutes were fulfilled they would have a right to State funds. Lassalle calculated that 100,000,000 thalers would be enough capital to begin with, and that with this money 400,000 workmen could be employed, these representing with their families a population of 2,000,000. Apart from undertaker's profit he counted on 5 per cent. interest on the capital, equally to 5,000,000 thalers annually, which at compound interest would double the capital in fourteen years, besides allowing 20,000 new workpeople to associate yearly. But a great advantage would accrue

[1] "Offenes Antwortschreiben," p. 20.
[2] "Arbeiterlesebuch," p. 52.

from the fact that trades work into each others' hands, the product of one being the raw material of another.   Thus the tanner works into the hands of the shoemaker, the cloth manufacturer into the hands of the tailor, the iron and steel worker into the hands of the machine constructor, so that it would not always be necessary to raise fresh capital when an Association was formed, for the new Association might be carried on with the credit of those existing.   Moreover, in time, Associations would combine, a distinct branch of industry having perhaps a single organisation in each town, so that over-production and commercial crises would be impossible.   Private trading would be supplanted, the profit-making middleman would disappear, and selling would be done in State bazaars.   Not only so, but a host of evils would vanish in the train of these superfluous institutions ; such, for instance, as unhealthy speculation, adulteration, deception, *réclame*, and Lassalle added, "obtrusive commercial travellers, payments to newspaper editors, and puffs of every kind."   The close connection of the State with production would also render it possible to establish a number of undertakings which now, though of great importance for the welfare and prosperity of the people, cannot be thought of.

Lassalle hoped to help not only the industrial but the agricultural population.   Peasant Associations would be formed, and the State would supply land for cultivation, and in this way the abolition of rent would be precipitated.   Moreover, the "small *bourgeoisie*," as he termed the class which includes State and public officials receiving small salaries, would be tempted into the ranks of the ordinary wage-earners by the prospect of more liberal remuneration.   Both in Industrial and Peasant Associations the mode of payment would be as follows : first, the wages usual in the particular place and industry would be given weekly, and at the close of the year the business profits would be distributed as dividend.   But how was the State to be induced to undertake the great task of supporting the Productive Associations ?   Lassalle saw a means of securing his end in the introduction of universal suffrage.   When the legislative bodies of the country were elected on the basis of a universal franchise, then only— but certainly then—would it be possible to realise the scheme.   For when the masses of the people were able to make their influence felt in legislation, they would become in reality, as they were already nominally, the State.   We find him telling the Leipzig Committee in 1863 that statistics showed 96¼ per cent. of the population to be then in a more or less distressed and needy condition. "To you, then, the needy classes, belongs the State, not to us, the higher classes, for it consists of you." Nevertheless, sanguine as he was, Lassalle did not venture to regard his Association scheme as a final measure. Fourier believed that when his teaching had once been accepted society would be reformed in ten years. Lassalle was not so confident. He admitted that the settlement of the social question would require generations—indeed, he once said five centuries—to its completion, and would be the result of a long succession of measures, each of which would have to be developed organically from its predecessors. He held, however, that the Associations would beat a path for further and more extreme reforms.

Lassalle introduced a perfectly new element into the Socialistic agitation of his day. His friend Rodbertus and his rival, Schulze— the latter, however, being no Socialist—stood upon purely economic ground, like Saint-Simon and Fourier. Lassalle followed the methods of Louis Blanc and Proudhon, and made politics part of his programme. He was indeed the first State Socialist in modern Germany. Analysing his theories, we find that the State which he seeks to inaugurate is thoroughly democratic. He wishes to do away with the class distinctions which have followed in the train of an advancing civilisation. These he holds to be out of date, and to be marked for extinction in the natural process of social development. Where there have been several estates in the past, there will only be one in the future, and the principle underlying it will be that of labour. The State will be society and society will be the State. In order to this change, a revolution in the economic order of things will be necessary. There must be capitalists and landowners no longer, for the State must supplant them. Production must be carried on under the direct auspices of the State, which will provide both the soil and the capital which are requisite. Thus the labourer will not have to support a recipient either of profit or interest, but will receive all the produce of his labour. Work will in this way be diminished and lightened, for the labourer's needs will easily be supplied when he only toils for himself and his family. Leisure will be had in abundance for intellectual and physical recreation, and while the lot of the labourer will be made happier, his life will be longer. Lassalle will secure to the individual as much independence of action as possible. Personal liberty will be complete within the limits imposed by his plan of State Socialism. Freedom of thought and speech will not be restricted, and the free Press will be made exclusively a means of public education. His views on this subject are original, and they have supporters amongst German social reformers in high places to-day, Professor Adolph Wagner amongst the number. Lassalle refuses to regard the news-paper as legitimately a business speculation. In his opinion its mission is that of a schoolmaster or a preacher. Thus he insists that a newspaper should be allowed to publish nothing but news. Adver-tisements turn it into "a public crier, a public trumpeter," and thus degrade its high functions. Public announcements must be published solely in official journals existing for the purpose, and conducted either by the Government or by the local communities. Then the news-paper will cease to be a lucrative speculation, and the journalist will follow a profession instead of a trade.

It is, however, pretty certain that Lassalle's views on the subject of the Press were coloured by the discourteous and often savage treat-ment which he received at the hands of a multitude of newspapers when engaged in agitation. He regarded as "literally true" the as-sertion of Prince Bismarck, that "the newspapers are written by people who have failed in their vocations," but he thought the con-demnation not half severe enough. For the Press of his day, indeed, he had the greatest contempt, for he believed that the worse a journal was, the more subscribers it had, though it never occurred to him that newspapers may after all be only what the public makes them. No anathema came more truly from his heart than the one which he pro-nounced in the hearing of a Rhenish meeting in 1863. "Hold firm," he said, "with ardent souls hold firm to the watchword which I give you: hatred and contempt, death and destruction to the Press of to-day! That is a daring watchword to be given by one man against the thou-sand-armed institution of the Press, with which even kings have vainly contended ; but . . . the moment will come when we shall dart the lightning which will entomb this Press in eternal night." [1]

Further, in the coming Social-Democratic State not only land and capital but all means of communication, and some, at any rate, of the banks will be in national hands. Direct taxation will take the place of

[1] " Die Feste, die Presse, und der Frankfurter Abgeordnetentag," (September, 1863).

O

indirect, to which Lassalle is thoroughly opposed. He holds that taxes
upon the necessaries of life, as well as those caused by the administration of justice, should be abolished, since in proportion to their earnings
the poorer members of society bear too much of the burden. He will,
therefore, have a system of direct taxation according to which everyone will be liable to pay imposts proportionately to his income. Lassalle's aim is throughout to engage the support of the State on behalf
of those who through deficiency in wealth, knowledge, or other social
advantages are unable to rely upon self-help. He will not hear of the
doctrine that the purpose of the State is merely to protect the personal
liberty and property of the individual. That idea of the " Manchester
men," [1] he says, may do very well as the basis of a night watchman's
functions, but it will not do for the State, whose duty it is to assist
and perfect the development of the race into a condition of freedom.
The whole history of mankind he regards as the history of a struggle
with nature—with the misery, ignorance, poverty, impotence, and
servitude in which man lived when he stepped forth into history. The
overcoming of this impotence means the realisation of freedom, which
has gradually been won for the individual. But without the State it
would not have been possible to carry on this struggle. The State,
however, is a union which increases a million fold the strength of all
its units, and this is why it has been able to do for its members what
they could never have done single-handed and isolated. Thus the
working classes—and the poorer classes of society in general—have
learned by instinct to place confidence in the State and to insist that
it shall fulfil its proper function, that of developing the liberty and
promoting at the same time the happiness and material welfare of all
subjects alike, regardless of condition.

So far Lassalle's economic views. Was he an original thinker or a
mere copyist, a mere adapter of the theories of others ? The answer
must be that he was the latter. Not, indeed, that he was a plagiarist.
It is no plagiarism to declare from the public platform doctrines with
which men of science are all familiar, unless the expounder claim to be
also author. And the " iron wages law " which lies at the very root
of Lassalle's teachings was in his day well known wherever Ricardo's

[1] "The Manchester men, those modern barbarians, who hate the State—not this or hat
particular form of State, but the State altogether—and who, as they here and there give us
clearly to understand, would like to abolish the State, to sell justice and police o the lowest
bidder, and to carry on war by public companies."—" Die indirecten Steuer. '

influence had spread. Not a few critics of Lassalle have laboured to show that he said nothing new. The task is a superfluous one. Probably Lassalle would have been the last man in the world to claim that his gospel was an original one. When he made his first appearance as the founder of the Universal Working Men's Association, he took care to support the "iron law" on the testimony of Ricardo, Smith, Malthus, John Stuart Mill, Say, and other distinguished men. The argument that he took the theory from others is in reality no argument at all. People do not usually enter into contention about matters that need no demonstration, but that is what has been done in this case. Lassalle advanced the wages law as a known economic doctrine, and gave authorities in support of his advocacy of it, and yet it has been found necessary to elaborate proofs that this doctrine, whose authorship he attributed to others, is not his own. In truth, he was not in need of theories. Of these there was a sufficiency. Lassalle was emphatically a man of deeds, and he took the theoretical groundwork which he found ready laid and built upon it a structure out of material likewise within hand's reach.[1] Karl Marx[2] charges him with having borrowed " all the general theoretical propositions in his economic works " from his published writings, and it may be granted that Lassalle was stimulated by this far deeper thinker. It is, however, very probable that the principal impetus and help came from his close friend Rodbertus, whose works he studied with something of a disciple's devotion.[3]

Beyond this, however, he had been schooled in English economic theories, and the influence of this part of his studies may be seen throughout his writings and published speeches. For England and English institutions, as representing the highest achievement in

1 " In economical science ingenious thoughts and systems do not come perfect into existence as the armed Minerva did from Jupiter's brain ; they rather develop. And he does enough who brings a train of thought to a certain conclusion."—G. Adler, " Rodbertus, der Begründer des wissenschaftlichen Sozialismus," (Leipzig, 1884), p. 16. So, too, L. von Stein, in his " Geschichte der socialen Bewegung in Frankreich von 1789 bis auf unsere Tage," (Leipzig, 1850), vol. i., p. 153, says : " Important theories never spring like an armed Minerva out of the head of a single person, but proceed in organic formation from long preparation, and require external circumstances in order to attain to external value."

2 Preface to " Das Kapital," vol. i., (Hamburg, 1867).

3 He tells Rodbertus on one occasion, in the year 1863, how ten years before he had read the third " Social Letter " " three times in succession, with my mental powers strained to the utmost and with constant self-discussion."

civil and personal liberty, Lassalle always showed great admiration. He was never weary of telling his audiences, whether in the assembly room or the Court of Law, how English freedom had "broadened down from precedent to precedent," how Cobden had converted a nation and slain a tradition mighty with the growth and strength of centuries, and how the English working classes bore a character for manliness and hardy independence unexampled in modern history. The influence derived by Lassalle from England in many ways was very considerable, and Marx might have remembered this when he spoke of wholesale plagiarism. He might also have remembered that it was only after long residence in England that he himself produced an important economic work. Had Marx not lived in this country he never would or could have written his epoch-making " Capital." Of that there can be no doubt whatever.

Lassalle's particular application of the theories which he found ready to hand led him to the Productive Association, and here again he has been charged with ploughing with the heifers of another. The Association does, in fact, bear great resemblance to the *atelier social* of Louis Blanc,[1] and it will not be wrong to conclude that Lassalle had this pro·totype in mind, though he carried the co-operative idea much farther than his French contemporary. The Productive Association had, how-ever, little or nothing to do—as was alleged in 1863[2]—with the *ateliers nationaux* established in 1848 by the Provisional Government, and abruptly discontinued after a few months' trial had proved their use·lessness. These *ateliers nationaux* were started and worked under the direct supervision of the State, and, moreover, they were not in-tended to supplant private industry, but to provide employment for the workpeople who could not find food. Both in origin and purpose, therefore, the French workshops differed radically from the Lassalle Associations. The latter were to be formed by voluntary association and not by State compulsion or even initiative : all the State was

1 " Organisation du Travail," 1840.—It is worthy of note that Leibniz nearly two hundred years ago proposed, amongst his other projects for the advancement of mankind, that artisans should be employed in national workshops, conducted on the principle of co-operation. It is very true that there is nothing new beneath the sun.

2 Lassalle published a refutation of the charge that his Productive Associations were identical with the *ateliers nationaux* of 1848 in a newspaper article, afterwards reprinted, the opening sentence of which ran, " Lying is a European Power." As to Louis Blanc's scheme, he contents himself with the remark that the views of this celebrated Socialist are very differ-ent from his own. The implied disavowal is not very ingenuous.

asked to do was to open its purse when called upon. "The free individual association of the working people," said Lassalle, "but this association made possible by the supporting and helping hand of the State : that is the only way offered to the working classes out of the wilderness." Further, the very *raison d'être* of the Associations was the absolute abolition of the undertaker and the capitalist. Not only were they to compete with private industry ; they were to supplant it, so that the producer might have undisputed command over the entire produce of his labour. Then, too, Lassalle intended to apply the same principle of association to the land, in order that it might together with capital and the instruments of labour pass out of the hands of the individual into those of society. Thus, while the idea of association with State help was not new, his own development was more thorough and more ingenious than any earlier attempts in the domain either of theory or practice. It may be said that his work led to no immediate results. Lassalle, it is true, did not live to see his abours crowned with the success which he confidently expected. But, apart altogether from the founding of a great social movement, the end of which no man can predict, Lassalle's agitation and writings have exerted an important influence upon the domestic policy of the German Government. It must not be forgotten that the principle which he placed at the head of his programme of social reforms, and which he enforced at various times in private discussion with Prince Bismarck—State intervention on behalf of the working classes[1] —has since become the groundwork of German social legislation, and that in no country in Europe has this principle been carried so far as in the country which Lassalle convulsed with agitation more than twenty years ago. Nor was the appeal for universal suffrage made in vain. Early in the year 1864, he predicted that before a year had passed the Prussian Minister President would have played the part of Sir Robert Peel, by reversing his policy, and that this demand would have been granted. The prophecy was too sanguine, but universal suffrage became law of the North German Confederation in 1867, and of the German Empire in 1871.

"This is what I have to say to you about the principle—and to-day we are only dealing with the principle—of proclaiming as our motto universal and direct suffrage for the avowed purpose of improving your social condition by legislation, by the intervention of the State," &c.—Speech at Frankfort, May 17th, 1863.

How far Lassalle was prepared to go in the abolition of individual property, and in overriding the acquired rights of the present proprietors, we cannot say with certainty, for his practice of taking one step at a time—of concealing his purposes until the proper time for their discovery had arrived—makes it difficult to judge of his ultimate ends. "Truth," he once wrote, "must be developed step by step." In his correspondence with Rodbertus, however, he speaks of the Productive Associations as a "transitional measure,"[1] and says that "the Association, proceeding from the State, is the organic germ of development which leads to everything else."[2] It is certain that he hoped, by means of the Associations, to get rid of the capitalist's profit and the landowner's rent, and thus in time to supersede as superfluous personal property in capital and land. Indeed, he went so far as to Germanise Proudhon's "*La propriété c'est le vol*" into the somewhat more euphemistic "*Eigenthum ist Fremdthum*," but he did not say in plain words whether he was prepared, in the words of Marx, to "expropriate the expropriators." Rodbertus claims him as a convert to his doctrine of income-property, but there is reason to believe that Lassalle was to some extent an unreadable book to this valued friend and correspondent, who once admitted that he had to do with "an exoteric and an esoteric Lassalle." A valuable light is thrown upon the esoteric views of Lassalle by the learned and exhaustive treatise in which he considers the theory of acquired rights.[3] In this, his greatest work, Lassalle speculates boldly in a domain of thought which for Socialists is one of the utmost importance. He inquires if, and to what extent, acquired rights can claim protection against the retroactive effect of new laws, and the conclusions to which he comes are pregnant with significance for the development of his economic theories. He lays down two propositions ; (*a*) "No law should be retroactive which only affects an individual through the medium of

---

[1] Letter of May 26th, 1863, in which he says: "My conscience as a theorist would not have allowed me to speak of a 'solution' of the 'social question' in connection with the Association scheme ; and to this I have referred briefly at Frankfort. It is now only a question of a transitional measure, not of a theoretical, final solution on principle, which you yourself only look for in five hundred years. That this solution will be gradually furthered and vastly facilitated by the Association appears to me incontestable."

[2] Letter of May or June (no month given), 1863.

[3] "Das System der erworbenen Rechte : eine Versöhnung des positiven Rechts und der Rechtsphilosophie " (Leipzig, 1861, 2 vols).

the actions of his will ; " and (*b*) " every law should be retroactive which affects the individual without the interposition of such a voluntary act ; which affects the individual directly in his involuntary, human or natural, or socially acquired qualities, or only affects him in that it alters society itself in its organic institutions." [1] He argues that the individual by his acts and by contract can only assure to himself or others rights if and in so far as the existing laws regard the substance of the rights as just. Thus he is able to advance the proposition that the sole source of right is the common consciousness and conviction of the nation. To every contract there must be added the tacit clause that the right therein stipulated shall and can only be valid so long as legislation regards it as permissible. The claim that an acquired right shall continue for all time, even when prohibitive laws permit it no longer, is nothing less than the claim of self-sovereignty for the individual. A right may be formed on the basis of legislation, but it only exists so long as this legislation continues unchanged ; he who makes any further pretension claims to be his own law-giver. This, says Lassalle, shows up the hollowness and illegality of the cries which will be raised when public opinion puts an end to the various existing forms of personal servitude, slavery, and forced labour, to hunting-rights, exemption from land tax, entail, and so forth. Thus the decrees of August 4th, 1789, by which the French National Assembly repealed all laws proceeding from feudal supremacy, violated no rights, for even if feudal privileges were regularly acquired, they could only be valid so long as national opinion did not call for a different law, and the storming of the Bastille was the expression of a change in the conscience and conviction of the nation, which change put an end to the old *régime*. It follows from this that the customs and traditions of the past cannot claim authority over the present ; or, as Lassalle elsewhere expresses himself, every age is independent and autonomous. [2]

Coming to the further question of compensation on the abolition of

[1] " System der erworbenen Rechte," vol. i., p. 55.
[2] Rodbertus questioned Lassalle as to how he would learn what the national opinion really is, holding that this could not be done either by votes of majorities or even unanimous votes. Lassalle answered : " You are right when you will not allow a majority or unanimity of votes to demonstrate what the spirit of the time is. How do I find this, then ? Well, I think very easily. What *you* by reason, logic, and science can demonstrate to yourself and to the age, that the age will wish. —Letter of February 17th, 1863.

acquired rights, he takes up a standpoint opposed to that of Savigny.[1] This famous jurisconsult said that indemnity should be given, and Lassalle answers that the giving of compensation is illogical, illegal, and unjust. There is, in fact, nothing to indemnify. It is only possible to stipulate for the validity of a right so long as the public conscience may approve of it, and when it does so no longer the right has had its day and ceases to be, for the limit of its validity has been reached. At the same time Lassalle takes care to lay stress upon the difference between the absolute prohibition of a right and the prohibition of a mode of its exercise. There may be cases where compensation will be allowable, viz., when the prohibition does not exclude all rights founded upon a certain legal title. In these cases, however, the compensation is really only a change from a prohibited to an unprohibited form of right. Thus in the case of the appropriation of land for the purpose of public buildings, not property itself, but a form of property in an individual case is prohibited, and land may continue to be acquired and held as private property. Here compensation must be given, but the compensation is mere appearance, the truth being that the prohibited form of property in a certain piece of land has been changed into the still unprohibited form of money-property. Prohibitive and compulsory laws may, therefore, be of two kinds. They may either determine that a right hitherto existing can no more be the property of the individual and can by no act of the will be made such ; or they may allow the right to continue as one which can be made the property of the individual, the only question being the form and condition which the connection of the individual with the substance of this right must take in order that the right may be lawful and valid. Prohibitive laws of the first kind apply to all existing contracts and all legal relationships, but those of the second class should never apply to existing legal relationships which may have been caused by individual actions of the will. If a law abolishes property altogether, or property in certain objects, it is no matter that the objects may have been acquired by inheritance or purchase, or in any other way ; they must still pass out of individual ownership.

In the second part of the work, Lassalle considers the right of

[1] Friedrich Karl von Savigny, born at Frankfort, February 21st, 1779, and became in 1810 a professor at Berlin University, where he continued for thirty-two years. Died October 25th, 1861.

succession as it existed in ancient times and now exists. He holds that the heir in the Roman sense was not heir of the property but the will of the dead, that the will of the testator was supposed to be perpetuated in the heir. The Roman idea of immortality was, in fact the testament. Dealing then with Germanic right of succession, Lassalle shows that it is a mixture of old Roman right, that of the testament, and old Germanic, viz., intestate succession. Germanic right of succession differed from Roman right in being in reality family right, for in substance the property of the testator was common family property during his lifetime, the appropriation only taking place, however, on his death. The Germanic nations borrowed the testament from the Romans, but without understanding its significance, regarding it rather as a formal disposal of the property of the dead. As, then, the family right of the early Germans has disappeared, and the true Roman testament has been discarded,—for no one believes any longer in the significance anciently attached to it,—Lassalle comes to the conclusion that the modern German testamentary right is nothing but a great misunderstanding and a theoretical impossibility.[1] [2] "This," he says, "is the fate of the Roman testament with the Germanic nations. Accepted by a national spirit which according to its own national idea interprets all inheritance as intestate, as the peculiar right of the heir, the character of the Germanic inheritance, the character of intestate right, is impressed upon testamentary right of succession, and the maxim necessary with intestate right, *le mort saisit le vif*, is extended to it."[3] And yet the modern testament has been said to be a natural right ; a natural right has been made out of a natural impossibility, out of a right which has never and nowhere existed. Property is now no longer family but personal property, and nowadays most systems of succession rest on the will of the State and society. The logical deduction is that the State and society can if they desire direct that the property of the dead shall be differently disposed of than it now is. It may appear somewhat singular that Lassalle did not refer during all his agitation to the startling doctrines

---

[1] " System der erworbenen Rechte," vol. ii, pp. 592, 593.

[2] One of Lassalle's critics, H. von Sybel, has met this argument with the analogy of royalty Nowadays people do not believe in "divine right," yet nations preserve the institution of royalty because they are convinced that constitutional monarchy is a beneficent form of government.

[3] " System der erworbenen Rechte," vol. ii, p. 594.

advanced in this work.   The explanation is only to be found when we bear in mind his great tenacity of purpose, which would not allow him to undertake fresh plans until the plans in hand had been realised. Had he lived long enough the time might have come when he would have gone back to the principles which he held to govern acquired rights and have sought to apply them.

CHAPTER XII.

DEVELOPMENT OF SOCIAL-DEMOCRACY.

THOUGH Lassalle's death was an irreparable loss for the Universal Working Men's Association, no one hinted at the idea of suspending operations. When the blow fell, branch organisations had been formed in fifty-two places, but many had already succumbed. The lists showed a membership of 4610, Barmen being most strongly represented (with 529 members), and Ronsdorf and Solingen following (with 523 and 500 respectively). Still, it would be far from right to regard this as the net result of Lassalle's labours. Although the Universal had failed to draw the working classes to itself, the principles which its founder and president had with unflagging zeal preached from the Rhine to the Oder had been eagerly accepted, and the foundations had been laid for a great and influential movement. Thus Lassalle's work must not be estimated by the membership of his Association ; it must be estimated by the later history of Social Democracy in Germany.

Meanwhile, it was necessary to take steps to prevent the fall of the democratic leader giving rise to anarchy in the camp. Bernhard Becker had been nominated by Lassalle as his successor in the presidency, and in November, 1864, the choice was confirmed by the Association. Dammer continued to be vice-president and Willms retained the office of secretary, while Schweitzer began at once to take a greater direct interest in the agitation. Becker was a complete failure. Not only did he fail to work amicably with Countess Hatzfeldt, who believed that her relationship to Lassalle imposed upon her the duty of keeping an eye on the progress of the movement, but—and this was his great failing—he lacked every qualification necessary to one who would be a leader of men. At first he tried despotism as Lassalle had done with such complete success, but the result was only to make himself look ridiculous. It was the old story of the ass in the lion's skin. When he found it impossible to have his way he took refuge in recrimination. Of Liebknecht he spoke as an "arch intriguer, who calls himself a Communist but is nothing but an ambitious, diabolical trickster, incapable of building anything up but always ready to destroy." Marx and Engels were included in the same condemnation, while Schweitzer was demolished in an egoistic outburst in which Becker said, "As to this Judas, working-men, I will crush this skeleton. I will shatter him like glass, since I alone amongst you represent Revolution and have revolutionary power in me." Evidently a man of this stamp was not in his proper place when occupying a post requiring the exercise of great tact, self-control, and self-sacrifice. The fall from the intellectual Lassalle to the bully Becker was a great one, and it seemed to augur ill for the future of the Association. Lassalle had proved himself a prince of agitators, and now his place was filled by a puppet. Towards his associates Lassalle had always preserved an attitude of cordiality, but Becker was unable to control his bad temper. Lassalle was vain, but it was a vanity which generally pleased and never seriously offended, for there was a great intellect behind it all; but his successor, with less justification than Anacharsis Cloots for his vanity, conferred upon himself the arrogant title of "President of Mankind."

A year after the catastrophe of Geneva signs of decay showed themselves within the Association, and even the foundation of an organ in the Press seemed unable to arrest disintegration. True to agreement, Schweitzer and Hofstetten had meanwhile issued on January 1st, 1865, the first number of the *Social-Democrat*, which was published in Berlin. Hofstetten furnished the money and Schweitzer the brains, and for a time the newspaper succeeded. It was not, however, recognised everywhere as the organ of the agitation, for Schweitzer had made himself many enemies—the Düsseldorf general meeting, indeed, expelled him from the directorate of the Association—and to this extent its influence was crippled. Nevertheless, with an able staff of contributors, including Marx, Engels, Liebknecht, Herwegh, Rüstow, Hess, and Wuttke, the *Social-Democrat* could hardly fail to prosper so long as it kept true to its aims, and in the end even the fulminating Becker withdrew the anathemas with which he had greeted its appearance. Schweitzer may be said to have drawn together the scattered bones of Social-Democracy and to have breathed fresh life into them. But towards the end of February a series of clever articles was published with the title "The Bismarck Ministry," in which Prussia was glorified, and the duty of settling the German question was imposed upon her. "Two factors are alone capable of action in Germany," said the concluding article, "Prussia and the nation. Prussian bayonets or the fists of the German *proletariat*—we see no third."[1] The democratic party was disgusted, and Schweitzer's chief contributors severed connection with the journal. The editor himself soon afterwards fell into the clutches of the law and was put into prison. His place at the head of the *Social-Democrat* was taken by Hofstetten, a man of no ability, who proved a very poor substitute.

But the Universal Association had other enemies to fear besides internal jealousies, and the greatest of them was rivalry without. No sooner did Lassalle disappear from the scene than Karl Marx, who was still in London, began to bestir himself. At the end of September, 1864, the famous International Working Men's Association[2] was established, and Marx was made its president. With the principles of this organisation Liebknecht, who in time won August Bebel over to his side, was in complete sympathy, and though he continued to profess allegiance to the more moderate proposals of the German Association he was known to be promoting the influence of the International. When the split occurred on account of the "Bismarck articles" of the *Social-Democrat*, Liebknecht came out in his true colours, and before many months had passed he was expelled from Prussian territory, and went to Leipzig. Reserving for the International a more detailed review, it will be well now to follow the history of the distinctly German movements further. The first general meeting of Lassalle's Association was held in December, 1864, at Düsseldorf, and the proceedings passed off very quietly. The second general meeting, held at Frankfort-on-Main at the end of November, 1865, was a stormy one, however, and one result was the overthrow of Becker, in whose place C. W. Tölke, of Iserlohn, was elected president. Tölke was a man of rough manners but of considerable common sense, and he did his little best to follow in the footsteps of his dead leader. He had, however, a fault which, in the eyes of friends of the International, was unpardonable : he was a monarchist. Indeed, he went so far as to call upon one occasion for cheers for the King of Prussia, an act which caused most good democrats to shrug their

[1] No. 28 of the *Social-Democrat*, which, for its effect in dividing the heterodox from the orthodox amongst the Democratic party, may be likened to No. 90 of the Oxford Tracts.

[2] See following chapter.

shoulders and pull long faces. Evidently Tölke was not the man to preside over the Association, and so when, tired of his honours, he resigned in the summer of 1866, the opportunity of replacing him was welcomed. At this time Schweitzer was in prison or he would probably have received the appointment, but as it was A. Perl, of Hamburg, was made president. During the succeeding months the Countess Hatzfeldt, who had all along kept a hand on the reins, interfered so objectionably with the affairs of the Association that a crisis came. The fourth general meeting, held at Erfurt at the end of December, 1866, repudiated the pretensions of this lady, and the consequence was that she formed without delay a rival association with Lassalle's statutes, and made one Försterling, of Dresden, its president. This organisation soon came to grief.

The wisest act of the Association after Lassalle's death was the election of Schweitzer to the presidency in May, 1867, at the Brunswick general meeting. The Association had got into very low water, and only a man of great ability and of strong will could now put an end to the disputes and rivalries which were hastening on dissolution. Had Schweitzer been Lassalle's first successor, the Association would have been growing stronger all the time of its increasing weakness. It was not too late to arrest decay, but complete restoration was now almost out of the question. Schweitzer proceeded to work at once in a business-like way. He restored the organisation of the Association, placed its finances upon a sound basis, and in time reduced confusion to order. The new president was, in fact, just the man for his position. He was educated and energetic, was a talented speaker, and, moreover, through personal intercourse with Lassalle, he understood the ideas of the late agitator as few of his associates did. Lassalle and Schweitzer had a good deal in common. Both were men of the world, both were full of resource and born administrators, and both were suspected at one time of being merely reactionaries in disguise. Liebknecht, indeed, declared that Schweitzer's imprisonment was only a feint, but later events showed that idea to be untenable. Where the new president came far short of his great predecessor was in his lack of real sincerity in the cause of the working classes. He had drunk the cup of pleasure and indulgence to the dregs, and the honey had become bitter in his mouth. Probably Schweitzer first took to politics as a distraction, though, when events forced him into prominence, he threw his whole energies into party warfare, and his later years certainly redeemed his earlier. In the first year of his presidency an important political incident took place which had momentous consequences for the Social-Democratic movement. Universal suffrage was granted for the election of the North German Reichstag, and before it the Constitutive Assembly. This deferred fulfilment of a prophecy made by Lassalle in 1864 was welcomed with jubilation. In the general elections the Socialists measured strength with the Conservative party in several constituencies, with the result that Schweitzer, Bebel, Fritzsche, [1] Hasenclever, [2] Försterling, and Mende were returned to the Reichstag, the party giving about 40,000 votes. The sixth general meeting of the Association was held in November, 1867, at Berlin, and the seventh in the following August at Hamburg. At the latter meeting, which was attended by delegates of 82 associations, representing 7192 members, two motions of importance were brought forward by the president. One declared that while industrial strikes were incapable of altering the ruling system of production, they were, if properly organised, a good means of promoting *esprit de corps* amongst the working classes, and of removing various social evils. The other motion related to the convocation of a congress of working-men for the purpose of establishing trades unions. The meeting adopted the strike resolution, but rejected the proposal to convene a congress. On Schweitzer threatening, however, to resign, it was agreed as a compromise that the president and Fritzsche should be allowed to call a conference not as members of the Association but as members of the Reichstag. This was at once done, the date of meeting being September 27th, and the place Berlin. The same month the Universal Association was dissolved by

---

[1] Friedrich Wilhelm Fritzsche, a cigar maker, born March 27th, 1825, at Leipzig. He emigrated to America. His Tobacco-workers' Association, founded in 1865, was the first Socialist Trade Union in the country.

[2] Wilhelm Hasenclever, author, of Dessau. He was born April 19th, 1837, at Arnsberg in Westphalia. Originally a tanner, but he early became journalist. In 1868 he was appointed treasurer of the Universal German Working Men's Association, two years later the secretary, and in 1871 the president. He became the president of the Socialistic Working Men's Party on its formation at Gotha in 1875. In 1881 he was expelled from Leipzig, where he followed the journalistic profession, and he has since lived at Wurzen, Halle, and Dessau. He has almost uninterruptedly sat in the Reichstag since 1869. Hasenclever is described as being thoroughly modest, good-natured, and gallant. In Parliament he opposed the granting of money for carrying on war with France, but as a Prussian militiaman he did his duty patriotically when with the besieging army before Paris.

the police at Leipzig, its seat, but Schweitzer formed another association with the same name and statutes at Berlin, and all went on as before. From this time may be said to date the pre-eminence of Berlin as a Socialistic centre.

All this time Liebknecht and his associates were doing their best to advance the interests of the International in Germany, and long before open hostility to Schweitzer was shown, they had endeavoured to undermine his power, and convert the Universal Association to their advanced principles. Finally, on March 28th, 1869, Liebknecht and Bebel appeared at the general meeting held at Barmen, and openly charged the president with being a reactionary. The design, however, failed, for of the fifty-six delegates present all but twelve voted confidence in their leader, and the rest remained neutral. Still, the Liebknecht party gained ground by this piece of strategy. Schweitzer, who this year again served two months in prison, resolved to checkmate the move of his enemies by having resort to Lassalle's old plan. He entered upon a political campaign of two months' duration, and received in all parts of the country warm tokens of attachment. When the ninth general meeting—held in Berlin—came round, his popularity seemed undiminished, but eighteen months later, in July, 1871, he resigned, and his resignation was followed sometime later by his expulsion from the Association on the charge of treachery. His own account of his withdrawal from the presidency was that he had grown weary of the never-ending intrigues, and had become convinced that the working classes could not be relied on for fidelity to their leaders. The *Social-Democrat*, Schweitzer's journal, ceased to be published on April 30th, 1871, and a younger organ belonging to him, the *Agitator*, was discontinued on June 1st of the same year.

It was a long time before Liebknecht and Bebel were able to secure a footing for the International in Germany, but as an introduction to the more advanced programme they drew up at a congress of Saxon working-men held at Chemmitz in August, 1866, a series of " demands of the Democracy." These demands were :—(1) Unrestricted right of the people to self-government. This implied universal, direct, and equal franchise with secret voting in all domains of State life (the Parliament, the Chambers of the individual States, the communal governing bodies, &c.), the abolition of the standing army and its substitution by a militia ; and a sovereign Parliament having absolute power to decide on questions of war and peace. (2) The unity of Germany as a Democratic State. There should be no hereditary central power—"no Little Germany under the guidance of Prussia, no Prussia enlarged by annexation, no great Germany under Austrian guidance, no Triad." (3) Abolition of the privileges of position, birth, and confession. (4) Futherance of the physical, intellectual, and moral training of the people. The school should be separated from the church and the church from the State, teachers should be given a worthier position, and schools should be established for their training, elementary schools should become free, and schools for higher education be provided. (5) The universal welfare to be furthered, and labour and labourers to be emancipated from all pressure and constraint. This demand comprised the amelioration of the position of the working classes, right of free migration, free choice of occupations, universal right of settlement in Germany, and State support of productive co-operative associations. (6) Self-government for parishes. (7) Promotion of a knowledge of the law amongst the people. This was to be effected by the independence of the Courts and juries, especially in political and Press trials, and by public and oral judicial trials. (8) Promotion of the political and social education of the people. This final demand comprehended a free Press, free right of meeting, and right of coalition. The Chemmitz programme attracted many adherents, and the two confederates felt that they had made a good beginning. As, however, the Universal Association was not to be turned out of its course, they looked in another direction. Bebel was originally a follower of Schulze-Delitzsch, and at the time of his alliance with Liebknecht he was the president of a Working Men's Association at Leipzig, founded on the principles of Schulze, from which, however, it had gradually departed. In the autumn of 1867, Bebel became president of the Union of Working Men's Associations, and the following year, at the annual congress, he was instrumental with Liebknecht in inducing a large majority of the associations to accept the programme of the International.

This was a substantial victory for Marx and his two lieutenants, for the International was now established in Germany. Thus Liebknecht and Bebel were encouraged to make renewed endeavours to detach Schweitzer's adherents, but for the present they were only slightly successful. In the following year, 1869, however, the Social-

Democratic Working-men's Party (*Socialdemokratische Arbeiter-partei*) was formed at Eisenach out of the "internationalised" Union of Working Men's Associations and the seceded members of the Universal. A conference was first called for August 7th. This was done by a manifesto, published by Liebknecht and Bebel in the former's *Demokratisches Wochenblatt,* wherein Social-Democrats were congratulated upon the progress which advanced views were making. This manifesto gives the key to a curious piece of party nomenclature. Liebknecht and Bebel spoke of their party as the "honourable Social-Democracy" (*die ehrliche Socialdemokratie*), and from that time the adherents of the International in Germany went by the alternative names of the "Honourables" and the "Eisenachers · The congress met, and did all that its promoters expected of it. Schweitzer conceived the plan of outvoting the adherents of the International, but the scheme completely failed. It is estimated that the two hundred and sixty-two delegates who avowed Internationalist principles at this congress represented 150,000 working-men, though two-thirds of them belonged to Austria and Switzerland. The shrewd and calculating policy which Liebknecht pursued, when promoting the principles of the International, is shown by a letter he wrote this year regarding the South German Democratic Party, whose progress towards Communism was too slow for many ardent disciples of Marx. Liebknecht refused to hurry the party, knowing that its advance was only a question of time. "Wait a little," he said, "and then the little people will be able to march to Basel ; but not now." The distance between the Eisenach and Basel programmes was too great. Meanwhile, every endeavour was made to secure a firm footing in Berlin. Liebknecht said at a popular meeting held in Vienna on July 25th, 1869 :—" The citadel of servitude in Prussia is Berlin. When we have stormed this citadel with the help of the Berlin working-men, —since the great battle for the emancipation of Germany is to be fought in Berlin,—where will the small Governments be that now stand in the way? With the Prussian Government they will all fall." But progress was difficult and slow, for Berlin was the seat of the Government and there the vigilance of the police was not to be eluded.

The Eisenach programme sets forth that the primary object of the Social-Democratic Working Men's Party is the establishment of the

Free People's State (*freier Volksstaat*).[1]   But that is not all.   The present political and social conditions are declared to be in the highest degree unjust, and for that reason they are to be combated with all energy.   A leaf is taken out of the book of the International when it is stated that " the struggle for the emancipation of the working classes is not a struggle for class privileges and prerogatives, but for equal rights and equal duties, and for the abolition of all class supremacy."   As the economic dependence of the working-man upon the capitalist is the basis of every form of servitude, the party will strive, by abolishing the present form of production, and by introducing the co-operative system, to secure for the labourer the full fruit of his exertions.   But political freedom is a prior condition of economic emancipation, and as the social problem can only be solved in a Democratic State various political demands are made.   These include universal, equal, and direct suffrage, with secret voting, for all men of twenty years, both in the election of Parliamentary and local administrative bodies ; direct legislation by the people, by which is understood the right of proposing and rejecting laws ; the abolition of all privileges of class, property, birth, and confession ; the substitution of a militia for the standing army ; the separation of the church from the State, and of the school from the church ; compulsory education in elementary schools, and free education in all public seminaries ; independence of the Courts, introduction of juries and courts of trade experts, public and oral judicial proceedings, and free administration of justice ; abolition of all Press, Association, and Coalition Laws, introduction of the normal work-day, the restriction of female and the prohibition of child labour, the abolition of all indirect taxes, and the introduction of a direct progressive income-tax and succession duty ; and finally the furtherance by the State of the co-operative system, with State credit for productive partnerships.

---

[1] The term *freier Volksstaat* hardly explains itself.   It will be well to quote Liebknecht's explanation as given during his trial in 1872.   "The idea ' free people's State ' is interpreted by a majority of our partisans as a Republic ; but does the intention of a forcible introduction of the same follow ?   No man has expressed opinions as to the mode of introducing it.   Let a majority of the people be won for our opinions and the State is of our opinions, for the people is the State.   A State without a king is conceivable, but not a State without a people.   The Government is the servant of the people . . . .   If the introduction of the Republic is legally determined on—as by a Parliament—and the existing Government resists it by force, in my view every citizen is bound to oppose force with force,"

The party adopted as its organ the *Volksstaat*, as the *Demokratisches Wochenblatt* was rechristened, and the work of propagandism was eagerly begun. In June, 1870, a second congress was held at Stuttgart and 66 delegates, representing 113 places and 13,147 members, were present. The Schweitzer party again tried to upset the meeting, but unsuccessfully. Liebknecht gave a glowing report of the work done, but while emphasising the importance of agitation, he recognised the inadequacy of strikes and similar non-political measures to the combating of the wages system. "Only with the fall of the present State in its entirety will a new system of production be possible. We must therefore overpower the State and found a new one, which shall know nothing of class domination, which shall tolerate neither masters nor slaves, and in which society shall be organised on a co-operative basis." Bebel proposed a resolution demanding the conversion of agricultural land into common property, and its lease by the State to associations which should be bound to cultivate it in a scientific way, and to divide the produce amongst the joint producers according to fixed agreement. The State was also called on to establish training schools for the agricultural population. As a transitional measure of confiscation it was proposed that fiscal lands, crown lands, ecclesias-tical and entailed estates, common lands, mines, and railways should be appropriated by the State. The greatest practical achievement of the congress was the union effected with the South German Demo-cratic party. In the same month that the congress was held Bracke issued to the party a manifesto on the subject of the French war, and as it was too national and patriotic Liebknecht was angry and protested. Bracke in his reply said : " Bebel and Liebknecht have estranged our hearts from them. If Liebknecht goes on in this way we shall at the end of the war have left a dozen incarnate Social Republicans and a number of Saxons, who, on account of their Particularism, are far fonder of the far-lying international idea than the near national idea, which since 1866 has, because of its black and white drapery,[1] become offensive to them." The dispute became so serious that Marx was asked to decide, and he naturally took Liebknecht's part, declaring for peace with France and non-annexation of Alsace and Lorraine. After Sedan and the proclamation of the Republic a reconciliation was effected between Liebknecht and Bracke, chiefly owing to the fact that

---

[1] Alluding to the Prussian colours.

the latter took part in the issue of a second " Manifesto to German working-men " in September, 1870, urging them to see that France was allowed to conclude an honourable peace, and to protest against annexation. This conduct was regarded as treasonable, and half-a-dozen members concerned—including Bracke, Bonhorst, and Spier—were arrested and taken in chains to Lötzen. Their trial came off in November of the following year, but as they had been incarcerated during the intervening time they were not further punished. In December, 1870, Liebknecht, Bebel, and Hepner, the responsible editor of the party organ, were also arrested for the publication of treasonable writings. They were tried early in 1872, Liebknecht being sent to prison for two years, and Bebel for two years and nine months, while Hepner was released. The anti-national policy pursued in the party camp was also pursued by the Socialists who held seats in the Reichstag. Holding fast to the idea of a Republic they voted against war grants, and opposed the *Kaiser* and *Reich*. The Reichstag was dissolved in December, and in the succeeding elections the Social-Democrats lost ground.

The congress of 1871, held at Dresden, was attended by 51 delegates, representing 81 places and 6,255 members. The attendance was smaller, as the war had seriously interfered with the organisation of the party. At this congress the question of the normal work-day came into prominence, and working-men were urged to strive for a legally fixed period of work, which should not exceed ten hours, and also to agitate for better protection against danger to life and person. The congress also expressed its approval of the Paris Commune, an act of bad policy, which alienated a large amount of sympathy from the Social-Democratic cause. Soon, however, auspicious events occurred, and the ground lost was won back again. Thus the economic crisis which prevailed in Germany after the war—the crisis which succeeded the historical *Gründungsera*, and which entailed untold misery on the working classes—told greatly in favour of the movement, and the years 1872 to 1874 witnessed a renewal of the growth which in 1870 had been checked. The congress of 1872 was held at Mayence in September. It was reported that the movement had suffered greatly from the war, but that the membership was again increasing, the accession of adherents during the past year having been 4,000. Hitherto the party had observed an attitude of strict neutrality on the question of religion, but it was now resolved, on the proposition of the Bavarian delegates, that members should be desired to withdraw from religious organisations. The next congress was held at Eisenach, the cradle of the party, in August, 1873, but it was only held here because permission to assemble at Nuremberg had been refused by the police. At this meeting 110 places and 9,224 members were represented, and it was reported that the party had secured a footing in 170 towns and villages.

In order to keep this story connected, it will be desirable to trace now the parallel course of the Universal Association, which we left at the resignation of Schweitzer. His successor was Wilhelm Hasenclever, simultaneously with whose election the *Neuer Social-Democrat* was founded. With the retirement of Schweitzer the Universal departed altogether from its programme. He, indeed, had been compelled by stress of circumstances to go farther astray than his judgment approved, but when his influence was no longer present to check the intemperate tendencies of the advanced section, these soon won predominance. The general meeting of 1872 was attended by 44 delegates from 98 places, though there were members in 145 places; and the meeting of 1873, held at Berlin, was attended by 61 delegates, though the organisation had members in about 240 towns and villages. In the following year ten members of the Social-Democratic party, three belonging to the Lassalle and seven to the Eisenach section, were returned to the Reichstag by 450,000 votes. Bebel and Liebknecht were still in prison, but they were nevertheless elected along with Hasenclever, Most,[1] Vahlteich, and others. Socialism was now becoming such a power in the State that the Government determined to be more

[1] Johann Joseph Most, born February 5th, 1846, at Augsburg, is none other than the notorious Anarchist of Chicago. In 1879, he established the famous or infamous *Freiheit* in London, and he now publishes the journal in America. He has written a number of small works for agitation, among them being "Die Kleinbürger und die Sozialdemokratie," "Die Pariser Kommune vor den Berliner Gerichten," "Die Bastille am Plötzensee," (a Berlin gaol), "Die Lösung der sozialen Frage," and "Die sozialen Bewegungen im alten Rom und der Cäsarismus." Most is known for his preaching of murderous doctrines. Only a short time ago, he stood up as the apostle of bloodshed on the occasion of the conviction and sentence of the Chicago Anarchists. But there was a time when he appealed to reason and not force. Thus he closed an address to Berlin working-men in 1876 with the words: "I appeal not to your fists but your heads. I do not recommend to you deeds of violence, but the thorough study of Socialism and the further propagation of the same. Think, and thought will conquer." ("Die Lösung der sozialen Frage.")

stringent, and the first evidence of this resolve was the uncompromising attitude taken up by the police in all parts. This was partly owing to the violent attitude of the Socialistic Press. Thus we find the *Volksstaat* addressing the wealthy classes in words like these: "Think what you will, do what you will, but know once for all—and this holds good for Germany as well as for Spain[1]—you will not escape the revolution : you have only the choice of an easy revolution by means of suitable legislative resolutions, or revolution by the dangerous means of force ; if the latter pleases you better, well and good, it is for you to decide." Doctrines of this sort did the movement no good, and during the summer of 1874 the Universal Association was often molested in Berlin. House searches were made in great number, and when Hasenclever, the president, removed to Bremen, the Association was declared by the police to be dissolved in Prussia under the Association Law of 1850, which forbade the combination of political organisations. The Social-Democratic Working Men's Party shared the same fate, and nearly all the trade associations which had been formed by Schweitzer came likewise beneath the bann of the law. Misfortune brought the two rival parties together, and negotiations for the drawing up of a common programme were entered into by Liebknecht and Geib for the Social-Democrats, and Hasenclever and his henchman Hasselmann[2] for the Lassalle party. Liebknecht's endeavours were at last crowned with success : the German Socialists were united in one body. A congress held at Gotha in May, 1875, completed the union. At this meeting 9000 members of the Eisenach party (representing 144 places), and 15,000 members of the Lassalle party (representing 148 places) were represented, the number of the delegates being 125. The programme then adopted became the basis of the great agitation which followed and extended to all parts of Germany.

The programme of the new Socialist Working Men's Party sets out with the proposition that labour is the source of all wealth and of all culture, and that as universally beneficial labour is only possible through society the entire produce of labour belongs to society as a whole ; while, with universal obligation to labour, each man has a claim upon the produce in accordance with his rational needs. But in

---

[1] Alluding to the revolution which began in Spain in 1872.
[2] Wilhelm Hasselmann, born September 25th, 1844, at Bremen.

the present society the capitalist class monopolises the means of labour, and the consequent subjection of the working classes is the cause of misery and servitude in all forms. In order that labour may be emancipated, society must own in common the means of labour, labour must be based on the principle of co-operation, and the produce must be justly distributed and employed for the publi good. This work of emancipation must be performed by the working classes themselves. Thus the party aims at establishing by lawful means a Free State and a Socialistic Society, at "shattering the iron wages law, abolishing exploitation in every form, and removing all social and political inequalities." Though confining its work within national limits, the party recognises the international character of the labour movement, and is resolved to fulfil all duties which may lead to the realisation of the universal brotherhood of mankind. As a way to the solution of the social problem, the party demands the establishment of Socialistic productive partnerships both for industry and agriculture with State help, and under the "democratic control of the labouring people." A series of demands is then advanced as the basis of the Socialistic State. These demands comprise universal, equal, and direct electoral rights, with secret and obligatory voting, for every subject who has reached the age of twenty years, and that not only for Parliamentary but communal elections. Moreover, the day of election and voting must be a Sunday or a holiday, so that none may be hindered by his work from taking part. Another demand is direct legislation by the people, who shall have power to decide questions of war and peace, and another is the substitution of a militia with universal service for the standing army. All exceptional laws, as the Press, Coalition, and Assembly Laws, and all laws restricting the free expression of opinion and free thought, are to be repealed. The administration of the law is to be gratuitous. The State is to provide adequate and equal instruction for the youth of the nation, and this instruction is to be free, while all educational seminaries are to offer gratuitous training, and religion is to be regarded as a private matter. A number of requirements are also made as the basis of society as distinguished from the State. Political rights and liberties are to be extended as much as possible in the sense of the foregoing demands. There shall be no indirect taxation, which falls especially heavily upon the popular classes, but a single progressive income-tax both for State and parish. The right of coalition shall be unrestricted. As to labour, a normal workday suited to the needs of society shall be fixed, and Sunday work shall be prohibited, as well as all juvenile work and such female work as may be objectionable on sanitary and moral grounds. Laws providing security for the life and health of the working man, sanitary control of artisans' dwellings, surveillance of mines, factories, workshops, and house industries by officials chosen by the workmen, and laws rendering employers responsible for the persons of their workpeople shall also be adopted. Finally, prison labour shall be subject to regulations, and complete self-control be given to all workmen's relief societies.

The energy with which agitation was carried on by the party may be judged from statements made in the report presented to the congress held at Gotha in August, 1876. During the first fourteen months of the party's existence 53,973 marks were placed at the disposal of the committee for the purpose of propagandism, and this amount was almost wholly " contributed by working-men who, under the pressure of the capitalistic mode of production and of the prevailing commercial crisis, are scarcely able to earn enough to provide the necessaries of life for themselves and their families." There were already 145 agitators at work, and the newspapers advocating the cause were 23 in number with 100,000 subscribers. The report, in fact, showed perfect organisation. In the following year it could be reported that receipts of 54,217 marks had been received and that the party had 41 newspapers, 13 of which appeared daily. The congress of the International held at Ghent in 1877 recognised the " magnificent organisation " of the German Socialist party, and recommended it as a model for other countries. The German Government also observed the perfection of this organisation and the success of the agitation which was being carried on, and already was devising means for checkmating both.

CHAPTER XIII.

THE INTERNATIONAL ASSOCIATION.

THOUGH not strictly a German organisation, the International Working Men's Association, or the "Red International," as it is often called, cannot be regarded as independent of German Socialism. Not only was a German Communist its founder, but it has exercised an incalculable influence upon the Socialist party in Germany, especially in the perfecting of its agitation and the moulding of its policy and its programme.[1] As early as the year 1840 endeavours had been made to bring the working-men of various countries together. In 1839 a number of German working-men were expelled from Paris, where their presence was considered dangerous, and they took refuge in London. Here they formed in the following year a "Deutscher Arbeiter-Bildungsverein," an association whose purpose was nominally the intellectual advancement of working-men, but which gave to political ends especial prominence. The statutes of this association were printed in several languages, and its members included, besides Germans, Englishmen, Hungarians, Poles, Danes and Swedes, for the most part political outlaws and malcontents. The association adopted the Chartist programme and corresponded with German working-men's organisations in France and Switzerland. But the "Deutscher Arbeiter-Bildungsverein" did not make any great stir in the world, and even when it took the name of the Society of the Fraternal Democrats its influence continued small. Fresh impulse was given to international co-operation by the publication of the Communist Manifesto of Marx and Engels, already mentioned, on the occasion of a conference of German Communists held in London in 1847. These

---

[1] Among the best German works on the International are R. Meyer's "Emancipationskampf," already referred to; Dr. E. Jäger's "Der moderne Socialismus" (Berlin, 1873); W. Eichkoff's "Die Internationale Arbeiterassociation" (Berlin, 1868); and C. Hillmann's small work with the same title (1871). Of French works may be named Edmond Villetard's "Histoire de l'Internationale" (Paris, 1872), which deals fully with the movement in France; Oscar Testut's "Le livre bleu de l'Internationale" (Paris, 1871); and Laveleye's "Le Socialisme contemporain" (Brussels, 1881).

two men, the Hengest and Horsa of modern aggressive Communism, were commissioned by the " League of Communists " with the drawing up of a programme for the party, and the Manifesto [1] was the successful result.

In this historic work stress is laid upon the social as distinguished from the purely national character of the labourers' question. All society is divided into the two great camps of the *bourgeoisie* and the *proletariat*, and it is the object of Communism to break down the wall of partition, and to place all classes on the same basis both by levelling up and levelling down, so that there may be only one all-embracing class. The Manifesto examines the mode of production which has given rise to the *proletariat*, whose growth keeps pace with the development of capitalism. Labour is bought by the capitalist like any article of trade, and like all commodities it is subject to the vicissitudes of competition and to all oscillations of the market. The price of a commodity is equal to the cost of its production, so that labour may be purchased for the cost of supporting the labourer and of propagating his species. The Manifesto says that the Communists do not form a special labourers' party independent of other labourers' parties. They have no interests which differ from those of the entire *proletariat*, nor do they advance particular principles according to which the *proletariat* must proceed. The only difference at all is that the Communists stand upon a social and therefore an international basis. They demand that private property shall be abolished, the *bourgeoisie* be hurled from its place of domination, equality be introduced in society, and the family cease to exist. It is often contended by critics more or less favourable to the Communist programme that the revolution proposed in the family relationship is not so great as it appears. Let us take the actual words of the Manifesto :

" Abolition of the family ! Even the most radical grow warm at this shameful intention of the Communists. But on what does the present, the civil, family rest ? On capital, on private gain. It only exists fully developed for the *bourgeoisie ;* but it is supplemented by the enforced childlessness of the *proletariat* and by public prostitution. The family of the *bourgeois* will naturally cease with the cessation of

[1] A preface to the third German edition of 1872 gives a short account of the origin of the Manifesto, which had up to that year been twelve times published in Germany, England and America.

this supplement; and both will disappear with the disappearance of capital. Do you charge us with desiring to put an end to the exploitation of children by their parents? We admit the crime. But, you say, we abolish the dearest relationships when we replace domestic by social training. Yet is not your training determined by society—by the social relationships amidst which you are brought up, by the direct or indirect interference of society, by means of the school, &c.? The Communists do not originate this interference of society in the training of children; they only change its character, they liberate the training from the influence of the ruling class. The talk of the *bourgeoisie* about the family and training, about the 'dear relationship' between parents and children, becomes all the more nauseous, the more, in consequence of industry being carried on upon a large scale, all family ties are broken for the *proletariat*, and children are converted into mere articles of trade and instruments of labour. ' But you Communists wish to introduce community of wives,' shrieks the entire *bourgeoisie* in chorus. The *bourgeois* regards his wife as a mere instrument of production. He hears that the instruments of production are to be exploited in common, and he cannot help thinking that community of wives will take place at the same time. He has no idea that the very thing in view is the abolition of woman's position as a pure instrument of production. Moreover, is there anything more ridiculous than the highly moral horror of our *bourgeois* at the official community of wives which the Communists are supposed to desire? The Communists have no need to introduce community of wives, for it has almost always existed. Our *bourgeois*, not satisfied that the wives and daughters of the *proletariat* are at their disposal—not to speak of official prostitution—find in the mutual seduction of their wives one of their chief pleasures. The civil marriage is in reality community of wives. At the most the Communists could be reproached for wishing to introduce an official and ingenuous, instead of a hypocritical and clandestine community of wives. Besides, it is self-evident that with the abolition of the present conditions of production, the community of wives to which they give rise, that is, official and unofficial prostitution, will disappear."

As transitional measures, leading up to the complete emancipation of the *proletariat*, the Manifesto advances: the expropriation of landed property and the employment of the rent for State purposes; a heavy

progressive tax ; the abolition of hereditary right ; the confiscation of
the property of emigrants and rebels ; the centralisation of credit in
the hands of the State by the establishment of a National Bank with
State capital and absolute monopoly ; the centralisation of the entire
transport system in the hands of the State ; the increase of national
manufactories and instruments of production, and the reclamation
and improvement of land according to a common plan ; equal compulsion to work on everyone ; the institution of "industrial armies,"
especially for agriculture ; the union of agriculture and industry for
the gradual removal of the distinction between town and country ; the
public and gratuitous education of all children, the abolition of juvenile labour in manufactories in its present form, and the association of
education with material production.

In conclusion, the Manifesto declares the policy of the Communists
to be that of combination with either friends or foe for the purpose of
combating the institutions against which they have declared war. Every
revolutionary movement aimed at the existing social and political
order of things will have their support. "Communists labour everywhere for the combination and reconciliation of the democratic parties
of all countries. The Communists disdain to conceal their opinions
and intentions. They declare openly that their purposes can only be
attained by the forcible subversion of all existing social arrangements.
Let the ruling classes tremble in view of a Communistic Revolution !
The *proletariat* has nothing to lose but its chains. It has a world to
win. *Proletariat* of all countries, unite ! "

The immediate success of the Manifesto was not great. The time
was hardly ripe for such a proclamation, and it only began to be famous a dozen years later. The League had later its seat at Cologne,
but it did not accomplish any great work. Until 1862 the Communists
were very quiet, but in that year events occurred to rouse them again
to activity. It was the year of the London Exhibition, and under the
auspices of the Emperor Napoleon III., a number of Paris working-
men visited the English capital. They were welcomed by a London
committee of artisans, and on this occasion the wish for a closer
union between the labourers of different countries was expressed on
both sides. Then the Polish insurrection broke out, and masses of
London and Paris working-men took steps simultaneously to manifest
sympathy with the insurgents. A deputation was again sent over

from Paris, and the result of this measure was a resolution to delay preparations for co-operation no longer. For some time the international idea was carefully given prominence in labour circles in various countries, and on September 28th, 1864, a congress of many nations was held in St. Martin's Hall, London, under the presidency of Professor Beesly. A committee was appointed, representing England, France, Germany, Italy, Poland, and Switzerland, for the drawing up of statutes for an International Working Men's Association, whose seat should be London. The German members of the committee were Marx and Eccarius, and the English members were twenty-seven in number. While Englishmen were chosen as president, secretary, and treasurer of the general council, corresponding secretaries were appointed for the affiliated countries, and Marx naturally received the office for Germany. At first the Association had the help of no less a man than Mazzini, but Marx and he were never friends, and it was soon seen that one of the two would have to give way and retire. Mazzini sought to establish the Association upon a thoroughly international basis, but the statutes he proposed were not suited to an organisation which intended to carry on active agitation. Moreover, he was too temperate a man for the International, and he failed to win great sympathy. Then Marx produced an inaugural address and a draft of statutes, and both were at once adopted. Marx thus found himself at the head of the organisation. This reverse was too much for Mazzini, and he withdrew from association with the movement, and did his best to prevent it from setting foot in Italy.[1] In his inaugural address Marx dwelt upon the want prevailing amongst the working classes, want which had continued undiminished since 1848, though the propertied classes had become more prosperous. He held it to be incontrovertibly proved that the perfection of machinery, the utilisation of science in industry and agriculture, the extension of markets, artificial measures like colonisation and emigration, as well as free

[1] Addressing a body of Italian working-men in 1871, Mazzini said he refused to co-operate with the International though pressed to do so. He said : " With this Association, founded in London several years ago, I have from the outset refused to co-operate. It is conducted by a general council, whose soul is Karl Marx. The latter is a German, a man of acute but destructive spirit, like Proudhon, of imperious temperament, and jealous of the influence of others. He believes strongly neither in philosophical nor religious truths, and, as I had reason to fear, hatred outweighs love in his heart, which is not right even if the hatred may in itself have foundation." Mazzini would thus appear to have assisted the founders of the Association only so long as he saw a chance of thwarting the Marx tendency.

trade were all unable to relieve the condition of the labouring population. Asking for a remedy, he found it in co-operative labour developed to national dimensions and promoted by State resources. But as the land-owning and capitalist classes would be sure to use their political privileges for the defence of their economic monopolies, the working classes must first acquire political power. They possessed one element of strength, that of numbers, but numbers without union were of no avail, and thus it was a paramount duty to combine for mutual defence and offence. "*Proletariat* of all countries," ended the address, "unite!" The statutes of the Association advance the claims of the working classes in a series of propositions. The emancipation of these classes, it is said, must be brought about by themselves, but the struggle for this emancipation does not signify a struggle for class privileges and monopolies, rather for equal rights and duties and for the abolition of all class domination. The dependence of the labourer upon the monopolist of the instruments of labour, the source of life, is at the root of all servitude, social misery, intellectual degradation, and political subjection; for which reason the economic emancipation of the working classes must be the great aim, and political movements must be subordinated to this aim. In the past all efforts on behalf of this emancipation have failed for lack of union amongst the labourers of different countries, and as this is not a local or even national, but in the widest sense of the word a social problem, the working classes should combine in an international organisation. The statutes declare that truth, justice, and morality are the basis of the dealings of members both with each other and all mankind. The watchword is "No rights without duties, no duties without rights."

It was not long before the International Association became a power which caused alarm to not a few European Governments. The first congress was to have been held at Brussels, but the Belgian Government refused to allow the meeting to take place, and the consequence was that a mere conference was held in London in September. The reports from the Continent were not very cheering. Italy had, owing to the influence of Mazzini, severed connection with the Association; in France the police were ruling with a high hand; in Belgium no one appeared to care to take the initiative; only in Switzerland were things prospering. The first real congress was held in 1866 at Geneva, and it sat from September 3rd to 10th. Sixty delegates of affiliated Working Men's Associations attended, seventeen being from France, seven from London, and several from Germany. Here the statutes were adopted, and the administrative machinery was properly set to work. In the discussion which took place on factory employment, it was demanded that children from nine to twelve years of age should not be allowed to work longer than two hours daily in factories and workshops, children of from thirteen to fifteen not more than four hours, and those between sixteen and seventeen years not more than six hours. In any case, proper care must be taken by the employer for the education of children working for him. Other resolutions were adopted in favour of Trades Unions, of direct taxation, of the abolition of standing armies, and the independence of Poland. An interesting point had to be settled in the consideration of the statutes. How was the term *proletariat* to be defined? Was it to mean hand-workers without head-workers, or was it to embrace both? It was a knotty as well as a delicate question to decide, for Marx and his associates could not be admitted to the Association if the word were given the narrower signification, as the French delegates desired. It was resolved to make the term comprehensive in the hope of gaining intellectual as well as numerical strength. Already the International was able to boast of quite a host of helpers in the Press. It had four organs in Germany—the *Social-Democrat*, Berlin; the *Deutsche Arbeiterzeitung*, Coburg; the *Nordstern*, Hamburg; and the *Correspondent*, Leipzig; six in Switzerland, four in Paris, two in London, and one in Belgium.

The second congress was held at Lausanne from September 2nd to 8th, 1867 A decidedly Communistic direction was taken by the proceedings this year. I· was resolved that the Association should aim at making the State the owner of all means of transport and communication—railways, canals, highways. A resolution was also brought forward calling for the abolition of hereditary rights and of private property in land and instruments of labour, but a decision was not arrived at on these questions. A qualified approval was given to the endeavours being made in various countries—especially Germany and England—to found Productive Associations for the labouring class, and as a means of raising wages the strike system was commended.

No sooner had the Geneva congress of 1866 been held, than the French Government sharpened its repressive weapons, and so closely were the adherents of the International pursued that before the year 1868 was out the French Association had to be dissolved. Still, the members of the expired organisation preserved their association with the parent society. Italy was now coming round, and a journal in Naples vigorously championed the cause of the International. The third congress took place September 5th to 11th, 1868, in Brussels. The delegates only fell two short of a hundred, and the countries represented were this year seven in number : Germany, England, France, Belgium, Switzerland, Italy, and Spain. This was essentially a Communistic co￭gress. At Lausanne it had been resolved that means of communication should be appropriated by the State. Now land, mines, quarries, forests, and telegraphs were added to the railways and canals : all must pass into the hands of the community, and by the community be employed for the universal welfare. Another blessing was pronounced upon strikes, but it was acknowledged that they could not be expected to make the working classes free and needed to be properly organised. Allied associations were recommended to take steps for the education of the working classes. At this congress, too, the cry of " The produce for the producer " was raised. Rent, interest, and profit of all kinds must cease to exist : labour must be rewarded with the entire produce.

The anti-religious tendency of the Association showed itself in the words with which the president closed the congress :—"We want no more Governments, for Governments oppress us by taxes ; we want no armies, for armies massacre and murder us ; we want no religion, for religions choke the understanding." More outspokenly anti-religious, however, was the programme of the " Alliance internationale de la Democratie Socialiste " formed at this time by the Nihilist, Michael Bakunin, of members who had seceded from the International. The rival organisation did not prosper, and it was dissolved in 1871. Both in 1867 and 1868 unfavourable reports were read to the congress from Germany. It was stated that progress was very slow, for branches of the association could not legally exist in the country.

Better prospects were offered to the International in Germany in the year 1869, when the Social-Democratic Party was formed at Eisenach with a programme based on the principles expounded by Marx. This year, indeed, the International flourished remarkably

Q

owing to the economic crisis which visited the industrial countries of
Europe, and from Germany, France, Belgium, and Italy the rosiest of
reports could be sent to the Council in London. Branches were also
established in Austria and Holland. This year's congress was held
at Basel, September 6th to 9th, and eighty delegates were present.
The resolutions adopted emphasised the necessity existing for the
abolition of private property in land and its conversion into common
property. The question of hereditary rights again came up, but no
decision was come to. The recommendation was issued to allied
associations that they should promote the formation of Trades
Unions, whose success in England made a great impression upon the
congress.

In 1870 occurred the war between Germany and France. It had
been decided to hold a congress in Paris in September, but events
prevented the assembling of delegates this year. But the International
was not slow to profit by the stormy occurrences of this memorable
year. Several manifestoes were issued relative to the war. The first,
which appeared on June 23rd,[1] declared the war to be for Germany
one of defence, and called upon the *proletariat* to see that it remained
such. On September 9th, when the German army, flushed with
victory, was advancing on Paris, an urgent appeal was issued to the
labouring classes of all countries to endeavour to prevent the war
from becoming a war of conquest, and another manifesto followed the
fall of the Commune. Marx actually claimed that the International
had a hand in the September Revolution, and he is said to have
planned risings in various parts of Europe, including the large towns
of Germany.

Neither in 1870 nor 1871 could a congress be held, but in the latter
year a conference took place in London, September 17th to 23rd.
The resolutions related chiefly to administrative and statutary questions.
It was reported that the International had now branches in Sweden,
Portugal, and Denmark. Long before this the German Social-
Democratic party had fully accepted the programme of the Association,
thanks to the zeal of Liebknecht and Bebel, and in 1871 Bebel publicly
declared that while the actual number of members in Germany was
only a thousand, all Social-Democrats were virtual adherents of the
International. It is, however, difficult to say how far the published

---

[1] War was formally proclaimed by France on July 19th, 1870.

reports of the Association are to be relied on when avowals like the following, which came to light during a Socialistic trial at Leipzig, have been made. Marx wrote to Bracke on March 24th, 1870 : " I beg you to remember that the report [respecting the state of the movement in Germany] is not written for the public, and *therefore* it exhibits the facts without varnish, and quite true to the actual state of things."

In 1872 a congress was held at the Hague early in September. Sixty-five delegates were present,—twenty-five representing German associations or bearing German names,—and thirteen countries took part, Germany, England, Ireland, Holland, France, Belgium, Denmark, Switzerland, Spain, Portugal, Hungary, the United States, and Australia. The congress was one of the most important held. An endeavour was made by one party to abolish the General Council, and by another to define its powers ; but Marx stood up boldly for his prerogatives, and by getting the seat of the Council removed from London to New York, he succeeded in preserving its functions and powers almost intact. Still, there was serious disagreement on the subject, and the breach thus caused was never properly healed. The minority of Spanish, Belgian, Dutch, and Jura delegates whose proposals Marx succeeded in defeating went so far as to enter formal protest against the decisions finally arrived at. One of the principal resolutions adopted at this congress urged the formation of the labouring classes into a political party, whose aim it should be to combat the existing social system with all energy. Before the delegates dispersed a meeting was held by invitation at Amsterdam, and Marx there made a speech in which he proclaimed in the plainest terms the doctrine of revolution. He said :

" We do not deny that there are countries, as America, England, and Holland, where working-men can reach their ends by pacific means. If this is true we must still acknowledge that in most Continental countries force must be the lever of our revolution : we must appeal to force in order to establish the supremacy of the working class." Then, referring to himself, he said, " I shall work away at my task, I shall not withdraw from the International, and the remainder of my life will, like the past, be devoted to the triumph of the social ideas which we are sure will one day bring about the rule of the *proletariat.*" The result of this congress was that the German delegates were divided into opposite camps, one part adhering closely to Marx, and the other seeking to check his power. The dissidents for a time withdrew from the International. This year an attempt was made by the Spanish Government to induce other Governments to combine for the suppression of the International, but England refused to unite, as English laws had so far not been transgressed, and the plan fell to the ground.

The succeeding congress was held at Geneva in September, 1873. On January 5th the General Council had suspended the Jura Federation for contumacy, and on the 9th it prepared to excommunicate on a larger scale by the adoption and promulgation of a resolution which declared that "societies or persons refusing to acknowledge the decisions of the congress, or knowingly neglecting duties imposed by the statutes and the orders of the administration, exclude themselves from the International Working Men's Association and cease to be members of the same." On account of this resolution federations in England, Belgium, Switzerland, Italy, and Spain ceded or were expelled. The General Council called a congress at Geneva for September 8th, and the excluded federations called a congress at the same place for the 1st of the month. The result of the rival congress was an attempt at reconciliation, but it proved futile. All that the seceded associations objected to was the dictatorial power reposed in the president Marx. Had this been broken down, the secession would not have occurred. The seceders decided to form a new International, and new statutes were drawn up, but the old name was preserved. In the new organisation branch associations were allowed greater independence of action, and the administrative power was restricted. The proceedings of his opponents must have been galling to Marx, for not only did the dissentients represent six countries, but his personal friend Eccarius had gone over to the enemy's camp. The second International began its career with every promise of success. Though the Universal Working Men's Association established by Lassalle in Germany had kept aloof from Marx, it cordially fraternised with his rivals, and sent a telegram of congratulation to the opposition congress. Oddly enough as it sounds, the seceders declared the old International to be defunct. This, however, did not prevent the holding of the congress called by Marx for the second week in September. This congress lasted from the 8th to the 13th of the month, and thirty delegates were present from Germany, France, England, and Switzerland. Favourable reports were presented from Germany, where a fortnight before an important Socialist congress had been held at Eisenach. It was stated that an unwearied agitation was being carried on in the country, and that Social-Democratic ideas were now propagated in " every village and out-of-the-way corner." The Socialist Press also did good work, the organs of the party including eleven ordinary newspapers, mostly appearing daily, and many trade journals. The political organisation of the working classes was again considered, and a resolution was passed for giving federate associations a free hand. It was also decided to hold biennial congresses for the future.

Of later congresses held at the instigation of Marx, the only one calling here for notice is that of Ghent. This was an International Socialist Congress and it met from September 9th to 15th, 1877. Delegates were present from Germany, England, France, Belgium, Denmark, Austria, Hungary, Switzerland, and Italy. It was a mixed gathering of extremists and moderates, of Marxians and independents. Liebknecht represented the Social-Democratic party of Germany, and continued true to his old leader. In this congress there was a lively debate on the question of the appropriation of not only land but all means of production by the State on behalf of society. This was the proposal of the adherents of Marx, who demanded that the State should alone regulate production and consumption. This was Communism pure and simple, and half-a-dozen years ago it would have satisfied everybody. But the followers of the Nihilist Bakunin were not contented ; they would accept nothing less than the total abolition of the State—in other words, absolute anarchy. This one of the delegates avowed, when he objected : "Communism is community and government, but Anarchism is community and anarchy," and this he wanted. Marx, however, won the day, and thus showed the world that his star was still in the ascendant, but the majority in his favour was small. It seemed as though the Communists were out-Marxing Marx in the extremeness of their demands. The proceedings of the congress made it clear that the half-heartedness with which participation in political life was formerly regarded, had entirely disappeared, for a resolution was passed urging the *proletariat* to employ all possible means of exerting an influence in politics with a view to ultimate social emancipation. A Universal Union of International

Socialism was formed, with an office in Ghent, and a manifesto was shortly afterwards issued to the Socialist working-men's organisations in England, France, Belgium, Denmark, Germany, Austria-Hungary, Switzerland, and Italy, in which the demands of earlier congresses were reiterated, and especial stress was laid upon the importance of political agitation, since "social emancipation is inseparable from political emancipation," and political action may be made "a powerful means of propaganda, popular education, and organisation." The manifesto ended with the old cry, "*Proletariat* of all countries, unite!"

The International had by this time become almost superfluous, for it had placed the Socialist movement in Europe upon such a firm basis that it could be carried on in the individual countries independently of any guiding organisation. Marx lived to see his labours in the cause of international co-operation completely rewarded, though when he died in 1883 the goal for which he had for half a century striven remained still out of sight. His Communism is yet a theory. Nowadays, the International Association is seldom mentioned in Germany, but in the United States it enjoys more or less success. A mass meeting held in New York shortly after the death of its founder vowed fidelity to the principles of the departed leader. "We pledge ourselves," said the meeting, "to keep his name and his works ever in remembrance, and to do our utmost for the dissemination of the ideas given by him to the world. We promise, in honour of the memory of our great departed, to dedicate our lives to the cause of which he was a pioneer—the struggle in which he left so noble a record—and never at any moment to forget his great appeal, 'Workmen of the world, unite!'" The same resolution was adopted by a large assembly at Chicago, where several Anarchists were executed last November for complicity in a series of heinous murders.

CHAPTER XIV.

THE ERA OF REPRESSION.

ANOTHER epoch in the history of German Socialism has now been reached, and it is the epoch of Repression, which began in the year 1878, when the German Reichstag passed the now celebrated Socialist Law. For years the Government had watched the progress of the movement with growing alarm and uneasiness. It had not only seen the Socialist party envelop the country with an agitation and an organisation unparalleled in German history, but it had also observed the gradual strengthening of the party in the Legislature of the Empire as well as in the Diets of some of the States. It had become at last a hydra exciting no less wonder than fear, and the Government resolved, if tardily, that an earnest attempt must be made to grapple with and overcome the monster. How far this decision was wise and how far the later measures have been just are not questions with which we have to do, seeing that we are dealing with pure history. Prince Bismarck has put it upon record that he first saw danger in the Social-Democratic agitation when in the first session of the new Reichstag a benediction was pronounced upon the Paris Commune. Up to then he had taken a lively interest in the movement, without regarding it as necessarily a source of peril to the State. But the time came when his opinions were to undergo a thorough change.

"It was the moment when in the assembled Reichstag either Deputy Bebel or Liebknecht in pathetic appeal held up the French Commune as a model of political institutions, and openly confessed before the nation the gospel of the Paris murderers and incendiaries. From that moment I experienced a full conviction of the danger which threatened us. . That appeal to the Commune was a ray of light upon the matter, and from that moment I regarded the Social-Democratic elements as an enemy against which the State and society must arm themselves."[1]

[1] Speech in the Reichstag, September 17th, 1878.

The Parliamentary strength of the Socialist party at the time we have reached may be shown by comparative figures, embracing the elections to the Reichstag from its constitution to the year 1877. The number of members in the Reichstag is fixed by article 20 of the constitution at 382, but from the election of 1874 the number has been 397 owing to the addition of 15 deputies from Alsace and Lorraine. In 1871 the Socialists returned only 2 members, exclusive of a member of the so-called *Volkspartei*, an insignificant section of the extreme Liberal Left, one of the first leaders of which, Jacoby, went over to Socialism. Three years later the Socialist members numbered 9 and in 1877 they had increased to 12. Saxony returned 2 Socialists in 1871, 6 in 1874, and 7 in 1877 ; Prussia returned 3 in 1874, and 4 in 1877 ; and in 1877 the Principality of Reuss a. L. returned one Socialist. The votes polled were as follows during these elections :

First ordinary voting for candidates contesting.

	1871	1874	1877
Total poll......	3,892,160	5,190,254	5,401,021
Socialist party	124,665	351,952	493,288

In point of numbers polled, the Socialist party in the last year took the fifth place amongst the fourteen parties returning candidates, while in point of Parliamentary strength its place was the eighth. The deputies returned by the Socialist party in 1877 included Liebknecht, Bebel, Hasselmann, Hasenclever, Most, Bracke, Fritzsche, and Vahlteich.

As early as 1871 Prince Bismarck had vainly appealed to the Governments of Europe to combine for the purpose of withstanding the enemy which confronted them. Naturally, therefore, the German Government seconded the proposals made by Spain in 1872 for the suppression by common European action of the International Association, which was rightly considered to be the root of the evil. The circular which the Spanish Foreign Minister addressed to the Powers on the subject was dated February 9th, 1872. It expressed the sanguine expectation that " in view of the urgency of the case," every State would be only too ready to take up arms against the universal foe. Lord Granville, however, speaking for the British Government, declined to co-operate, as such a step would be contrary both to the letter and the spirit of the British law. Foreigners, he said, in a despatch of March 8th, were secured by law an unrestricted right of residence in England, and so long as the law of the country was not violated it would not be possible to interfere. This attitude of the British Government gave displeasure to more than one of the Powers, and the semi-official *North German Gazette* of Berlin grumbled loudly in an article published on April 17th. Here, however, the matter dropped for the time being. The German Government next tried to reach the Socialist agitation by means of a gag upon the Press. In May, 1874, when the Imperial Press Law was under consideration, a provision was introduced which would have enabled the Executive to place a severe check upon the publication of objectionable prints. This provision was to the effect that any person who held up disrespect for the law as " something allowable or meritorious " would be liable to two years' imprisonment or, if extenuating circumstances existed, to a fine of 600 marks. The Reichstag, however, declined to sanction this proposal and also another of a more mildly repressive kind, holding that they struck at the root of the freedom of the Press. Two years later the Government made another attempt in the same direction, proposing that the excitement of various classes of the population to acts of violence and attacks upon the institutions of marriage, the family, and property—whether by speech or writings—should be punishable. Again, however, the Reichstag was obdurate.

What finally brought the Legislature over to Prince Bismarck's views, when argument and persuasion proved futile, were acts which threw all Germany into perturbation. On May 11th, 1878, while driving in the Linden, in Berlin, with his daughter the Grand Duchess of Baden, the Emperor William was shot at by a young man named Hödel, an ignorant fellow of low character. Two shots were fired from a pistol but both failed to take effect. The scene of the attempted assassination was near that of the attempt of Blind upon Bismarck on May 7th, 1866. The nation was horrified, and it was quite in accordance with its passionate desire that somebody should suffer, that two days later an Anti-Socialist Bill was introduced in the Reichstag. The conviction was widely shared that Hödel, who three months later suffered death at Berlin, was an instrument of the Social-Democratic party, and natural conclusions were drawn from the fact that when captured photographs of Liebknecht, Bebel, and other prominent Socialist leaders were found on his person. The coercive law—" Law for the check of Social-Democratic excesses " (*Gesetz zur Abwehr socialdemokratischer Ausschreitungen*)—was debated during May, at a time when the Anarchist Most was being prosecuted in Berlin for libelling the clergy. The Socialist Deputies denounced the proposals as an "unexampled attempt on popular freedom," and indeed they were extreme. Associations and prints which furthered the ends of Social-Democracy might be prohibited by the Bundesrath, whose prohibitions should be notified to the Reichstag, which had a power of veto. The circulation of objectionable prints in public streets, roads, and places was forbidden, and while offenders made themselves liable to severe punishment the publications were to be confiscated. The right of public meeting was also restricted. The Government was defeated ; the Reichstag by a majority of 251 votes to 57 rejected the first paragraph of the bill, and the measure was consequently withdrawn. No sooner had the Reichstag refused to pass the law than another attempt was made upon the life of the aged sovereign. This time the would-be assassin was a Dr. Karl Nobiling, who on June 2nd, 1878, fired at the Emperor from an upper window in the Linden and severely wounded him. Great as was the indignation of the nation before, it was now infinitely greater, and the cry for repressive measures against the Socialists became general. Yet so far were many people from comprehending the strength of the foe which they desired to overcome, that proposals such as the expulsion of all Social-Democrats from the country and the refusal of employment to all persons avowing Socialistic principles were commonly advocated. The Chancellor thought he knew of a more excellent way of dealing with the difficulty , he would take steps to suppress agitation. A general election took place, and the constitution of the new Reichstag was such as to enable Prince Bismarck to carry out his will. In the assembly of 1877 there was a strong Liberal majority, but the election of 1878 showed a decided reaction. The German Conservatives increased their strength from 40 to 59, and the Imperial party (Free Conservatives) advanced from 38 to 57, while the National Liberals fell from 128 to 99, the Liberals from 13 to 10, and the Progressists from 35 to 26. The Socialists only succeeded in retaining 9 of their 12 seats, and their aggregate poll in the first elections fell from 493,288 to 437,158 votes. With such a Reichstag, Bismarck could do pretty nearly as he liked.

Another law was now proposed—the " Law against the publicly-dangerous endeavours of Social-Democracy" (*Gesetz gegen die gemein-gefährlichen Bestrebungen der Socialdemokratie*). The bill as introduced consisted of twenty-two clauses, and as approved it gave to the Executive and the police, as will shortly be seen, very extensive powers. The statement accompanying the bill in which the Government justified the powers sought for referred to the two attempts made upon the Emperor, the result of which was a firm conviction on the part of the Federal Governments that repression was imperative. This *Begründung* also set forth :

"The endeavours of Social-Democracy are aimed at the practica realisation of the radical theories of modern Socialism and Communism. According to these theories the present system of production is un-economical, and must be rejected as an unjust exploitation of labour by capital. Labour is to be emancipated from capital ; private capital is to be converted into collective capital ; individual production, regulated by competition, is to be converted into systematic co-operative production ; and the individual is to be absorbed in society. The Social-Democratic movement differs greatly from all humanitarian movements in that it proceeds from the assumption that the ameliora-tion of the condition of the working classes is impossible on the basis of the present social system, and can only be attained by the social revolution spoken of. This social revolution is to be affected by the co-operation of the working classes of all States, with the simultaneous subversion of the existing constitutions. The movement has especially taken this revolutionary and international character since the founda-tion of the International Working Men's Association in London, in September, 1864. . . . It is, in fact, a question of breaking away from the legal development of civilised States, and of the complete subver-sion of the prevailing system of property. The organisation of the *proletariat,* the destruction of the existing order of State and society, and the establishment of the Socialistic community and the Socialistic State by the organised *proletariat*—these are the avowed aims of Social-Democracy. The well-organised Socialistic agitation, carried on by speech and writings with passionate energy, is in accord with these ends. This agitation seeks to disseminate amongst the poor and less educated classes of the population, discontent with their lot as well as the conviction that under the present *régime* their condition is hopeless and to excite them as the "disinherited" to envy and hatred of the upper classes. The moral and religious convictions which hold society together are shattered ; reverence and piety are ridiculed ; the legal notions of the masses are confused ; and respect for the law is destroyed. The most odious attacks and abuse which are levelled at the German Empire and its institutions—at royalty and the army, whose glorious history is slandered,—give the Socialist agitation in this country a specifically anti-national stamp ; for it estranges the minds of the people from native customs and from the Fatherland. The representations which are given, both by spoken and written word, of former revolu·tionary events and the glorification of well-known leaders of revolution, as well as the acts of the Paris Commune, are calculated to excite revolutionary desires and passions, and to dispose the masses to acts of violence. . . . The law of self-preservation, therefore, compels the State and society to oppose the Social-Democratic movement with decision ; and, above all, the State is bound to protect the legal system which is threatened by Social-Democracy, and to put restraints upon Socialistic agitation. True, thought cannot be repressed by external compulsion ; the movements of minds can only be overcome in intel·lectual combat. Still, when such movements take wrong ways and threaten to become destructive, the means for their extension can and should be taken away by legal means. The Socialistic agitation, as carried on for years, is a continual appeal to violence and to the passions of the masses with a view to the subversion of State and social order. The State *can* check such an enterprise as this, by depriving Social-Democracy of its most important means of agitation, and by destroying its organisation ; and it *must* do this unless it is willing to surrender its existence, and unless there is to grow up amongst the population the conviction either that the State is impotent, or that the aims of Social-Democracy are justifiable. . . . Social-Democracy has declared war against the State and society, and has proclaimed their subversion to be its aim. It has thus forsaken the ground of equal right for all, and it cannot complain if the law should only be exercised in its favour to the extent consistent with the security and order of the State."

Such was the heavy indictment brought by the Government against Socialism on the momentous occasion of its demand for exceptional coercive laws. The debate which took place on the bill was one of historical importance, for Prince Bismarck expounded his economic and social views with a freedom and candour which astonished many, and paved the way for an open avowal of the policy of State Socialism. The debate on the first reading was begun on September 16th, and it lasted two long days. The Socialist party endeavoured to clear itself of complicity in the two attempts on the Emperor, but it was answered that even although Hödel and Nobiling might not have been the emissaries of the party, the very essence of Socialism and Communism was hatred of the ruling classes. Bebel declared :

"We wish to abolish the present form of private property in the instruments of production and means of labour, as well as in land. That is a fact which we have never denied. But so far Social-Democracy has never forcibly taken or destroyed private property to the value of a nickel *Fünfer'* [5 *Pfennig* or about $\frac{1}{2}$d.], nor does it wish to attack private property with the intention of ruining the individuals."

On this ground he opposed a bill that proposed to attack the legally-acquired property of Socialists and their sympathisers by the confiscation of newspapers and publications. He twitted Prince Bismarck for associating with Socialists like Lassalle, an act which could only serve to confirm the working classes in the belief that their Socialistic convictions were right, and instanced Rodbertus, Von Thünen, Rau,[1] Lange, Schäffle, Roscher,[2] Wagner, Samter,[3] Von Scheel,[4]

---

[1] Karl Heinrich Rau, born November 23rd, 1792, at Erlangen, counts as one of the classical political economists of Germany. He became professor at Heidelberg in 1822, and remained there until his death, which occurred March 18th, 1870. His chief work is "Lehrbuch der politischen Ökonomie," which since his death has been remodelled by his pupils Adolph Wagner and Erwin Nasse, the latter professor at Bonn.

[2] Wilhelm Roscher, professor of political economy at Leipzig, where he last year celebrated his seventieth birthday in the midst of a large circle of admiring disciples. He was born October 21st, 1817, at Hanover, and in 1843 became professor a Göttingen, his *alma mater*. Since 1848 he has taught at Leipzig. Roscher is the founder of the historic method in Germany. He has been a very fertile writer.

[3] Adolf Samter, political economist and author, born at Königsberg, March 2nd, 1824. Until 1878 he was in the Prussian State service, but on account of his pronounced Socialistic opinions, or rather the advocacy of them, he lost his position. Samter is a defender of the nationalisation of the land.

[4] Hans von Scheel, a writer of repute on social-political questions, was appointed to an academic chair at Bern in 1871.

Brentano,[1] and Schmoller,[2] as political economists whose writings all had more or less a Socialistic tendency. In reply, however, to Bebel's profession of the pacific character of his mission, Count
Eulenberg could quote from "Unsere Ziele," a work now prohibited,
wherein Bebel considers the contingency of violent developments, and
euphemistically says that the social question will not be "settled by
the sprinkling of rose water." Prince Bismarck repudiated the charge
that he had formerly been in communication with Social-Democrats,
to whose number he refused to reckon Lassalle, and complained that
distinction should not be made between honourable endeavours to
improve the condition of the working classes, and "that which we are
to-day compelled to our sorrow and pain to understand by the idea of
Social-Democracy." Surely men like Rodbertus were not to be
placed on the same level with Nobiling and the Nihilists. The bill
was referred to committee, and the second reading was fixed for
October 9th. It was proposed that the measure should continue in
force until March 31st, 1881. The second debate was even more
animated than the first. On October 9th the Chancellor said :—

"I will further every endeavour which positively aims at improving
the condition of the working classes . . . As soon as a positive
proposal came from the Socialists for fashioning the future in a sensible
way, in order that the lot of the working-man might be improved, I
would not at anyrate refuse a favourable examination to it, and I
would not shrink from the idea of State help for the people who would
help themselves." He charged the Socialists with being a party of
pure negation : their programme was simply subversion and annihila-
tion. For eleven years the Reichstag had had Socialists in its

[1] Lujo Brentano, professor of political economy at Strassburg, was born December 18th,
1844, at Aschaffenburg. In 1868 he travelled in England for the purpose of studying the
labour question here, and especially the working of trades unions. Thus he was led to in
vestigate the history of our guilds, the result being a work published in 1871 with the title
Geschichte der englischen Gewerkvereine," forming part of his "Arbeitergilden der
Gegenwart." He has written other works upon phases of English political and social life.

[2] Gustav Schmoller, professor of political economy at Berlin. Born June 24th, 1834, at
Heilbronn. First filled an academic chair at Halle (1865), and then at Strassburg (1872).
Schmoller has devoted great attention to the history of the German guilds. His views on the
Socialistic question are contained in a little work bearing the title "Über einige Grundfragen
des Rechts und der Volkswirthschaft," which was published in 1874 as a reply to an attack
by Professor von Treitschke upon the tolerant critics of Socialism ("Der Sozialismus und
seine Gönner.")

midst, and he challenged anyone to point out a single positive thought uttered during that time : they had heard nothing but dark, vague promises, whose fulfilment was impossible. Referring to the atheistic tendencies of Socialism, he said :—

"If I were to come to the unbelief which is attributed to these people : well, I live a life of abundant activity, and am in a well-to-do position, but all this would not make one wish to live a day longer if I had not what the poet calls the 'belief in God and a better future.' Rob the poor of that, for which you cannot compensate them, and you prepare them for the weariness of life which shows itself in acts like those we have experienced."

The bill became law on October 19th—after Liebknecht had declared that it could "neither be made better nor worse," and the Progressist leader, Richter, had said, "I fear Social-Democracy more under this law than without it," and on the 21st it was promulgated. The division showed 221 members to be in favour of the measure, and 149 against it. This business having been transacted, and thus the only object of its convocation fulfilled, the Reichstag was at once prorogued. The Socialist Deputies had done their best to thwart the passing of the measure, but it had been a hopeless struggle from the first.

The Socialist Law prohibited the formation or existence of organisations which sought by Social-Democratic, Socialistic, or Communistic movements to subvert the present State and social order. The prohibition also extended to organisations exhibiting tendencies which threatened to endanger the public peace and amity between classes. Registered relief associations might be dissolved if thought necessary, and the same applied to independent unregistered relief associations, but first of all an extraordinary system of control and supervision must be adopted by the police authorities on suspicious symptoms showing themselves. While local associations were subject to the authority of the police, foreign organisations could only be prohibited by the Imperial Chancellor, and in all cases prohibition was to affect the entire federal territory. In the event of an association being prohibited, its funds and effects were to be sequestered, and after its affairs had been properly liquidated, the money was to be applied according as its statutes or the law might direct. Appeal was allowed against the prohibitory acts of the police.

The right of assembly was also greatly restricted. All meetings in which Social-Democratic, Socialistic, or Communistic tendencies came to light were to be dissolved, and even meetings which might be expected to show such tendencies could be prohibited, request for permission to assemble being pre-supposed. In this respect public festivities and processions were regarded as meetings, the police being here again the empowered authority. Further, Social-Democratic, Socialistic, and Communistic publications of all kinds were to be interdicted, the local police dealing with home publications and the Chancellor with foreign ones. Prohibition must be announced by letter, together with the reasons for the step, and right of appeal was allowed. Stocks of prohibited works were to be confiscated, and the type, stones, or other apparatus used for printing might likewise be seized, and, on the interdict being confirmed, be made unusable. The collection of money on behalf of Social-Democratic, Socialistic, or Communistic movements was forbidden, as were public appeals for help.

Coming now to the penal provisions of the law (Sec. 17 *et seq.*), any person associating himself as member or otherwise with a prohibited organisation was liable to a fine of 500 marks or three months' imprisonment, and a similar penalty was incurred by anyone who gave a prohibited association or meeting a place of assembly. The circulation or further printing of a prohibited publication entailed a fine not exceeding 1000 marks or imprisonment up to six months; and, similarly, contraventions of the provisions regarding the collection of money entailed penalties of half this severity, while unwitting contravention was in either case punishable with a fine not exceeding 150 marks or detention. As all prohibitions were made public, no excuse was allowed for ignorance. Convicted agitators might be expelled from a certain locality or from a Governmental district, and foreigners be expelled from federal territory. Innkeepers, printers, booksellers, and owners of lending libraries and reading rooms who circulated interdicted publications might, besides being imprisoned, be deprived of their vocations. Persons who were known to be active Socialists, or who had been convicted under this law, might be refused permission to publicly circulate or sell publications, and contravention of a prohibition, or of the provision against the circulation of Socialistic literature in inns, shops, libraries, and newsrooms, was punishable with a fine of 1000 marks or imprisonment for six months.

But the kernel of the law was the 28th section, which conferred upon authorities exceptional and extreme powers when the existence of Socialistic organisations was held to endanger the public security. Here the police were made subject to the Executive Government, and the powers granted were only valid for a year at a time. The provisions were four in number, and their application constituted what is known as the minor state of siege.[1] They ran as follows :—

"(a) Meetings may only take place with the previous sanction of the police, but this restriction does not extend to meetings held in connection with elections to the Reichstag or the Diets ; (b) The circulation of publications may not take place without permission in public roads, streets, squares, or other public places ; (c) Persons from whom danger to the public security or order is apprehended may be refused residence in a locality or Governmental district ; (d) The possession, carrying, introduction, and sale of weapons within the area affected are forbidden, restricted, or made dependent on certain conditions."

All ordinances issued on the strength of this section were to be notified at once to the Reichstag, and to be published in the official *Gazette*. Contravention of the foregoing provision entailed a fine not exceeding 1000 marks or imprisonment up to six months.

[1] The *état de siège* dates from the revolutionary orgies of 1791 in France. It was first introduced in Saxony amongst German States ; then in Prussia (July 4th, 1851), and was finally incorporated in the Imperial Constitution of 187. (article 68). From the state of siege, in which military law supervenes, was derived the "minor state of siege" (in German, *kleinerer Belagerungszustand*):

R

Social-Democratic literature of all kinds, from the daily newspaper to the pamphlet and the hand-bill for circulation in the streets, and the yearly turn-over was reckoned at 800,000 marks or nearly £40,000. The organisation was perfect and seemed to be incapable of subversion. If, therefore, the Socialists saw themselves confronted by a formidable enemy whose strength had still to be put to the test, they were by no means disposed to lose heart. They rather nerved themselves for a severe struggle, and prepared for the worst which the full exercise of the new legislative powers might bring. One of the first things which the Government and police did was to place Berlin in a minor state of siege on November 29th, and meanwhile a plan of campaign was organised for the combating of Socialist organisations and agitation in the several States most seriously affected. Societies were dissolved, meetings prohibited, newspapers suppressed, miscellaneous publications confiscated, and before many months had passed nearly fifty agitators had been expelled from the capital. Soon Prince Bismarck attempted to grapple with Socialism in the Reichstag itself. Here the Socialist Deputies were free to utter their opinions and expound their doctrines without let or hindrance, and when the public platform was refused to them they took good care to turn the Parliamentary tribune to advantage. The Reichstag became, in fact, a last place of refuge. Here, at any rate, the pursued Socialist knew that he could claim the right of sanctuary, and at first the right was quietly conceded. It is hardly to be wondered at that the Socialist Deputies turned liberty of speech within the walls of Parliament into licence. They did not hesitate to say that when they spoke it was not with a view or a desire to convince their listeners but to reach the ears of the outside world. The publication of Parliamentary reports being privileged, journals with Socialistic tendencies were able to reproduce in full the speeches in which Bebel, Liebknecht, and their fellows preached the principles of a movement which the Government had just been given a commission to suppress.[1]

There was only one way of meeting this new danger, and it was by

[1] The *Volksstaat* wrote as early as the year 1874:—"The Social-Democratic party is a revolutionary party. If it allows itself to be decoyed upon Parliamentary ground it ceases to be a revolutionary party—ceases, in fact, to exist. We take part in the Reichstag elections and send representatives to the Reichstag solely for purposes of agitation. The strength of our party lies in the people, in the people lies our sphere of operations. Only in order that we may address the people do we ascend the tribune of the Reichstag."

restricting the privileged publication of reports or by silencing the speakers by getting rid of them. While the Chancellor tried the former plan, the Berlin police authorities tried the latter and attempted to seize two obnoxious members while literally holding to the horns of the altar. On February 18th, 1879, a letter was read to the Reichstag in which consent was sought to the imprisonment and prosecution of Hasselmann and to the expulsion from Berlin of Fritzsche on account of their violation of the provisions of the new law. The section of the law to which the Deputies had become amenable was the twenty-eighth, in accordance with which the police wished for power to act. During the debate on the second reading of the bill a speaker had proposed that this section should apply also to Deputies, but a voice cried out "The constitution!" and no attempt was made by the Government to act on the suggestion. Members were thus protected against the police by the thirty-first article of the constitution, which provides that no Deputy can be arrested for debt or for any offence, unless he be taken in the act of commission or on the following day, without the sanction of the Reichstag. The proposal roused quite a storm of opposition, and Professor Gneist,[1] the constitutional historian, was one of the boldest leaders of the resisting party. The Reichstag, by a great majority, refused to grant the powers sought, but an un-easy feeling prevailed in the Socialist camp that the police should have dared to play such a game.[2] Then Prince Bismarck showed his hand. On March 4th, a bill was introduced giving the Reichstag power to punish any member who abused his Parliamentary position. The court which should award punishment was to consist of thirteen persons—the president and vice-president of the assembly, and ten members to be chosen at the beginning of every session—and the punishment was to have three degrees of severity : censure by the House, obligation to apologise to the House, and exclusion for a fixed period. It was also proposed that the House should, when it was

[1] Rudolph Gneist, born August 13th, 1816, at Berlin, where he is a respected professor. He was elected to the Prussian House of Deputies in 1859 and to the German Reichstag in 1871. He is a gifted speaker.

[2] On January 14th, 1882, the same question arose again. A Socialist Deputy for Hamburg, Dietz, was that day arrested at Stuttgart. The matter was at once introduced in the Reichstag by the Socialist members, and a resolution was passed by a large majority calling upon the Chancellor to request all Federal Governments to instruct courts to communicate with him immediately on the arrest of a deputy during the sitting of the House, so that the latter might learn the fact and the particulars. Dietz was released the same day.

found desirable, prevent the publicity of its proceedings. In the course of the three days' debate England and English freedom of debate were frequently extolled, but Prince Bismarck reminded members of the power which the British House of Commons reserved to itself, and which was enforced by the utterance of the words, " Mr. Speaker, I see strangers in the House." He asked that the measure might be passed for two years, for he hoped in that time to place an effective barrier against the spread of Socialistic agitation. Not only were the Ministerial proposals warmly opposed in the Reichstag, where the desired precedent was thought too dangerous to be tolerated, but out of doors the cry of " Freedom of debate " was also taken up heartily, and the *Maulkorbgesetz* or Muzzle Bill was defeated.

While the Government was bracing itself up to the task of crushing the hydra, the extreme members of the Socialist party began to clamour for a more aggressive policy. The existence of a group of men disposed to violence was especially made clear at a secret onference held in September, 1879, at Wahren, near Leipzig. Here Most and Hasselmann were all for force. Hasselmann advised revolution outright. He acknowledged the certainty of failure, yet he argued that the blood that would be shed would help on the cause. Most, who early in 1879 established the *Freiheit* in London, with the motto "All measures are legitimate against tyrants," advocated murder, outrage, and rapine. The columns of this print were filled, issue after issue, with incitements to crime and instructions as to the preparation of instruments of destruction, while war was declared against "princes and ministers, statesmen, bishops, prelates, and other dignitaries of the various churches, a large part of the officers, the greater part of the higher bureaucracy, divers journalists and advocates, and finally all important representatives of the aristocracy and *bourgeoisie.*" The *Social-Democrat* was now appearing at Zurich, and it did its best to fan the flame of discontent and violence. The Wahren conference was guided by sober counsels, and all it did was to resolve on carrying on an energetic though secret agitation. It was proposed to hold a congress in June of the following year at Rorschach, in Switzerland, but it was at the last moment postponed on it becoming known that Most and Hasselmann intended to be present and to endeavour to force a revolutionary programme on the party. An important congress was, however, held at Wyden, near Ossingen, in Switzerland, on

August 20th-23rd, and fifty delegates were present from Germany, but neither Most nor Hasselmann appeared. It was found that the adherents of these men were a strong body, and the congress became divided into Government and Opposition. The former persisted in preserving an avowedly pacific policy, while the latter demanded the adoption of a revolutionary programme, along with the establishment of a party organ of as radical a tone as the Socialist Law would tolerate, and the reorganisation of the directorate of the party. The congress, however, refused to be led by the nose by the trumpeters of Most and Hasselmann, both of whom were disowned, and decided to agitate peacefully but energetically in all electoral districts ; to collect funds for propagandism ; to place the direction of the party in the hands of the Socialist Deputies, who were to be assisted by a committee of control, acting as a tie between leaders and followers ; to hold regular congresses for the future ; and to keep up communication with associates abroad. The principal result of the Wyden congress was the severing of the revolutionary limb from the Socialistic body. Most and Hasselmann were rejected, and Bebel and Liebknecht were adhered to. While the Socialist party was pretending to desire a peaceful development of events, its now official organ, the *Social-Democrat*, was declaring that "only by a violent subversion can the Democratic State be attained." Indeed, the manifesto issued just after the congress belied the assumed attitude of passive resistance. This declared the firm resolve of the Socialist party to continue the struggle for the emancipation of the oppressed and plundered classes of society, and for the overthrow of the present "insane and criminal" State and social system, in spite of all opposition and persecution. It then stated that while German Social-Democrats adhered to the principle of adopting peaceful and lawful means for the accomplishing of their ends, it was "self-evident" that unless the ruling classes "surrendered their privileged position voluntarily and without compulsion," they would be justified in resorting to any measures that might be found expedient. In other words, if society did not reform itself the Socialists would undertake the work and make it bear the cost. The manifesto added : "This is now our position in Germany. Our antagonists, the Government and the *bourgeoisie*, are so infatuated that they are making any pacific development of affairs absolutely impossible, and are thus forcing matters to a necessarily and inevitably violent issue. The present political and economic rulers of Germany do not wish for negotiation or mediation, but for a war of extermination. Well, if they wish it they shall have it, and to the full, but the responsibility will fall on their own heads." "Be sure, in any case, of this," concluded the manifesto, "wherever the struggle for the emancipation of the working classes from political and social bondage is carried on, you will find the German Social-Democracy on the spot, with advice and assistance, with sympathy and energetic help, eager and ready for the combat. Long live International Socialism!"

On March 13th, 1881, the Emperor Alexander II. of Russia was assassinated by Nihilists, and a few days later the German Emperor wrote to his faithful Chancellor, urging him to lose no time in bringing before the Governments of Europe the necessity of combining against the forces of anarchy and destruction. "The great crime of the 13th," said the Emperor,[1] "forces the conviction upon me anew, that the time has come for checking the incitement, now extending all over Europe, to attempts on political grounds upon sovereigns and persons of all conditions. In my opinion this can only be done by common action on the part of the Great Powers. . . . The chief thing is to induce England, Switzerland, and France, which have hitherto offered asylum to the perpetrators of political murders, to enact laws for putting an end to this mischief. The task is no easy one, since these countries have hitherto had no such laws. England is, however, now bound, owing to the proceedings within her own shores, to alter her legislation in this domain, in order to be able to act more vigorously. The present would therefore be a favourable moment for winning England over to acquiescence in an international proposal. It would be more difficult with France and Switzerland. You know what I think of these attempts, and you know that police measures are no protection, as the murder of the Emperor Alexander has again proved, but the general weal of the States and their peace will be at stake unless this conduct be conjointly opposed by the Powers." If any sovereign in Europe had a right to consideration in such a matter it was the aged Emperor of Germany, whose life had three times been imperilled, and who had once at least fallen severely wounded to the pistol of a desperado.

Prince Bismarck at once opened negotiations with foreign Govern-

[1] See speech by Prince Bismarck in the Reichstag, May 9th, 1884.

ments. The Russian Government, as most nearly affected, owing to the spread of the Nihilist movement, was asked to take the initiative by convening a conference of representatives of the Powers, the German Chancellor promising to do all he could to further the object of such a meeting. Accordingly the Government in St. Petersburg nvited the chief States to a council at Brussels. Germany and Austria immediately expressed willingness to take part, but France made her assent dependent on that of England, and England, for reasons which only Englishmen can be expected properly to appreciate, declined to participate. Switzerland and other countries also insisted on the co-operation of the two great Western Powers, but this co-operation being out of the question, the conference was not held. Prince Bismarck then tried to bind the three Eastern Empires in a league against anarchy, and the negotiations were continued for some time, but Austria eventually backed out, and the net result of months of diplomacy was that Germany and Russia concluded an extradition and dynamite treaty for themselves.

Meanwhile the election of 1881 took place. The Socialists fought against great odds. Liberty of meeting and of speech was restricted, the distribution of literature was dangerous, and the collection of money for electioneering purposes was difficult, yet a triumph awaited the party. In 1878, when the two attempts on the Emperor had created a violent revulsion in the national mind, the Socialist Deputies fell from 12 to 9 and the Socialist vote decreased 56,000. The election of 1881 gave the party again 12 Deputies, while diminishing its support at the polling booths by over 125,000 votes, the exact figures being 437,158 votes in 1878, and 311,961 in 1881. It must not, however, be concluded that this represented the strength of the cause. The repressive legislation and the vigorous policy pursued by the police prevented the real position of the party from being known. Still, an addition of three members in the Reichstag was a substantial victory. Towards the expenses of the election the party received 13000 marks from America, collected by Fritzsche, who went thither for assistance, and the same amount from a Jewish banker in Germany who had already given considerable help. When the time came for the prolongation of the Socialist Law, whose duration only lasted until March 31st, 1881, the Government did not find it difficult to secure assent, though the parties which had opposed the measure in 1878 did the same thing again. A report presented to the Reichstag in November of this year stated that the minor state of siege had been extended to Altona, Harburg, Hamburg, and Leipzig. The admission had to be made that the Socialist movement had not been seriously checked, for not only did the old organisation continue in force, but agitation was energetically carried on both by meetings and the circulation of prints, notwithstanding all the vigilance of the police. The Saxon Government reported that agitation was carried on with great ardour in Leipzig and the large towns, in spite of the suppression of newspapers, and the expulsion of obnoxious persons. What the native Press could not do, was done by journals like the *Social-Democrat* and *Freiheit*, which were smuggled into the country in large numbers. Socialistic literature had even been introduced into garrisons. As for the associations, there was no grappling with them, for no sooner were suspected organisations dissolved than others "with innocent-sounding names" took their place, and funds for the agitation were raised by means of concerts and public entertainments. The Saxon authorities were, indeed, in despair. The next report presented to the Reichstag, bearing date December 5th, 1882, was equally discouraging. It stated: "The position of the Social-Democratic movement in Germany and the other civilised countries is unhappily not such as to admit the hope of its being suppressed or weakened. The interruption and check naturally caused in the organisation of German Social-Democracy by the introduction of the Socialist Law, and by the adoption of exceptional measures in the chief seats of the movement, are, together with the embarrassment and uncertainty which resulted from these measures and from the vacillating attitude of many of the leaders, being overcome. From the last Reichstag election, which afforded the party a welcome, and as it proved an effective means of strengthening the organisation, a renewed breaking out of the movement must be dated. The hope that the movement would, owing to the social-political legislative proposals, take a quieter character has not been fulfilled. At first it seemed as though the more moderate views which were showing themselves would gain the upper hand, but after the utterances of the chief leaders it must now be admitted, that a proper appreciation of the endeavours of the State to promote the welfare of the working classes is hardly to be expected as yet from the Social-Democratic party." The report spoke of the activity with which agitation was being carried on by means of newspapers and other publications. During three months no fewer than 13,000 copies of the *Social-Democrat* had been confiscated in various parts of the country. It was evident, moreover, that the views of Most were spreading rapidly, owing largely to the agitation of the International Association, which had been endeavouring to win over the Polish population of Prussia. Both in Berlin and Leipzig, said the report, the agitation was increasing, notwithstanding that there had been many expulsions, eighty persons being expelled from the latter town during the period June 29th, 1881, to May 15th, 1882. What was thus said by Government reports was said, in more reserved terms, by Minister von Puttkamer on December 14th, 1882 :—"It is un-doubted that it has not been possible by means of the law of October, 1878, to wipe Social-Democracy from the face of the earth or even to shake it to the centre."

This year a conference of the party was held at Dresden, when the social policy lately entered upon by Prince Bismarck was discussed. [1] As early as February, 1879, the Emperor, in the speech from the throne read at the opening of the Reichstag, gave the assurance that the Government would not stay its hand at purely repressive measures, but would devise social reforms which might improve the condition of the working classes, and this assurance was several times repeated during the following two years. Finally, on February 15th, 1881, the definite statement could be made that a measure for the insurance of workpeople against accident would shortly be laid before the Reichstag, and during the same year Prince Bismarck foreshadowed bills for the insurance of working people against sickness and against want in old age. These promised reforms were very ungraciously received by the Socialist members, Bebel's criticism of the Accident Insurance Bill introduced on April 1st being that the Socialists did not suppose it would hurt them. The Dresden conference, however, went farther than this, for it decided to "reject State Socialism un-conditionally so long as it is inaugurated by Prince Bismarck, and is designed to support the Government system." A section of the party

---

[1] The endeavours of Prince Bismarck to grapple, by means of reforms, with the difficulties presented by the social problem meet with appreciative treatment in a work which is at once a biography of the Chancellor and a history of modern Germany, "Prince Bismarck, an historical biography," (London, 1885), by C. Lowe, M.A., (vol. ii., chapter xiv., pp. 433-460.

was, nevertheless, disposed to treat the Government fairly, inasmuch as it had shown a desire to conciliate where hitherto only coercion had been offered ; but the "*Aut Cæsar aut nullus*" adherents of the Socialist State would hear of no compromise. In August of 1882 a three days' conference was held at Zurich, and at the end of the following March a congress assembled at Copenhagen. The place of meeting was kept an absolute secret up to the last moment. Even the delegates themselves did not know until train time whether they were to meet in Switzerland, Belgium, Sweden, or Denmark. There were sixty delegates present, and a very encouraging report was presented to them. It was stated that the Socialist Law had but little interfered with agitation, though new methods had now to be resorted to. Contributions were being liberally given, and from August 5th, 1882, to February 28th, 1883, the agitation fund had received the addition of 95,000 marks, apart from 150,000 marks expended locally in relief and on the elections. The *Social-Democrat* was said to have four times as many readers as at the time of the Wyden congress. The congress recorded its disbelief in the honourable intention of the new reform party in Germany, as well as in its ability to carry out efficacious measures. "The congress . . . is convinced that the so-called social reform is only to be used as a tactical means of diverting working-men from the true way. It is, however, the duty of the party and its representatives in Parliament to look energetically after the interests of the working classes when proposals are brought forward for improving the economic position of the people—without regard to the motive—but, self-evidently, without for a moment abandoning any of the Socialist demands." Other questions debated were the advisability of abandoning the religious question, which had always been a source of greater or less disagreement ; measures for gaining the sympathy of the rural population, and for interesting students and the educated classes ; and also the expediency of disavowing the Anarchist party more decidedly than hitherto. It is evident, too, though the meagre official protocol does not say so, that the congress was exercised on the subject of trade organisations, for soon afterwards it was seen that these coalitions were being formed all over the country just as after Schweitzer's Berlin congress of 1868. The party Press and the leaders took up the question vigorously, while the police quietly awaited the development of this new move. As to principles the Copenhagen congress cannot be said to have advanced anything new. But it was not, indeed, principles that the Socialist party needed—of these it had more than enough—what was felt to be necessary was still more energetic agitation, and this lack was at once supplied.

On the other hand, an event occurred during this year which roused the authorities to increased vigilance. This was the Niederwald plot against the Imperial family, the existence of which was discovered in September. Various arrests were made, and the trial took place at Leipzig, two men, avowedly Anarchists, being in December, 1884, sentenced to death. In the early part of this latter year the Socialist Law was prolonged for two years until September 30th, 1886, and the Government succeeded on May 15th in passing a law against the " criminal and publicly-dangerous use of explosives," a measure which received general support. The accounts given by the several Federal Governments of their stewardship under the Socialist Law were not more sanguine than before. Agitation continued to be carried on with undiminished zeal, the circulation of prohibited newspapers defied prevention, money was collected in large amounts, and meetings were held in spite of police prohibition and espionage. As before, Berlin, Leipzig, Hamburg, and other places were in a minor state of siege, but although the local authorities thus acquired greatly increased powers, it was impossible to check the movements of the enemy. Bebel was perhaps right when he declared in the Reichstag on March 20th that the Socialist party was nowhere more numerous or better organised than in the districts where the minor state of siege had been proclaimed, and that the party Press had never been more serviceable than then, for though the *Social-Democrat* was published abroad, its circulation was far larger than before the passing of the coercive measures, and it was now able to furnish the agitation with considerable funds. He referred to Prince Bismarck's State Socialism as follows :

" I will frankly tell you something. If anything has furthered the Social-Democratic agitation and the Social-Democratic tendency, it is the fact that Prince Bismarck has to a certain extent declared for Socialism and social reform ; only we are in this case the master, and he is the scholar. People are saying everywhere : when to-day Prince Bismarck with his great authority comes forward and not only acknowledges the existence of a social question—which was a few years ago emphatically denied by the ruling parties—but declares for Socialism, and regards it as his duty to introduce measures on the subject, then it may well be concluded that Social-Democracy is at bottom right."

He also made use of the significant words : "The fathers of the Socialist Law are also the fathers of Anarchism in Germany," words which, if they were intended as a disquieting prophecy, have fortunately had no fulfilment as yet. On the same occasion Liebknecht rang the changes on the word revolution. He said:

"It has been said that it is hoped to put an end to social revolution by social reform. But is there any essential difference between social reform and social revolution? What is social reform? A proper and true social reform is only that which fundamentally removes the evils of society as it now exists. Wherein consist these evils? . . . They consist in the wrong relationship between production and consumption and in our present wages 'system. From these causes springs the unequal distribution of wealth—wholesale poverty on the one hand and great wealth in few hands on the other. He who takes up the question of social reform honestly must place the lever here, at this wrong relationship between production and consumption, and abolish the exploitation of the working classes by capital. That is social reform, and, carried out thoroughly, social revolution. What the Imperial Chancellor is summing up as social reform has nothing to do with real social reform. What is the Sick Fund Law? A police law for the regulation of a part of the poor law system. What is the Accident Law? Exactly the same thing—a police law for the regulation of a part of the poor system. And what is the great law which still hovers befor us in the misty future, the law for the support of the infirm and old? Exactly a police law of the same kind for the regulation of a part of the poor system. Since all those persons who are to receive support under the Sickness Insurance Law and the Accident Insurance Law and the proposed law providing for age do already receive support under our present poor law, only it is in another form. Thus this is not solving the social problem ; it is not even breaking the way for social reform ; and with *this* kind of reform you will certainly not obviate a violent settlement of the question."

What follows might appear to offer an unfavourable commentary upon the supposed pacific direction of the Liebknecht-Bebel school :

"So far," said Liebknecht, "you have not succeeded in destroying our organisation, and I am convinced that you never will succeed. I believe, indeed, it would be the greatest misfortune for you if you did succeed. The Anarchists, who are now carrying on their work in Austria, have no footing in Germany—and why? Because in Germany the mad plans of those men are wrecked on the compact organisation of Social-Democracy, because the German *proletariat*, in view of the fruitlessness of your Socialist Law, has not abandoned hope of attaining its ends peacefully by means of Socialistic propaganda and agitation. If—and I have said this before—if your law were not *pro nihilo* it would be *pro nihilismo*. If the German *proletariat* no longer believed in the efficacy of our present tactics ; if we found that we could no longer maintain intact the organisation and cohesion of the party, what would happen? We should simply declare—we have no more to do with the guidance of the party ; we can no longer be responsible. The men in power do not wish that the party should continue to exist ; it is hoped to destroy us—well, no party allows itself to be destroyed, for there is above all things the law of self-defence, of self-preservation, and if the organised direction fails you will have a condition of anarchy in which everything is left to the individual. And do you really believe—you who have so often praised the bravery of the Germans up to heaven when it has been to your interest to do so—do you really believe that the hundreds of thousands of German Social-Democrats are cowards? Do you believe that what has happened in Russia would not be possible in Germany if you succeeded in bringing about here the conditions which exist there ? "[1]

The Government secured the prolongation of the Socialist Law, but while applying this law with great stringency it did not falter in the attempt to pacify the working classes by the passing of social measures of the kind Liebknecht ridiculed. On June 15th, 1883, a Sickness Insurance Law was passed for workpeople employed in mines, salt works, quarries, factories, smelting and other works, as well as on the railways and in the inland shipping trade. This was supplemented by an instalment of the Accident Insurance Law on July 6th, 1884. Prince Bismarck, indeed, went so far as to proclaim the doctrine of a right to work (*Recht auf Arbeit*) and astonished both friends and foes by the pronounced Radicalism of his views on the social question.[2]

---

[1] Speech in the Reichstag, March 21st, 1884.

[2] "Give the working-man the right to work," he said in the Reichstag on May 9th, 1884, "as long as he is healthy, assure him care when he is sick, assure him provision when he is old. If you will do that, and not fear the sacrifice or cry out at State Socialism directly the

He showed that he had broken for ever with the doctrine of *laissez-faire* as he preached that it was the duty of a State pretending to be Christian to care more for the weak and less for the strong amongst its citizens. Nothing could exceed the earnestness with which the Chancellor enforced the pressing importance of social reforms during these early years of the State Socialistic era, but so far as the Social-Democratics were concerned he found but little sympathetic response. This did not, however, give him discouragement, for he refused to regard the working classes and the Social-Democrats as identical. " Our working-men," he said, " are not all, thank God, Social-Democrats, and are not all indifferent to the endeavours of the Federal Governments to help them, and perhaps not to the difficulties which they have to contend with in Parliament." In this year another general election took place and it afforded the Socialist party an opportunity of demonstrating a strength which no one had believed to exist. The campaign was entered upon with extraordinary vigour, and the result was that, in spite of all the difficulties incidental to the vigilant enforcement of the Socialist Law, no fewer than twenty-four seats were won, or double the number of 1881. Ten seats were won in Prussia, five in Saxony, two in Bavaria, one in Hesse and six in minor States.

In Berlin two out of the six places fell to Socialists, and in Hamburg and Breslau two out of three. The number of votes polled was 549,990,

---

words ' provision for old age ' are spoken ; if the State will show a little more Christian solicitude for the working-man, then I believe that the gentlemen of the Wyden programme will sound their bird-call in vain, and that the thronging to them will greatly decrease as soon as working-men see that the Government and legislative bodies are earnestly concerned for their welfare." Then, answering the sneer of an opponent, he said, " Yes, I acknowledge unconditionally a right to work *(Recht auf Arbeit)* and I will stand up for it as long as I am in this place. But here I do not stand on the ground of Socialism, which is said to have only begun with the Bismarck Ministry, but on that of the Prussian Common Law." [This states expressly : " It is incumbent on the State to provide for the support and care of those citizens who are unable to provide sustenance for themselves and cannot obtain the same from other private persons who are by special laws made responsible." Then : "To those who lack means and opportunity of earning a livelihood for themselves and those belonging to them, work suited to their powers and capacities shall be appointed."] " Was not the right to work," proceeded Bismarck, " openly proclaimed at the time of the publication of the Common Law ? Is it not established in all our social arrangements that the man who comes before his fellow citizens and says, ' I am healthy, I desire to work, but can find no work,' is entitled to say, ' Give me work,' and that the State is bound to give him work ?" He would have great public works undertaken if it were necessary in the interest of the unemployed, for it was a duty.

an increase of 238,029, so that even judging by electoral results the party could now claim a tenth part of all the votes cast in the country, but the real voting strength was far greater, for in a multitude of cases no candidates were brought out where the Socialist vote was considerable. The alarming story told by the elections produced a great effect in Government and police circles ; and the war of extermination was carried on with greater determination than ever. Between October 1st, 1884, and September 30th, 1885, seventy-six meetings were dissolved in Berlin alone, and as many more were forbidden. In spite of this it was reported to the Reichstag that an extraordinarily vigorous agitation was still carried on. Industrial associations were formed in large numbers, and the careful secrecy preserved baffled the powers of the police. The history of the year 1885 was made more exciting by the murder at Frankfort-on-Main of a high police official named Rumpff by the Anarchist Lieske, and the judicial measures which followed. This year also a split occurred in the Socialist camp, and at one time it promised to attain serious dimensions. The cause was the support given by the Socialist Deputies to the Government's mail steamship subvention scheme, which passed the Reichstag in the spring. There was a little plain speaking on both sides, but the breach was eventually healed.

On January 21st, 1886, the Socialists in the Reichstag brought in a bill for the repeal of the Explosives Act. The proposal was, of course, defeated, but the Government's request that the Socialist Law might be prolonged was two months later agreed to, and the measure was extended until September 30th, 1888. During the debate which took place on this latter question Liebknecht again professed that he had no sympathy with violence. "The Government may be sure," he said, "that we shall not, now or ever, go upon the bird-lime, that we shall never be such fools as to play the game of our enemies by attempts. Yes, it would be your game : it would be exceedingly agreeable to you—we know that well." Yet the Socialists were as defiant as ever. "I will tell you this : we do not appeal to your sympathy ; the result is all the same to us, for we shall win one way or the other. Do your worst, for it will only be to our advantage. And the more madly you carry on, the sooner you will come to the end ; the pitcher goes to the well until it breaks." [1]

[1] Speech of April 2nd, 1886.

Bebel was more warlike than his friend Liebknecht, and an expression used by him roused Prince Bismarck to an unusual outburst of indignation. Either with or without ulterior design, Bebel said that if such a crisis occurred in Germany as in Russia, there would be murder. This brought the Chancellor to his feet in a rage, and he deduced from the words said a declaration of the justifiableness of assassination. "Herr Bebel," he exclaimed, "says 'The monarchy would certainly be affected if you employed the measures which are customary in Russia.' The monarchy !—that is with us the monarch, so that coming in immediate connection with the reference to the murder of the Emperor Alexander, this is a direct threat of the murder of the German sovereign ! . . . It is a direct threat of the murder of the Emperor, of the repetition of the Hödel and Nobiling attempts which you [the Socialists] seek to repudiate. It depends on your own theoretical judgment whether our institutions are sufficiently Russian to justify the murder of an Emperor. You leave it to the individual to pass judgment over the State, the monarchy, customs, and over all our institutions and our laws. You hold the individual to be under certain circumstances justified in committing murder. That is the enormous difference which divides you from the rest of mankind and qualifies you to be the object of exceptional laws." [1] The Government sought prolongation for five years, but this was out of the question, as the Clericals took sides with the Progressists in opposing a longer term than before. The majority on the second reading was 27, and that on the third reading, on April 2nd, was 32. It is significant that the Ministerial majority had fallen very low. In 1878 the Socialist Law was passed by 221 votes against 149, a majority of 72 ; and now it was prolonged for two years by 169 votes against 137, a majority not half so large. In July a somewhat sensational

[1] Speech of March 31st, 1886. It should be explained that the word *treffen* which Bebel used is ambiguous, and from the context might be understood to mean either that the monarchy would be "affected" or "struck at." Bebel's words, spoken on March 30th, were as follows: " Herr von Puttkamer calls to mind the speech which I delivered in 1881 on the debate on the Socialist Law a few days after the murder of the Czar. I did not then glorify regicide. I declared that a system like that prevailing in Russia necessarily gave birth to Nihilism and must necessarily lead to deeds of violence. Yes, I do not hesitate to say that if you should inaugurate such a system in Germany it would of necessity lead to deeds violence with us as well. [A Deputy called out: 'The German Monarchy?'] The German monarchy would then certainly be affected, and I do not hesitate to say that I should be one of the first to lend a hand in the work, for all measures are allowable against such a system."

Socialist trial took place at Freiberg, when nine Socialists, including the six Deputies, Bebel, von Vollmar,[1] Dietz,[2] Auer,[3] Frohme,[4] and Viereck [5] were charged with taking part in a secret and illegal organisation. The result of the trial was that all the accused were sentenced to imprisonment for six or nine months, Bebel and four Parliamentary associates receiving the heavier penalty. Several of the Deputies were reported on their release to have suffered severely from incarceration.

At the end of November, reports were presented to the Reichstag on the working of the Socialist Law in Berlin, Altona, and other places. It was stated that agitation continued to be carried on with unflagging zeal, and that the prohibition and dispersal of meetings had frequently to be resorted to in the metropolis, where " social-revolutionary agitations and Anarchist movements threaten public security." Up to date 172 refusals of residence in Berlin were in force.

[1] Georg Heinrich von Vollmar, born March 7th, 1850, at Munich. He was a lieutenant in the Bavarian army as early as 1866, when he went through the Austrian campaign, but he withdrew from service in 1867. He took part, however, in the Franco-Prussian war as a higher official in the field telegraphic department and was severely wounded near Blois. Invalided, he devoted himself to philosophical, economical, and political studies and became a Socialist. After several years of authorship and journalism his political principles brought him a year's imprisonment and expulsion from Dresden (1878). In 1879 he proceeded to Zurich and carried on his studies further both there and later in Paris. He was in 1881 returned to the Reichstag and the following year he resumed residence in Germany, but in 1883 he was imprisoned. Last year he was unable to regain a seat in the Reichstag. He has written several small works on Socialistic subjects and has contributed largely to newspapers.

[2] Johann H. W. Dietz, printer and bookseller, of Stuttgart, born October 3rd, 1843, at Lubeck. He was expelled from Hamburg under the Socialist Law in 1878. He has sat in the Reichstag since 1881 for a Hamburg division.

[3] Ignaz Auer, a saddler of Schwerin, in Mecklenburg, born April 19th, 1846, in Bavaria, a Catholic Socialist. He has been successively expelled from Dresden, Berlin, Hamburg, Altona and Harburg. He was elected to the Reichstag by a Saxon constituency in January, 1877, but was defeated in the election of the following year. In 1880 he succeeded in winning a seat, and he continued to sit in the House until 1887.

[4] Karl J. E. Frohme, author, of Bockenhelm, Frankfort, born February 4th, 1850, at Hanover. Has travelled in Switzerland, Holland, Belgium, Austria, Denmark, and England, and since 1870 has been an avowed Socialist advocate, in which capacity he has several times been imprisoned. He has sat in the Reichstag since 1881. His principal literary achievement is a work on the development of the institution of property, but he has written many *brochures* for the purposes of agitation.

[5] Louis Viereck, a Munich journalist, born March 21st, 1851. He studied medicine at Marburg, and after the French war, during which he did voluntary hospital service, he studied jurisprudence and social science at Berlin, entering the State service in 1873. In 1878 he became a journalist. He has travelled in many countries, including England, Scotland and the States.

During this year further progress was made with the accident and sickness insurance schemes, which it was found desirable to carry out piecemeal. The only other incident calling for mention is the issue of an unpopular decree by Herr von Puttkamer, the Minister of the Interior, rendering strikes of workpeople difficult. For some time the Socialist Deputies strove to secure the recall of the ordinance, but its author stood firm, and the matter ended with the addition of a new word to the Socialist vocabulary, the not too graceful word *Puttkamerei*.

In February, 1887, the Reichstag was dissolved on the Army Bill, which it refused to accept, and the patriotic spirit aroused led to a reaction similar to that of 1878. On this occasion the National Liberals and Conservatives united in support of the septennate, and this coalition of forces naturally affected some of the other parties very seriously, and the Socialist party most of all. The Socialists were also handicapped in that their movements were carefully watched by the police, who rigorously made use of all the powers given by the law of 1878. Electoral agitation was in most places next to impossible, for meetings were forbidden, the circulation of pamphlets and leaflets was made illegal, and proper house-to-house visitation was in the nature of the case impracticable. These modes of electioneering were, of course, pursued to some extent in the teeth of law and police, but the odds were after all very heavy. During the four weeks preceding the election, the Government *Gazette* published prohibitions of 106 publications, 88 of them being electoral leaflets, while during the first quarter of the year the Berlin police dissolved or prohibited nearly forty meetings, made fifty domiciliary visits, and apprehended or expelled seven persons. Yet, in spite of all difficulties, the Socialists polled 763,128 votes, or 213,138 more than in 1884, an increase of nearly 39 per cent., though the aggregate increase in the number of votes cast in Germany was only 33 per cent. The number of Deputies returned fell, however, from twenty-four to eleven. The total number of valid votes cast in the first elections was 7,540,938, (the number of persons qualified to vote being 9,769,802, with a population of 46,855,704), so that 10·1 per cent. fell to the Socialist party. The Socialists took the fifth place numerically amongst Germany's eleven political parties. The results of the Berlin elections were very startling. Of the 232,362 valid votes cast in the first elections 93,335 or 40 per cent. fell to the Socialists, an increase of 24,425 or 35 per cent., though the number of

persons qualified to vote only increased about 10 per cent. The
Socialist vote was nearly twice as large as in the year of the passing
of the Socialist Law. It was not, however, in Prussia that the
Socialists so seriously lost in Parliamentary strength, for the Prussian
Deputies only fell from ten to eight. The decline was chiefly attributable
to the total extinction of the party in Saxony, which in 1884 returned
five Socialists, and in the minor States, with the exception of Hamburg,
which still retained its two Socialist members. And yet Saxony, with
no Socialist Deputy, polled 149,270 votes, or 28·7 per cent. of the
aggregate poll, against only 87,786 votes in 1881. Indeed, in Saxony
the Socialist voters increased during this period considerably more
than the total number of qualified voters. The results of the elections
showed some curious inconsistencies. With proportional representation
the Socialists would have had forty instead of eleven members, and
as a fact the Imperial Party (Free Conservatives) with a less vote
returned forty-one members. Nevertheless, the Socialists were
thoroughly satisfied with their moral victory, and the party Press
raised loud shouts of exultation, and spoke of the " mighty growth " of
the proletarian vote. " Have we any need to doubt the future ? "
asked the Berlin *Volksblatt* ; " no, the old parties may divide the old
property class as they like, but the future belongs to none of them." The
Socialist Deputies returned included Bebel, Grillenberger, Hasenclever,
and Singer.[1]

It cannot be uninteresting to give here a few figures showing the
distribution of Socialism in Germany as indicated by this election :

States, &c.	Population on December 1, 1885.	Votes given in the first elections. Total valid.	Socialist. No.	Percentage of whole.	Socialist members returned.
Prussia	28,318,470	4,530,500	393,635	8·7	8
Bavaria	5,420,199	827,327	54,774	6·6	1
Saxony	3,182,003	519,358	149,270	28·7	—
Wurtemberg	1,995,185	326,798	11,437	3·5	—

The *Volkspartei*, an extreme democratic party, polled 45,803 votes,
or 14 per cent. of the whole vote of Wurtemberg.

[1] Paul Singer, a tradesman of Berlin, whence, however, he was expelled under the Socialist
Law in 1886. Born January 16th, 1844, a Jew. He has been a member of the Reichstag
since 1884, having been returned in that year by a Berlin division, which he still represents.

States, &c.	Population on December 1, 1885.	Votes given in the first elections. Total valid.	Socialist. No.	Socialist. Percentage of whole.	Socialist members returned.
Baden	1,601,255	275,537	13,088	4·8	—
Hesse	956,611	168,063	18,913	11·3	—
Mecklenburg-Schwerin	575,152	100,151	5,653	5·6	—
Saxe-Weimar	313,946	53,964	3,097	5·7	—
Mecklenburg-Strelitz	98,371	11,229	268	2·4	—
Oldenburg	341,525	52,852	2,359	4·5	—
Brunswick	372,452	61,412	12,550	20·4	—
Saxe-Meiningen	214,884	34,078	4,659	13·7	—
Saxe-Altenburg	161,460	28,251	4,078	14·4	—
Saxe-Coburg-Gotha	198,829	32,171	9,105	28·3	—
Anhalt	248,166	39,100	3,448	8·8	—
Schwarzburg-Sondershausen	73,606	11,505	920	8	—
Schwarzburg-Rudolstadt	83,836	14,093	1,167	8·3	—
Waldeck	56,575	6,444	—	—	—
Reuss older Line	55,904	9,930	4,079	41·1	—
Reuss younger Line	110,598	18,615	6,455	34·7	—
Schaumburg-Lippe	37,204	7,321	172	2·4	—
Lippe	123,212	21,244	359	1·7	—
Lübeck	67,658	12,732	4,254	33·4	—
Bremen	165,628	27,884	7,743	27·8	—
Hamburg	518,620	96,860	50,972	52·6	2
Alsace-Lorraine	1,564,355	253,517	673	0·3	—
Total for the Empire	46,855,704	7,540,938	763,128	10·1	11

And here a few words upon a phenomenon which has hitherto received little attention. It is a fact of much significance that in the Catholic parts of the Empire Socialism does not wield anything like the power which it can boast in those parts where Protestantism predominates. This is undoubtedly due in great measure to the greater solicitude shown by the Catholic priesthood for the masses—indeed, the Protestant Church has acknowledged its neglect in this respect— though another factor of importance is the industrial character of most centres of Socialism. The following figures relating to Prussia are also taken from the election returns for 1887, the population being based on the census of December 1st, 1885. Districts in which industry prevails over agriculture are indicated by an asterisk. The districts regarded as Protestant are those in which at least 60 per cent. of the population are Protestants ; so, too, with Catholic districts.

PROTESTANT DISTRICTS.

Governmental Districts.	Population. Protestant.	Catholic.	Socialist votes.	Socialist members.
*Königsberg	78·2	20·8	8,174= 5·5	—
Gumbinnen	97·3	2	49 —	
*Berlin	87·1	7·6	93,335=40·2	2
*Potsdam	96·8	2·7	26,636=11·7	—
*Frankfurt	97·1	2·3	12,811= 7·8	—
*Stettin	97·8	1·2	8,062= 8·3	—
Köslin	97·0	1·9	— —	—
Stralsund	98·6	1·2	116= 0·4	—
*Liegnitz	82·9	16·5	6,611= 3·7	—
*Magdeburg	95·3	4·1	22,935=13·4	—
*Merseburg	97·7	2·1	14,674= 8·9	—
*Erfurt	76	23·4	5,702= 8·3	—
Schleswig	98·5	1·1	39,876=21·5	1
*Hanover	86·9	12·4	31,086= 8·1	1
*Minden	61·8	37·1	4,845= 6·2	—
*Cassel	81	16·6	13,709=11·4	—

The average percentage of Socialist votes is here 9·7.

CATHOLIC DISTRICTS.

Governmental Districts.	Protestant.	Catholic.	Socialist votes.	Socialist members.
Posen	26	71·0	226= 0·1	—
*Oppeln	9·1	89·3	294= 0·1	—
Münster	10·6	88·7	243= 0·3	—
Coblenz	33·6	64·8	327= 0·3	—
*Cologne	15·3	83·1	9,625= 7·6	—
*Treves	18·6	80·4	— —	—
*Aix-la-Chapelle	3·7	95·4	1,244= 1·3	—
Sigmaringen	3·5	95·5	— —	—

The average percentage of Socialist votes is here 1·21. Even taking the industrial districts alone, the percentage is only 2·25 against 9·7 in the Protestant districts. Taking Prussia altogether, the population was 64·6 per cent. Protestant and 34 per cent. Catholic, and the Socialist votes numbered 4·8 per cent. In Bavaria the bulk of the population is Catholic. An analysis of the election returns gives the following results :—

Governmental Districts.	Population. Catholic.	Protestant.	Socialist votes.	Socialist members.
Upper Bavaria	94·4	5	17,432 = 12·2	—
Lower Bavaria	99·2	0·7	270 = 0·3	—
Palatinate	43·2	54·8	5,060 = 4·1	—
Upper Palatinate	91·3	8·4	1,011 = 1·4	—
Upper Franconia	42·2	57	7,552 = 9	—
Central ,,	22·3	75·8	17,771 = 16·2	I
Lower ,,	79·9	17·7	2,073 = 2	—
Swabia	84·9	14·4	3,605 = 3·2	—
Totals	70·8	28·1.	54,774 = 6·6	I

The total number of votes cast in the first elections was 827,327 (apart from 1,305 spoiled votes). Where the Protestants were in excess of the Catholics the Socialist vote was on an average of 9·7 per cent., and where the Catholics predominated this vote only averaged 3·8 per cent. In Saxony the population was 96·8 per cent. Protestant and 2·8 per cent. Catholic : the Socialist vote was, as we have seen, 28·7 per cent. In Wurtemberg the population was 69·2 per cent. Protestant and 30 per cent. Catholic, and the Socialist vote was 3·5 per cent. In Baden the Catholics numbered 62·7 per cent. and the Protestants 35·6 per cent., and the Socialists voted 4·8 per cent.

CHAPTER XV.

PRESENT ASPECT OF THE SOCIALIST MOVEMENT.

FOR twelve years a stringent law held in check the public agitation of Socialism, but the party grew by leaps and bounds. The Socialist Law failed, in fact, of its purpose, for it was dictated by a short-sighted estimate of the results of coercion, and by an unwarranted depreciation of the resource of those who were to be coerced. The end came in 1890 at the instance of the Emperor William II. In that year, the last year of his Chancellorship, Prince Bismarck proposed to embody the Socialist Law, as a permanent statute, in the penal code of the Empire. Another provision in the bill which marked departure from the earlier measure was the proposal to give to the Government the power of expelling not only, as hitherto, from districts proclaimed to be under the minor state of siege, but from Germany altogether, subjects whose Socialistic proclivities might render them publicly obnoxious. This latter proposal was the great stone of stumbling at which one party of the Reichstag after another hesitated during the debates on the bill. Had the then Chancellor agreed, as his friends asked him, to withdraw the expatriation clause, he might have secured a majority for the measure, but he refused either to do this, or to take part in the discussions. The bill, shorn of its expulsion clause, passed its second reading by a majority of five votes, but it was ultimately rejected, on January 25th, by 169 votes against 98.

It was regarded at the time as singular that the speech with which the Emperor dissolved the Reichstag the same evening made no mention either of the Socialist Law or of the Government's defeat. Yet the omission was not accidental ; it had a deep significance. For already the courageous decision to abandon exceptional legislation had been formed in the mind of the new ruler. Prometheus was at last to be unbound.

The election took place in February, 1890, and, when the final results were known, it was found that the only party which could speak of triumph was the Socialist party. They left the Reichstag numbering eleven ; they returned numbering thirty-five, and had later a further addition. Prince Bismarck said in 1884, when the Socialists had won greatly at the polls, that although they had then returned "their second dozen" members, he would "give them a third." The third dozen was now completed. But more significant than this increase of Socialist members was the increase of Socialist voters, for of the seven million men who voted in the first ballots, a million and a half supported Socialist candidates. In other words, with proportional representation, the Socialist members of the Reichstag would have numbered 85 out of 397. The Socialists, indeed, polled more votes than any other party.

The doomed law had still validity for six months, and its provisions continued to be quietly, though faithfully, enforced. Yet, as the time of expiration drew near, no attempt was made to secure the prolongation of the measure. Without further appeal to the supporters of coercion in the past, without even the suggestion of compromise, the Government allowed the law to run out its sands. On September 30th, 1890, just twelve years after its birth, the Socialist Law died a natural death. Social Democracy had conquered, after all. "The Imperial Chancellor thinks he has got hold of us," said Bebel on one occasion in the Reichstag, "but, the fact is, we have got hold of him." The boast was no hollow one. After a long and desperate struggle with the indomitable pertinacity of a coalition which had brought to perfection the art and science of secret agitation, the Government abandoned the weapon to which it had once attributed the strength and virtues of the invincible Excalibur. "The Socialist Law has fallen," exclaimed Liebknecht, as he began a speech of congratulation in Berlin, "The Socialist Law has fallen, and the Red Flag is mounting up."

The " Prisoner of Chillon " regained his freedom with a sigh, for he had " learned to love despair." Not so the Social Democrats of Germany. Yet it must be allowed that they made very tolerant use of their restored liberty. The eve of emancipation saw the re-gathering in Berlin of many of the expelled victims of the moribund law. From east and west, from north and south, they came back to the scene of agitations which for most of them had meant the hard severing of friendships, the sacrifice of home, even the loss of livelihood. It was a glad, mad evening for the Socialistic workman of the metropolis. For the first time for ten years he dare avow his Socialism with impunity. He might now restore the portraits and busts of his heroes— Marx, Lassalle, Liebknecht, Bebel—which he had so long been compelled to treasure in secret. He might again read literature the possession of which had been forbidden him on pain of imprisonment. For him the police had no longer terror. The spectre of the vigilant spy ceased to trouble his imagination and his tranquillity. He needed no longer to whisper with bated breath thoughts which his fellows in other lands known to him might proclaim from the house-tops. He was free again, and once more he felt himself a man. As midnight approached, great gatherings were held in all parts of the city to celebrate the victory which had been won. When twelve o'clock sounded, roar after roar of triumphant acclamation testified to the intense relief and joy experienced by the working classes. There was no disturbance, only much cheering, much congratulation, much singing of the " Marseillaise," and much waving of red flags. To complete the celebration, a medal was struck " in memory of the famous victory won by the people's cause "—let it be added—against tremendous odds. And so the era of repression reached its close.

Within a few days a congratulatory gathering of the party was held at Halle, the result of which was the convening in the following year (1891) of a formal Congress (Parteitag) at Erfurt, at which the official programme was revised, and given its present form.

The succeeding elections of 1893 and 1898 have peculiar interest, since in them the Socialists were able to resort to the free and open agitation of old. In the former year 1,786,738 votes were cast for Socialist candidates, of whom 44 were elected, a number increased later to 48 by bye-elections. The election of 1898 showed further remarkable progress, for the party made an addition of eight to their Parliamentary representatives.   This election, in fact, made the Socialists the second party in the Reichstag in point of seats—being only surpassed by the Ultramontanes—while in point of votes they came out at least half a million ahead of any rival faction, having polled about 2,135,000 votes, or one-fourth of the total number recorded.   Even in Berlin, where they had to surrender two seats to the Radicals, they were the only party that could boast an increase of votes as compared with 1893.

More significant still, however, was the progress which the Socialists made in the rural districts, where, until latterly, they have almost vainly striven to gain the ear of the electorate.   East Prussia is one of the most agricultural parts of the Empire, and, traditionally, one of the most Conservative ; yet while in 13 rural constituencies of this province the Socialist candidates nine years ago polled just 236 votes between them, and while their aggregate vote in these same constituencies was only 11,816 in 1893, the number rose in 1898 to 29,338.   In one constituency the five years' increase was from 660 to 3,178, in another from 1,392 to 3,564, in another from 225 to 3,539.   Taking the whole province, with the exception of the town of Königsberg, the Socialist vote was 12,368 in 1893, and in 1898 31,774—an increase of 19,406.   Again, in the essentially pastoral kingdom of Würtemberg the increase was from 42,000 to 62,000, or nearly 50 per cent.   In the kingdom of Saxony, while all parties together only polled 12,386 votes more than in 1893, the Social-Democratic vote increased 28,534 (from 270,654 to 299,188), being as nearly as possible one-half of the aggregate vote of all the seven parties which put forward candidates.   In Bavaria and Schleswig-Holstein the increase of Socialist votes was 10 per cent., in Hanover 20 per cent., and in Mecklenburg 46 per cent.

Yet while the elections told so emphatically in favour of Social Democracy, it is significant that never before did the "parties of civil order" manifest so serious or so general a determination to join forces in resistance to the onslaught of a common enemy.   In the first ballots the watchword was, of course, "*Sauve qui peut*," and as most of the factions which confronted each other did so with a genuine hope of success, it was only here and there that agreement was come to, outside the groups closely allied in principle and aim, to combine in this sense.   But no sooner were the first elections decided than from the headquarters of every party the injunction was issued that wherever Social-Democratic candidates were in the field, no effort should be spared to inflict upon them crushing defeat. Even parties so self-centred as the Conservatives and the Ultramontanes did not hesitate to unite with their antagonists in pursuance of this end, while in not a few Rhenish and other Catholic districts Ultramontane candidates were supported both by Radicals and National Liberals where Social-Democratic success was the only other alternative.

The two principal leaders of the Social-Democratic party in Germany —in fact, the only members of the party to whom the term leader can properly be applied—are now Wilhelm Liebknecht and August Bebel. Both men have lived eventful lives and have suffered often and severely for the sake of their cause. Already we have seen how they worked hand in hand on behalf of the International Association and how they gradually came to the head of the German Socialist movement. A few biographical facts may well be added here. Of Lieb-knecht not even enemies venture to say that he seeks interested and ambitious ends. Mehring's verdict is the following : " A fanatic, with all the good and bad sides of one, Liebknecht is personally a very estimable man, whose private life is in all respects exemplary. Un-like Lassalle, Marx, and Schweitzer, he was born poor and he has remained poor ; he is contented with mere necessaries so long as he can devote himself to his work, and he despises the most honourable gains which might turn him from his life's purpose. In this respect he is irreproachable ; the reproach of sordid motives in the low sense of the word cannot be brought against him. But when his cause is at stake it will be difficult to find in Germany the man who can use the most poisoned and contemptuous weapons with equal indifference."[1] Liebknecht was born at Leipzig on March 29th, 1826. He studied at the Universities of Giessen, Berlin, and Marburg, and at one time he thought of following an academic career, but scientific and social studies made him a politician, and when the first Baden insurrection broke out in 1848, he took arms in the Republican cause. The enter-prise failed wofully, and he was captured and flung into prison, where he remained from September until the following May. We next find him as a fugitive in Switzerland, but this country he soon exchanged for England, which was his home from 1850 until 1862. During this

---

[1] "Die Deutsche Socialdemokratie, ' pp. 89, 90.

time he was much in the society of Marx and Engels, and he embraced the former's views with enthusiasm. In August, 1862, he returned to Germany and became a chief writer for the *North German Gazette* before it was converted into a Ministerial organ, confining himself to foreign politics, as he had lost touch with domestic affairs. A month later, Count von Bismarck was called upon to form a Ministry, and the journal went over to the Government. Liebknecht at once resigned his position, though great inducements were held out to him in the hope that he would stay. His next move was to join Lassalle's agitation. A letter written by the secretary of the Universal Association to the president in December of this year expresses doubts as to the new convert's trustworthiness, but these were soon set at rest. The last clinging suspicion that he was a reactionary was dispelled in the summer of 1865, when he was ordered to quit Berlin and Prussia. Taking up his residence at Leipzig he conducted a democratic journal until it was suppressed in September, 1866. A little later he ventured to return to Berlin without permission, and the penalty for this act of defiance was his imprisonment for three months. In autumn of 1867 he was returned to the North German Diet by a Saxon constituency, and from that time until the present he has been one of the greatest supports of the German Socialist movement in the manifold capacity of journalist, author, agitator and Parliamentary Deputy, and he may now be regarded as the commander-in-chief of the Social-Democratic army. He entered the New Reichstag in 1874 as member for a division in Saxony, and this division he represented until 1881, when he was elected in the Grand Duchy of Hesse. The reaction of 1887, however, cost Liebknecht his seat, though his rival's majority was small. He has suffered other imprisonments than the one named. In December, 1870, he was apprehended on a charge of high treason and was detained in prison until March following. In 1872, he was with Bebel sentenced to two years' imprisonment for publishing treasonable writings during the French war. In 1881 he was expelled from Leipzig under the Socialist Law.

Liebknecht cannot be regarded as an original thinker. He is, however, a man of high intellectual attainments and his several published works are more than mere compilations for propagandism. Especially deserving of mention is " Zur Grund- und Bodenfrage," a work on the land question, expanded from a lecture and first published in 1874.

Yet, though not claiming the authorship of new theories, Liebknecht has done a great deal to popularise the political and social theories of men like Marx and Lassalle. He is through and through a Communist and a Republican, and he is determined upon realising his ideals by hook or by crook—by fair means if possible, but if not by fair means then by foul. "I am a Republican," he wrote in 1869, "the fact that I live in a monarchy does not make me a Royalist. We acknowledge the supreme power, but only as a fact which we shall tolerate until that power no longer possesses power. We do not sit idle, but use every weapon which the ruling power has left us in struggling with that authority."[1] And again, "Socialism is no longer a question of theory but simply one of power, which can be settled with no Parliament, which can only be settled in the street or on the battlefield."[2] He works for the subversion of the monarchical principle and for the establishment of a Free People's State. In this State all subjects will stand upon the same level : there will be no classes and no privileges. The political revolution will necessarily entail a social and economic revolution. Society will come into possession of the land and instruments of production, and the labourer will receive the produce of his labour. In all these theories he stands upon the ground of Marx, at whose feet he sat so long. Upon one occasion he explained his standpoint to the Reichstag as follows :—

"You reproach us with desiring to introduce community of goods and to abolish private property : we on the other hand say that modern society already has community of goods in the bad sense of the word and is abolishing property ; that is, the produce of labour, which belongs to the labourer, is taken from him, the real proprietor is expropriated, and the end of the matter, the revolutionary conclusion, must be that which Marx has put into the formula, the expropriators— those who have stolen the real property, which is the produce of labour, from the true owners, the labourers—will themselves be ex propriated." Unlike many Socialist agitators, Liebknecht has all along recognised the importance of winning the rural population. So long ago as 1869 he wrote to one of his associates : "We do not need the peasantry in order to bring about a revolution, but no revolution can take place if the peasantry are against it."[3] Thus while others

[1] " Über die politische Stellung der Socialdemokratie."
[2] *Ibid.*
[3] Letter of November, 1869, to Bracke.

have confined attention to the industrial classes, he has sought to induce the rural labourer to take an equal interest in the Socialist movement, and he has also represented strictly rural or semi-rural constituencies in the Diet. Like Marx and Lassalle, Liebknecht has been a careful student of English literature, and among his favourite authors are Macaulay, Mill, and Lord Beaconsfield, all of whom have exercised influence upon him. His admiration of Disraeli is, indeed, boundless, and we find him expressing it not only in his writings but in Parliament. He gives the author of "Coningsby" and "Sybil,"—works which, from beginning to end, he does not hesitate to take *au sérieux*—credit for having "studied the social question and understood it up to a certain point, and for having drawn a picture of the social condition of England a generation ago which for truth and skill surpasses any of Zola's achievements." A year ago the publication of a German translation of "Sybil," done by Frau Liebknecht, was begun in a Berlin democratic journal, and in an introduction written for the work Liebknecht pronounced the following verdict upon the author of the novel, a verdict which, coming from such a quarter, is noteworthy. "Disraeli," he said, "is the first statesman who recognised the importance of the social question, and who practically interpreted politics as the science of society. A novelist, he hated the *bourgeoisie*, but he nevertheless saw that it would be madness to hinder *bourgeois* development. Still, he did not wish to see the *bourgeoisie* in the State. His ideal was a monarchy of the people ; the government to be exercised through sovereign and Parliament, and the working class taking part as a counterbalance against the middle class, the *bourgeoisie*. In regard to Chartism and the movements of the working classes, Disraeli professed a Radicalism which in Germany would have caused him to savour of Socialism. The fact is, that all that has of late been said respecting State Socialism and the duties of the State towards the 'poor man' was said twenty times better by Disraeli forty years ago."

August Bebel—or Ferdinand August Bebel, to give the name in full—is a man of far coarser mould. By occupation a master turner, and an author through force of circumstances, his character possesses none of the traits of refinement which mark that of his intellectual coadjutor. Bebel is a plain, blunt man, a Mark Antony of an inferior class, but he can claim the high merit that he does not try to appear what he is not, Yet if Bebel lacks in culture, he has abundant energy and will, and the Social-Democratic movement would fare ill if it lost the services of this champion. Bebel was born near Cologne, on February 22nd, 1840, and was educated first at a village and afterwards at a Sunday school. He passed through the industrial grades of apprenticeship and journeymanship, and spent his *Wanderjahre* in South Germany and Austria from 1858 to 1860, settling down in the latter year at Leipzig. Always reflective and observant, and fond of improving his mind, he gained both in knowledge and experience of the world by his travels, and when he began to give attention to labour movements, he secured a ready ear amongst his fellow workmen. Originally Bebel had no Socialistic tendencies. He was for some time an adherent of the Schulze-Delitzsch school, and took a prominent part in the promotion of working-men's associations on a political and educational basis, being, in fact, a leading member of the organisation which called Lassalle into public life. On the establishment of the Universal Association, however, he became a violent opponent of Lassalle, and by the influence he was able to exert upon the working-men's associations did him great injury. In 1865, he was elected president of the Leipzig association, and two year later of the Union of German Working Men's Associations, a congeries of labour strength which, in association with Liebknecht, he took over to the International camp, thus hastening the conversion of the entire German democratic party to advanced views. Up to the year 1866, he held an entirely anti-Socialistic position, but the influence of his patron Liebknecht soon showed itsel:, and now his views illustrate the adage, *plus royaliste que le roi.* He was returned to the North German Diet by a Saxon constituency in 1867, and he continued in the German Imperial Parliament until 1881. In that year he was defeated, but two years later he obtained a seat in a by-election, and he was returned in 1884, and again last year for a division of Hamburg. In his last contest he received 52·5 per cent. of the votes cast, and thus overcame the combined strength of two antagonistic candidates. His prison record is a heavy one. In 1869 he was detained three weeks for disseminating doctrines dangerous to the State. In December of the following year he was apprehended on a charge of high treason, and was kept under arrest for over three months pending investigations. The trial came off in March, 1872, and he received sentence of two years' imprisonment, which he served at Huburtusburg. July of the same year saw an addition to this penalty of nine months, for the offence of leze majesty. Finally, the Freiberg trial of July, 1886, led to his being deprived of liberty for a further nine months on account of complicity in a secret and illegal (*i.e.*, Socialist) organisation.   Repeated imprisonment has given Bebel ample leisure for authorship, and a number of works have left his vigorous if unrefined pen.   Chief among them are " The German Peasant War," [1] "Woman in the past, present, and future," [2] and "The Mohammedan-Arabian Period of Civilisation in the East and Spain," [3] while smaller writings published for the purpose of agitation are "Christianity and Socialism," "The Parliamentary activity of the German Reichstag and the Diets," and "Our aims."   Nearly all Bebel's works are interdicted in Germany.

Bebel once summarised his views in a sentence which, so far as he spoke for himself, is as true as it is short.   "We aim," he said, "in the domain of politics at Republicanism, in the domain of economics at Socialism, and in the domain of what is to-day called religion at Atheism." [4]   Here we see Bebel as in a mirror.   He is a Republican and a Socialist, and he is proud of it ; he is without religion, and he is never tired of parading the fact, even having himself described in the Parliamentary Almanacs as " *religionslos.*"   Like his colleague Liebknecht he is a warm admirer of England, of which he has spoken as "this model of a Constitutional State, this free England," and he is prepared to do anything in order to win for the German working classes the freedom enjoyed in this country.   Of all latter-day Socialists he has with least reserve proclaimed the doctrine of force.   The following passage from " Our Aims " shows Bebel in what for him is a favourable light :—" There are only two ways of attaining our economic ends.   The one is the gradual supplanting of the private undertakers by means of legislation, when the Democratic State has been established. . . .   The other and decidedly shorter though also violent way would be forcible expropriation, the abolition of private undertakers at one stroke, irrespective of the means to be employed. . . . If it should come to force, there could be no doubt whatever as to which side would win in the measuring of physical powers.   The

---

[1] " Der deutsche Bauernkrieg mit Berücksichtigung der hauptsächlichsten sozialen Bewegung des Mittelalters." (Brunswick, 1878).

[2] " Die Frau in der Vergangenheit, Gegenwart, und Zukunft," (Zurich, 1883).

[3] " Die mohamedanisch-arabische Kulturperiode in Orient und Spanien," (Stuttgart, 1884),

[4] Speech in the Reichstag, March 31st, 1881.

masses are on the side of the labouring population, and so also is moral right. Only let the necessary insight be gained by the masses, and the struggle is decided. But there is no need to be horrified at this possible use of force, or to cry murder at the suppression of rightful existences, at forcible expropriation, and so forth. History teaches that, as a rule, new ideas only assert themselves through a violent struggle between their representatives and the representatives of the past, and that the champions of the new ideas have endeavoured to strike the latter blows as mortal as possible." Then, after referring to the French Revolution of 1848, he adds : " We thus see how force has played its part in various periods of history, so that it is not without justification that Marx exclaims in his work 'Capital,' in which he describes the development of capitalist production : ' Force is the midwife of every old society which is in labour with a new. It is itself an economic power.' " Bebel's economic theories need not detain us, for they are not his own. It is, however, worth while glancing at the model Socialistic State which he has sketched, and the perfection of which is only to be understood when we bear in mind his contention that "Socialism is the true representative of culture, civilisation, and morality. It is the only guarantee for human progress, for the liberty, equality, and fraternity of mankind."[1] The primary conditions of the Socialistic State are the abolition of personal property in land and the means of production and communication, the universality of labour, the equality of all members of society, and the secularisation of all social institutions. Production must be carried on upon the principle of association, the basis of association being the individual commune. When this mode of production is adopted, the distinction between employer and employed—a relationship which is to Bebel that of ruler and oppressed—will disappear. Labour is a social necessity, and so every member of society who can work must do so. The duty will, however, be all the pleasanter from the knowledge which a worker will have, that what he is doing for others these are doing for him. As all the subjects of the Socialistic State will naturally strive to facilitate and economise labour, an impetus will be given to the making of technical improvements and inventions, and the time thus gained will be employed partly in the production of new commodities for the satisfaction of new needs, and partly in intellectual

[1] " Die parlamentarische Thätigkeit des deutschen Reichstags."

T

pursuits. When labour is compulsory for both men and women, a healthy spirit of emulation and a lofty pride in toil will spring up. No capable man will be exempted from engaging in a certain class of industrial or agricultural labour, though choice of occupation will be free. Not even the learned members of society will escape. The distinction between head work and hand work will be abolished, and philosopher and ploughman will take their places side by side as producers for society. The scholar, the man of science, the artist, the musician may go their own ways in the afternoon, but it is on the express understanding that they do a fixed amount of muscular work—whether it be brick-laying, hedge-clipping, soil-turning, or wood-chopping—during the morning hours. And, moreover, as Bebel takes care to say, for the sake of sages who may be absent-minded, they must do this physical work diligently (*fleissig physisch arbeiten*), for that will both benefit society and their own digestive organs. It follows that there will in future be no distinction between "higher" and "lower" kinds of labour.

Now-a-days a mechanic thinks himself superior to a day labourer, but in the Socialistic State there will be no respect of labour, as there will be none of persons. As only work of social use will be performed, all kinds of labour which fulfil this requirement will be of equal value to society. It may be expected that all unpleasant and offensive work will in time be performed mechanically, but until the requisite machines are invented, everybody must take his turn at this work, so that there may be no such thing as false shame or contempt for useful labour. The unit of the State will be the family, families will be grouped in communes, and the communes will elect local administrations on the principle of universal suffrage for both sexes. The central administration at the head of the State will not be a Government possessing executive power, but a guiding and directing organisation. Thus the State as now understood will disappear, and with it all the present political machinery, Ministers, Parliaments, standing army—for this a national militia will be substituted—police and gendarmes, law courts and lawyers, prisons, customs and revenue departments, and the rest. Political crimes and indeed crimes of any kind will be unknown. Robbery will cease because every man wil be able to supply his needs by honest work. There will be no vagabonds ; perjury, forgery, fraud, and fraudulent bankruptcy will exist no longer, since the abolition of private property will remove the cause of these crimes ; incendiarism will never be committed, since the possibility of hatred will be taken away ; and as for murder, why, asks Bebel, should there be murder when no man can enrich himself at the expense of another ? Altogether the condition of society will be angelic. One great requirement must, however, be fulfilled. The training of youth must be radically altered, and this will involve new family relationships. Free marriage or rather free love is to be introduced, woman being economically and socially independent, and politically equal with man. The training of children will become the duty of society, which will take charge of infants as soon as they can leave their parents and will bring up the sexes together. The views which Bebel represents on this subject, and which are but a debased imitation of Plato, are, as set forth in detail, not less opposed to common sense than repulsive to moral instincts. Education will be provided gratuitously, and on a liberal scale, but the State must have nothing to do with religion. Holding this to be hostile to progress, he would like to see it suppressed, but such an act would be opposed to the Socialistic principles of equality and freedom. All, therefore, that he can fairly require is that the State shall give no sanction or help to religious institutions or agencies. Until the Socialistic State is realised, he demands that Ministers for Public Worship shall lose their offices, and that the money thus saved shall be applied to the purposes of education and culture. The physical training of the young is to be carefully looked after, and he proposes that just as children are prepared in school for their vocation, so they shall be taught how to discharge the military duties of citizens. If boys learned military exercises during school years little further training would be necessary at a later time, and barrack life and parade service would be superfluous. The citizen army of the future will be far superior, both in technical efficiency and moral status, to the standing army, and it will be a less drain on the physical strength and the resources of the nation. But, further, in order that time, labour and expense may be spared, and the Socialistic idea be developed to the fullest extent, great warehouses and magazines will replace shops, and the work of the household will no longer be done independently, but collectively in vast establishments for feeding, cooking, washing, bathing, and heating. Woman, thus relieved of the duties at once of wife and mother, will be set to work for society in various useful ways. For society is to be regenerated in such a way that all its members will be mutually dependent and helpful, and all will pursue the common end of universal happiness.

Such are the two men who now stand at the head of the German Social-Democratic movement. There are other more or less prominent leaders, such as Herren Hasenclever,[1] Von Vollmar, Singer, Grillenberger,[2] Auer, and Dietz, but above all these Liebknecht and Bebel tower head and shoulders. The one is the complement of the other ; separate they would both lack the qualities requisite to the direction of a great party, but together they make up as much of a Lassalle as suffices to preserve unity in organisation and resolute energy in agitation.

INDEX.

U

Wirth, Moritz, 83, 84 ; Max, 149.
Wolff, Wilhelm, 95, 120.
Wurtemberg, political disturbances in, 20, 21, 25.
Wuttke, Heinrich, 142, 220

Zachariae, H. A., 69,

Cowan & Co., Limited, Printers, Perth.

www.ingramcontent.com/pod-product-compliance
Lightning Source LLC
Chambersburg PA
CBHW031400270326
41929CB00010BA/1260